Instrumental Music Teacher's Survival Kit

Ready-to-Use Guidelines, Lessons & Exercises for Teaching Beginning Band Instruments

Randy Navarre, DMA
Photographs by Louis Cipollini

Parker Publishing Company
Paramus, New Jersey 07652

Library of Congress Cataloging-in-Publication Data

Navarre, Randy.
 Instrumental music teacher's survival kit : ready-to-use guidelines, lessons & exercises for teaching beginning band instruments / Randy Navarre ; photographs by Louis Cipollini.
          p.   cm.
Includes index.
ISBN 0-13-017821-7
          1. Bands (Music)—Instruction and study—Handbooks, manuals, etc. 2. School music—Instruction and study. I. Title.
          MT733.N28 2001
          784'.071—dc21   00-068450

Publisher: Win Huppuch
Production Editor: Mariann Hutlak
Interior Design/Formatting: A-R Editions, Inc.
Composition: A-R Editions, Inc.

© 2001 by Parker Publishing Company

Printed in the United States of America

10 9 8 7 6 5 4 3 2 1

ISBN 0-13-017821-7

PARKER PUBLISHING COMPANY
Paramus, NJ 07652

www.PHedu.com

About the

INSTRUMENTAL MUSIC TEACHER'S SURVIVAL KIT

This practical resource gives new and experienced band directors and instrumental music teachers ready-to-use guidelines, lessons, and activities for organizing an effective instrumental music program and for introducing students to 12 beginning band instruments. Even if you have never played or taught a particular instrument before, the *Kit* provides virtually all of the information you need to successfully teach the first five lessons with that instrument, from the various techniques for producing sounds on the instrument to time management.

For quick access and easy use, materials are printed in an $8\frac{1}{4}$" × 11" format that folds flat for photocopying and is organized into the following seven parts:

1. Preparing for Instrumental Music Lessons
2. Teaching Beginning Band Instruments
3. Planning Charts and Reports
4. Conducting
5. Surviving the Beginning Band Concert
6. Band Method Review
7. Final Tips and Suggestions

You are free to photocopy any of the music scores, charts, and other aids in this resource for use with individual students and groups.

Part 1, "Preparing for Instrumental Music Lessons," offers practical suggestions and materials to help you prepare for music lessons. This section covers mental preparation, selecting a beginning band method, and physical environment, each of which will greatly influence the outcome of the initial lessons and lay the foundation for students' progress in mastering the instruments.

Part 2, "Teaching Beginning Band Instruments," is the heart of the *Kit*. It provides a step-by-step guide for teaching each of the beginning band instruments: flute, clarinet, saxophone, trumpet, F horn, low brass (trombone, baritone horn, tuba), drums, bells, and double reeds (oboe and bassoon). Since the most effective teacher is one who can say the same thing in many different ways, this resource offers several ways to instruct students how to produce a sound on each instrument. Each instrument section is complete and self-contained.

At the end of each instrument section is a troubleshooting chart which should help teachers find quick cures for problems. Each section also includes a beginning fingering chart for that instrument. The fingering charts give two fingerings for many notes. The first note is the preferred and more commonly used position and the second is the chromatic fingering. The chromatic version should be used only when the musical passage demands the use of that fingering. Often chromatic fingerings entail some intonation problems. Music is provided for the first five lessons for each instrument. The lessons are tailored for specific instruments. After the students have played the music for the first five lessons in this resource, they should easily be able to continue with most commercial band methods chosen by the teacher. Additional musical exercises that may be very helpful in teaching students are also included.

Part 3, "Charts and Reports," provides charts and sample schedules that you may use as is or adapt for the specific situation. Also included are instructions on how to make up a chart and the factors to keep in mind while constructing it.

Parts 4, 5, and 6 will help guide you in giving effective concerts right from the start. These cover everything from using the baton and teaching as a conductor to concert program planning and etiquette, and also include a beginning band concert. The last section, "Final Tips and Suggestions," offers a medley of special tips to help you with a wide range of related topics, from personal education to retention, budgeting, and other subjects.

I hope this resource will be an effective tool for instrumental music teachers and band directors just starting their careers as well as for those who have been in the profession for many years.

Throughout the *Kit* the gender of the student changes. At no time does the author mean to imply that a particular gender should play a particular instrument. For the purpose of easier reading, one is chosen for each instrument. There is no such thing as a girl or boy instrument, and no one instrument is designed more for one gender than the other.

—Randy Navarre, DMA

About the Author

Randy Navarre (D. Musical Arts, University of Maryland) has been active in music education since 1973, starting as a music teacher in the Philadelphia public schools. His experience ranges from developing instrumental music programs at the grade-school level through teaching music majors in college and directing clinics for school band directors.

Dr. Navarre is the founder and director of Northeastern Music Programs, Inc. (NMP). NMP provides general and instrumental music programs to schools in the areas of southeastern Pennsylvania, southern New Jersey, and northern Delaware. His responsibilities include recruiting new schools, recruiting students, supervising and guiding music teachers, and running day-to-day business operations. An affiliated company, Northeastern Music Publications, Inc., which Dr. Navarre founded and continues to direct, specializes in publishing music for school bands and orchestras.

In addition to teaching and operating NMP, Dr. Navarre performs as a classical saxophonist in concerts and festivals in the United States and Canada and plays with various orchestras, including the Philadelphia Orchestra. He has written several compositions that are published and performed throughout North America, Europe, and Asia, and his articles have appeared in *The Saxophone Journal, The Instrumentalist, BandWorld,* and *Fanfare* magazines.

Dr. Navarre also offers clinics on teaching all beginning instruments, recruiting, developing the inner ear, and score reading. These clinics are given in colleges, state music educators' conferences, music stores/clinics, and provincial music educators' meetings in Canada. For availability and fees, please contact Randy Navarre, DMA, P.O. Box 517, Glenmoore, PA 19343; phone: 610-942-2370; fax: 610-942-0660; e-mail: randy@nemusicpub.com.

Contents

Instrumental Music Teacher's Survival Kit

## Part 1

Preparing for Instrumental Music Lessons

. . . .

Mental Preparation

To become a good teacher, one must want to teach. As obvious a statement as this may seem, it does not always apply in the case of music education. Many young teachers just starting their careers want to be performers and take a teaching position only to secure an income. After several years, they realize that teaching is the vocation in which they will spend most of their lives, and they will enjoy it. Very good players make wonderful teachers. In fact, a band or orchestra cannot perform any better than the teacher can perform or imagine how to perform a composition. The better the teacher can play his or her own instrument, the better the band or orchestra will perform.

One must realize that teaching is sharing the love of music. The students will enjoy music only as much as the teacher enjoys sharing music with the children. The music teacher must know his or her craft very well in order to become a great teacher. As the teacher gains experience, he or she will quickly communicate this knowledge to the students. Conveying joy in being there and sharing music is what will make the students want to come to your class every day. Be enthusiastic! Let them know you are aware of every little accomplishment and success. And remember this: No matter how bad a day you are having, some of your students may be in a worse position than you. Give every student a smile a day. This may seem trite, but students will realize that when you are having a bad day and things are not going well, you are not blaming them. The students should want to come to band no matter what is happening in your personal life. Your intense concern for them and wanting to have fun making music are your best recruiting tools.

Selecting a Beginning Band Method

Many factors must be taken into account before choosing a method for teaching instrumental music lessons. The number of days a week your group will meet for lessons, the number of band rehearsals per week, whether the groups will meet in small groups or very large sections, and whether you are able to meet with like instruments only, are just a few of the factors to consider in choosing a band method.

1

Some of these factors may not be within your control. For example, you may be in a school that does not allow for individual or group lessons. If you meet only with a full band rehearsal, you must choose a heterogeneous band method that you feel best accommodates all instruments. You may be in a situation where you can give group lessons as well as band rehearsals daily or weekly. During the lessons, you may choose to use methods that cater to individual instruments. This resource provides the first five lessons for you. The lessons are designed to cater to the problems of the individual instrument, but also allow you to use the band method for your full band rehearsals. After the first five lessons in the *Kit,* you should be able to pick up with the fifth lesson in most commercial band method books. All the lessons in the *Kit,* except for those in the flute section, are written so that you may use either a band method book or the lessons included in this resource. Because of the complex nature of teaching flute, and because few if any commercial band methods give the flute student the correct start needed to develop a good basic beginning, it is advisable to use the lessons in this resource.

The following are instrumental and general concerns to consider when choosing a band method.

Appearance

There are a few very important questions to ask when choosing a band method book: Does the band method look like it will be fun to play? A nice shiny bright cover with pictures of the instruments may be very important to students. If their first impression is positive, they will be excited. Though one cannot always tell a book by its cover, the cover can sell the book and sell excitement. This is not the only consideration, but it is an important one.

How much text is included in the book? If the first several pages are all words, with few pictures and no notes to play, the student may think it is too difficult to play an instrument. If it looks complicated, it *is* complicated. That will be the mental attitude of the students.

How quickly do the students play the instrument? If you remember back when you first signed up for band, the main reason you signed up was to play the instrument. Do not choose a method book that requires students to wait days or weeks to start playing their instruments while they are singing and clapping rhythms. It is important to do these things, but not in place of playing an instrument. It is incredibly important that all students play at least one note on the first day and, if at all possible, part of a song. If you lose their enthusiasm in the beginning, they will drop out of the band before the end of the first three months. You need to nurture their excitement in the first lessons. When their progress slows down in a couple of months, their enthusiasm will carry them through this period until their coordination develops, and they can play more songs. **The book must look like fun, be fun, and teach the students all at the same time.**

Introduction

Try to find a book that has pictures of young students playing their instruments properly. This will help the students at home remember how to sit up straight and form proper embouchures. (You may make photocopies of pictures from this resource and hand them out to your students.)

Rhythmic Beginning

Starting with quarter notes is easier for young students than starting with whole notes. Most band method books start with whole notes and move quickly to quarter notes. However, it is easier to play four quarter notes and count to four at the same time than to try and hold a note for four foot taps. This is an abstract thought, and can be difficult for young beginners. Also, many students, especially flute players, will not be able to hold the note for four beats, thus giving them the misconception that they are not completely successful on their first attempt to play their instrument. A quick and easy success is essential for young students. You do not want to lose their early enthusiasm. There are many good methods starting the lessons with whole notes. If you choose one of those, you may want to consider starting your students with the lessons in this text.

Flute

The students should play high notes such as B, A, and G above the staff. If the book has pre-lessons, it should include these notes. Starting with high notes causes a more closed aperture, which will develop a more focused and clear sound. D, C, and B♭ are notes starting too low, and the fingerings are more difficult for beginners to play. At least the first three notes should be G, F, and E♭, so students will develop a better sound in the early stages of learning to play. If you use the Flute lessons in this resource, they will develop a good embouchure and not delay the progress of the flute students. After the first five lessons in the *Kit,* students will be able to resume with the band method you are using for your band rehearsal. Some books start with low B, A, G. If you wish to use the beginning lessons in these books, have the students play the notes high instead of low as written.

Oboe

The best notes with which to begin are B, A, and G. Once students can play those notes successfully, the next notes in the book should not be too difficult. Notice the range in the early part of the book. The oboe is one instrument that you would not want to have the students playing too high too quickly, because the intonation will be unbearable. The muscle development should be more gradual for high notes.

Bassoon

Bassoon is another band instrument that does not fare well with heterogeneous band method books. The first notes in these books often have difficult hand and fingering positions. It is best to start with the notes E, D, and C, and play lower notes in the first few lessons. Avoid playing an F or higher in the first few lessons. That would be similar to having a clarinet player crossing the break within the first five lessons. The lessons presented in the *Kit* will provide a better start for bassoons than the lessons in most commercial band method books.

Clarinet

Whether the first notes are E, D, and C, or G, F, and A, the clarinet player should do well. A major concern with teaching clarinet is how the book introduces crossing the break. Few if any method books address this properly. Clarinets should play songs with low notes before trying to play the high notes. This resource gives a good supplement that has proven to be very effective in teaching young students to play over the break.

Saxophone

The easiest starting notes for the saxophone players are B, A, and G. However, they really can handle the first few pages in most beginner books. Students will find success more easily, however, if the first note is not D. D requires that all fingers be wrapped around the saxophone without pushing down any of the side keys—an almost impossible act for a student with small hands.

Trumpet

Trumpet players will have a more successful start beginning with higher rather than lower notes. G, F, and A are very good notes on which to start (in that order). The notes are not really high, but require the player to start with more tension and then relax. Some students have difficulty playing G and A in method books that start with E, D, and C for their first notes.

F Horn

In most band method books, the F horn receives poor treatment. This is not intentional, but because of the transposition of the F horn, and the ranges of the other instruments, lessons often start on very high or very low notes in heterogeneous band method books. Neither is ideal for the young beginning player. A problem some students have with starting the F horn is playing the correct pitch. Because the fundamental tone is so low and the beginning range is so far away from the fundamental, valves are of little help to students in playing the correct pitch. F horn students must be good listeners. If they do not listen to themselves and the other students playing around them, they will have a difficult time playing and being successful on this instrument. The more academically successful the student is, the better that student will be able to play the F horn, as well as the oboe and bassoon.

Good starting notes are E, D, and middle C. These notes are not too difficult to hear and are not too high or too low. Many method books show both high and low notes on the same staff, which is very confusing to a young student. It is difficult enough to start reading notes during the first few lessons for any instrument, but having to see two sets of notes at the same time and block out or ignore the top or bottom notes is asking too much of a beginning player. Anything that looks complicated may scare a child and thus make the lesson seem more difficult than it really is. The lessons in the *Kit* are easy to read and work around the notes that are easy to play for a beginning student. It is recommended that students start on the F or single horn as opposed to the double horn. They do not need to consider two sets of fingerings as they are learning an instrument for the first time. The B♭ horn is fine as a starting instrument, but the F horn is more common. Many contemporary methods provide only F horn books.

Trombones and Low Brass

Basically, the low brasses have the same problems as the trumpet. It is best to start playing notes around F, E♭, and G, and then relax the embouchure to lower notes.

Drums

A major problem with most band method books is the slow rate of rhythmic development for young drummers. Drummers often become bored very quickly with band, thus becoming the conduct-problem section that band directors are always complaining about. Try to find a band method that advances the drums to more complex rhythms as soon as possible. Also, rudiments are extremely important for young players, but very few method books introduce rudiments until the second book. If the band method does not teach the rudiments from a very early stage of development, then, as a band director, you should add that instruction for the student. It will be fun, and the drummers will enjoy their instruments more. The rudiments are included in this resource. Have the students finish the first band method book as quickly as possible, and study from a drum method book. You may start a drum method book while the students are still playing in the beginning band method. The drummers must advance rhythmically in order to enjoy playing and staying in the band.

Bells

It is a great idea to demonstrate the bells when recruiting. Many students studying piano would make excellent mallet players. They do not want to be drummers! Most band methods have a bell or mallet percussion book. There is no range problem with bells, so the major concern is picking a band method that is fun to play.

Musical Advancement

Some band methods start very slowly and tend to progress slowly throughout the book. Try to find the right balance for your group. You should start eighth notes at least by page fourteen or fifteen. The type of songs included in the book is a very important consideration when choosing a band method. The songs should be fun while benefiting students' musical education. Classical melodies should be introduced in the first book. An introduction to dynamics should take place by at least the middle of the first book. Consider using supplements. There is no rule that states you must use only one beginning band method. Further, it is not necessary, nor is it necessarily advisable, to use the same method for all supplements and advanced methods. A band director may choose one Book I method, a different publisher's beginning band arrangements, and another's method for Books II and III. The method book you choose is a tool. You may wish to use several tools to advance your students. Experiment and try different methods. You may find that one method that works very well in one school does not work efficiently or effectively in another. Do not limit yourself to the same band method for all of your teaching career. In addition to becoming boring and not much fun for the teacher, using the same method year after year may cause the students to miss out on a method that will advance more quickly than the present method you are using. Keep in touch with new ideas. It will be fun and educational for all.

Classroom Setup

Classroom setup will depend on your situation. If you are an itinerant teacher you may have to teach group or private lessons in classrooms, storage rooms, or the gymnasium, or if you are really lucky, a music room. Having a music room will be the exception, however.

For small groups in a classroom situation, you may wish to have the chairs in a straight row or in a semicircle like that shown in Fig. 1-1. The advantage of a semicircle is that it allows you to get to students quickly in order to help them. It also gives them an atmosphere similar to that in a band situation. However, you may not have space to set up your room in such a fashion. As many an itinerant teacher has learned, you may be in one classroom (sometimes very small) for one or two periods and then be asked to move to another room, or the gym, for the next few lessons. You will have to quickly set up the chairs and stands while students are entering the room. Consider the fastest and most efficient setup for each situation. Since time will be limited, you cannot spend more than a few minutes setting the chairs and stands in place. Whenever possible, have the students help you.

Figure 1-1
Small Group Lesson

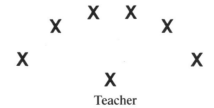

Teacher

If you are in a band hall teaching group lessons, you may choose to have students sit in their instrument sections or in the first row (Fig. 1-2). It should not matter which position you choose as long as you can quickly and easily help the students and keep control of the class. This is an important consideration. You do not want to put students in a position where you cannot easily see them, or put them too close to distractions such as percussion equipment. This is especially important during the first few lessons when students may be attending the class without an instrument.

Figure 1-2
Large Group Lesson

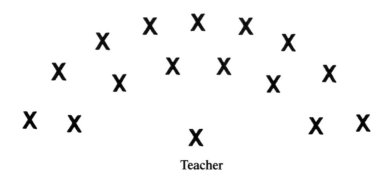

Teacher

The main considerations when designing your seating chart for full band rehearsal is your instrumentation and the strength of certain instrumental players. Figures 1-3 and 1-4 show various seating arrangements for a band rehearsal and concert. The fact that some instruments are missing is intentional. There will be situations where you may have no low brass or other instruments. The charts are suggestions that may be helpful to you. However, it is up to you to decide where the students should sit to produce the best possible ensemble sound. There is no right or wrong way to set up your band. If the students can play the music, and you have taught them to listen and play in tune, your band will sound good.

Figure 1-3
Band Rehearsal
Small Band

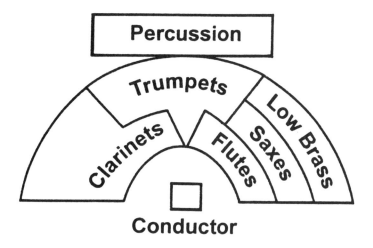

Note: Always put flutes up front or no one will be able to hear them.

Figure 1-4
Band Rehearsal
Large Group

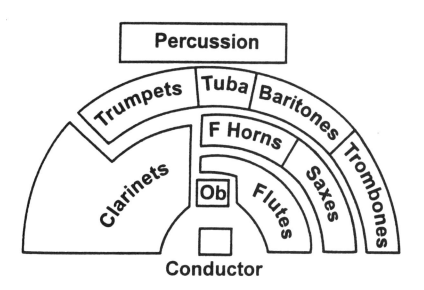

There is no set pattern for band chairs. You may need to put the F horns in front of the saxes or the percussion directly behind the clarinets. The final decision will be made according to the space available and how well certain sections play. If risers are available, put the trumpets first and on the highest risers. Put all low brass on risers if possible. If enough risers are available, you may wish to put F horns next to trumpets.

Teaching the Beginning Band Instruments

. . . .

Part 2 of the *Instrumental Music Teacher's Survival Kit* provides detailed guidelines, musical exercises and troubleshooting tips for teaching 12 basic band instruments: flute, clarinet, saxophone, trumpet, F horn, low brass (trombone, baritone, and tuba), drums, bells, oboe, and bassoon. Each instrumental section is complete and self-contained, including illustrated procedures and music for the first five lessons in a particular instrument, a troubleshooting chart with specific solutions to a variety of problems students experience in learning how to play the instrument, a fingering chart, and a quick checklist of key points covered in the first five lessons for that instrument.

For the teacher's convenience, directions for the flute, clarinet, saxophone, trumpet, low brass, and drums are organized for group instruction by lesson. They allow for new beginners up through Lessons 3 or 4, but assure the steady progress of "advanced" players. Directions for the other instruments, for which there are generally fewer beginners, are topically organized. The suggested music for each lesson is separately printed on one or more pages accompanying the particular lesson except for the F horn, bells, oboe, and bassoon, in which case it follows the lesson text. All of the music pages, and any other page of this resource, may be photocopied as many times as you need them for individual or group instruction.

BEGINNING FLUTE LESSONS

All of the instrumental music lessons in this resource except for the flute lessons have been written with the idea that the text can be accompanied by music from either a beginning band method book or the music pages provided here. Due to special concerns in teaching beginning flute lessons, however, I strongly encourage you to use the music written for these lessons. Because method books must be concerned with all instruments playing the same notes at the same time, they do not give adequate attention to the special needs of young flute players. If you use the first five lessons in the *Kit,* your students will be able to continue in the band method of your choice without delaying their progress. In fact, because their embouchures will be in such good condition, they will move very quickly through your chosen band method.

Flute Lesson 1 (Fig. 2-1)

Prepare the room in advance of the students' arrival. Chairs should be set up in a row, semicircle, or whatever style you like. That, in part, may be determined by how many students there are in the class. On the first day, you may have no idea how many students will show up for the flute lesson. Most likely only a few will have their instruments, but you may have to contend with more students. If necessary, set the chairs in two rows. Place six to eight chairs in the first row and the rest in the second row. If you know who is coming, have name tags taped to the backs of the chairs.

When the students enter the room, have the students with instruments sit in front. (If there are name tags, they should find their names.) Students with instruments should be in the first row. You may have two rows of students with instruments if there are more than six to eight students in the class. For future lessons, try not to have more than six flutes in a class. This will enable you to devote more time to each student, and the class will progress quickly. Inform the students not to open their cases until you have given them permission. This is a good time to state the rules. Let them know the deadline for obtaining an instrument, class conduct, the rules for returning to the regular classroom, and any penalties involved. Penalties may include detention, phone call to parents, and, if a problem continues, removal from the band program.

The first instruction to the students is how to distinguish the top of the case from the bottom of the case. As simple as it may seem, students do not consider this unless you tell them. The top of the case is usually the section with the brand name on it. However, some flutes have the brand name on both the top and bottom of the case. The handle is always on the bottom of the case. Some instrument manufacturers put handles on both the top and bottom of the case. In that situation, the latches will flip up to release the case. Tell the students not to open the case upside down because the instrument will fall out and possibly be damaged. The students should put the cases on the floor in front of them or to the side of their chairs. Students should not try to balance the cases on their laps while removing the instrument (Photo 2-1).

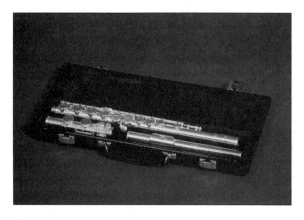

Photo 2-1

During the first lesson, and throughout the first week of practice, the students should play only the head joint. It is very important that they understand the reason for this. This practice will help to ensure that the muscles in their lips develop so they can obtain a good sound on the flute. If they try to hold the entire flute on the first day while making a sound, they will be too concerned with holding the flute up to their lips and will not be able to concentrate on making a good sound. It is important that you win their trust on this. Playing the entire flute during the first week will make it more difficult for students to become good flute players. Flute students should not worry about falling behind on lessons with the other instrumental students. Even though other instruments will be assembled and played on the first day, the flute students will quickly catch up with all the other classes, and will most likely pass them before the end of the school year. However, if they do not learn to make a good sound from the beginning, it will be very difficult to play the instrument, and it certainly will not be fun.

Embouchure

Instruct the students one at a time. The flute is not a soda bottle nor should it be played like one. The student should put his lips together. Tell him to close his mouth completely, but not tightly, the way he does when he should be listening to the teacher in class but instead is daydreaming. Have the student blow the

Figure 2-1
Music for Flute Lesson 1

Teach this lesson without showing the music to the student. Students should concentrate on producing a good sound. Attempting to read music will distract from all that is needed to produce a good sound.

High note.

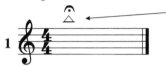 — This symbol indicates a high pitch, but no note in particular.

The note is sustained for a comfortable length of time. Counting is not necessary for the first note.

Head joint only.

Indicating a high pitch, but not a particular note.

Students should play the note four times in a steady count. All students not playing should count out loud with the band director.

indicating low note

Follow the same procedure as above.

Head joint only

Practice playing high and low.

Practice playing high and low notes, using the tongue to separate the notes.

Name your song:

ASSIGNMENT: Practice with the head joint only.
Play both high and low notes. Be able to control the sound so you can play high and low when you mean to.
Use your tongue to separate the notes.
Make up a song using high and low notes. You do not have to write out the notes.
Teacher: Be Enthusiastic at All Times!

air out through his lips (Photo 2-2). The lips should open as the air stream blows an opening for the air to escape. Do not pucker the lips, and do not smile. The opening in the lips is a result of blowing the air, not making any special shape. All of this is done without the flute up to the lips. After the student blows the air out properly, the teacher places the head joint up to the student's lips (Photo 2-3). Instruct the student not to blow until you tell him. Center the flute to the student's

Photo 2-2

lips. The top lip should not be over the opening of the flute. A natural position is the best so that the air blows over the hole. Not all the air will go directly into it. The student should use the syllable "pu," not "who," to blow the air out of his mouth. This will keep the aperture as small as possible. If the student has a teardrop lip, you may need to move the head joint into a position where the air stream will flow directly over the opening. The air stream will be split, so you will not be able to adjust the mouthpiece where the student may use all of his air. Never tell a student he or she has a teardrop lip. The student should not be made to feel that something is wrong with him or her. Also, the parents may call you, or, worse, the school board or their lawyer, to question your ability as a teacher and complain about the damage you have caused the child. After several lessons, you may offer the child with a teardrop lip the opportunity to change to another instrument. Some children will quickly take advantage of the opportunity to change to another instrument, and others will want to stay with the flute. The frustration may eventually be too much for some students, but there are students who will find the best embouchure for the flute and learn to play it very well.

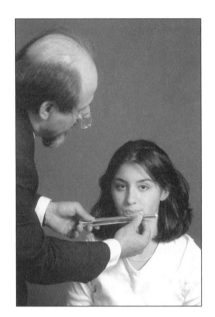

Photo 2-3

As soon as the student makes a sound, enthusiastically praise him. It does not have to be a perfect sound. Praise any sound he gets. Flute students need praise at this time. Build the student's confidence quickly by letting him know he is doing well. Once he gets a sound, have him do it again. You are still holding the flute, so if needed, adjust it to improve the sound. When the sound is at its best, have the student play the note several times in a row. Then remove the mouthpiece from his mouth, and quickly put it back into position and have him play again. He should get a sound easily. If not, move the mouthpiece into its proper position and have him play again. Then have the student put his hands at each end of the head joint, as shown in Photo 2-4. Be careful that his right hand does not cover up the opening at the end of the flute. Have him play again while both of you are holding the flute. Once he gets a sound, remove your hands from the head joint and ask him to play again. If he does not get a sound, push the head joint against his lower lip with your finger or thumb (see Photo 2-5). Often a student will not push the head joint firmly against his lip. Your gesture of adding pressure with your finger will let him know how firmly he must push the flute mouthpiece against his lips. After he has produced a good sound several times, ask him to put the head

Photo 2-4

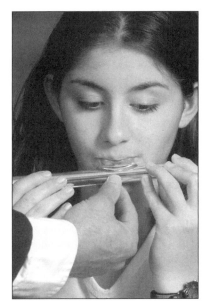

Photo 2-5

joint in his lap. Then quickly ask him to put it back up to his lips and play. You want to do this quickly so he will remember where to put the opening of the mouthpiece to his lips. The opening of the flute should be close to or on the bottom portion of his lip (see Photo 2-4). It should not go below his lips or close to the aperture of his mouth. Push the flute up against his lips if he needs your assistance. Once he has produced a good sound, ask him again to put the flute in his lap and back up again and play. Do this several times in a row, so he will remember where to put the mouthpiece against his lips. This procedure should be done for every student in the class. You must move quickly. Try to devote enough time so every student can produce a good sound.

If a particular student has a problem getting a sound out of the head joint no matter what you do, then go on to the next student. Tell her you will get right back to her, but you want to keep things moving and she will get a sound today. If you work too long with one child, it may embarrass or humiliate her, and you could end up with a crying child. By going on, you also allow her to see how and what other students are doing to produce a sound. When you get back to her, she may produce a tone for you. Not every student will have the same or as good a sound. That is okay. The sounds will improve with practice. You must be encouraging to everyone!

If the class is small, you may have time left. You may show them how to make different sounds by putting your hand over the end of the head joint and making the sound of a tugboat (Photo 2-6). Different sounds can also be made by putting the finger deeper into the head joint making a slide whistle sound. "Mary Had a Little Lamb" may be played by using the index finger and inserting it into the opening of the head joint. If you can, play the song for the students and give them a chance to try to play the song. It is doubtful that anyone will be able to play the song, but they will have fun making sounds with the head joint.

Regardless of whether you have the students play "Mary Had a Little Lamb" using the head joint only, it is important to have them practice making both high and low tones using the head joint alone. Ask a student to make a high sound, then a low sound. Make sure the students can distinguish the difference in the two pitches. Ask the stu-

Photo 2-6

dents which tone is high, and which tone is low. This will develop both the ear and the embouchure. You may make a game out of this by asking the students to hold a high note as long as possible with a good sound. Have a contest to see who can hold the note the longest. Do the same with the low notes. You may even ask students to make up their own songs with the head joint using a combination of high and low sounds. This can be a great deal of fun for the students while they strengthen their embouchures, better develop their ears, and extend their imaginations. It should also make the first week of practice more enjoyable.

Regardless of how much time you have left, do not have the students play the entire flute. Continue to work with the head joint and practice making better sounds with the head joint only. Though it will be tempting to play the entire instrument, it is extremely important that students play the head joint only for the first lesson and for the first week of practice. You may show them how to assemble the instrument. However, do this only so they will not damage the instrument when they get home and show it to their parents. It is important that they understand that playing the head joint only will strengthen the muscles in their lips. Thus, they will have a better sound, become better flute players, and have fun playing the flute.

Always give a specific assignment. Tell the students to practice with the head joint only for at least 10 minutes a day. (They may practice longer.) Suggest that they practice 10 minutes alone in their room, or wherever they may practice, and then practice during the commercials while watching television. Even if they do not produce a sound when they get home, it is extremely important to keep trying. Remind them to push the flute mouthpiece against their lips to help produce the sound. Even if they do not get a sound all week, they must keep trying. Everyone made a good sound in class, so they will all make one again, but they must keep trying in order to make the muscles in their lips strong enough to play the flute. As the students leave the room, tell them how pleased you are with their sound today, and that you look forward to seeing them next week.

Flute Lesson 2 (Fig. 2-2)

One common problem with teaching group lessons is that while some students are scheduled for their second lesson with their instruments, and are ready to advance, other students are receiving their instruments for the first time. It is important to keep all the students busy and interested. You do not want to forget about one student while you are busy trying to correct the problems of another.

When the students enter the room, have the students who played the previous week take out the head joint only. One at a time, have each student make a sound with the head joint. As you review with these students how to obtain a good sound, remind the new students how to tell the top of the case from the bottom of the case. The instrument case should be put on the floor to remove the head joint. All the students who played the prior week, who shall be referred to from now on as advanced, should make a sound before you proceed with the beginners.

Show all the students the three parts of the flute. Introduce the head joint, body joint, and foot joint to the students. The advanced students are the only students who will assemble the flute; the beginners should watch. You will need to stress to the beginners that for the first week they will play only the head joint, just like the students who started the previous week. Then they will quickly catch up with the other students. Developing a good sound first is extremely important and must be done without the entire flute.

Instrument assembly is very important. However, before teaching the students to assemble the instrument, check new flutes for packing materials, such as small corks, that may still be in between the keys and braces between the body and rods of the flute. The first two pieces to be put together are the head joint and the body joint. Demonstrate how to put these two parts together. Tell the students that they will hold the body part above the keys and the head joint at the bottom away from the mouthpiece. The two parts should come together fairly easily by twisting the two parts back and forth as they are pushed together, as in Photo 2-7. (You should demonstrate this to the students.) Then line up the hole of the head joint with the first key on the body as shown in Photo 2-8 on page 16. The only proper and accurate way to line up these two parts is to use your eyes. Do not use the lines at the edge of the body and head joints which may be on some flutes. After you have demonstrated this, have the advanced students put these two parts together. You should help the students as they perform this task.

After the advanced students have put these two parts together, direct your attention to the new students (now referred to as beginners). Have each beginner make a sound using the head joint only.

Photo 2-7

Figure 2-2
Music for Flute Lesson 2

Teach this lesson without showing the music to the student. Students should concentrate on producing a good sound. Attempting to read music will distract from all that is needed to produce a good sound.

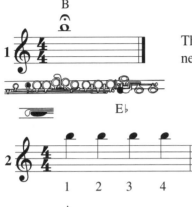

The note is sustained for a comfortable length of time. Counting is not necessary for the first note.

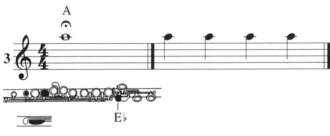

Students should play the note four times in a steady count. All students not playing should count out loud with the band director.

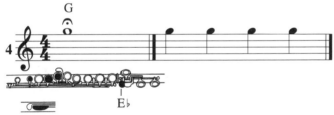

Follow the same procedure as above.

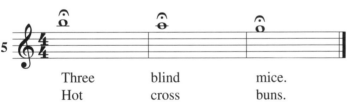

Follow the same procedure as above.

First song. Counting rhythms is not necessary the first time. A quick accomplishment is paramount.

Three   blind   mice.
Hot   cross   buns.

Mary Had a Little Lamb

ASSIGNMENT: First, hold each note, then play each note four times.
Play "Three Blind Mice" or "Hot Cross Buns."
Challenge: Who can play "Mary Had a Little Lamb" using the three notes learned today? The teacher may play the song as an example.
Be Enthusiastic!

Follow the same procedures you used with the students the previous week. It is extremely important that you emphasize to them the importance of practicing with the head joint only for one entire week.

As soon as all the new students have made a sound on the head joint, continue to show the students how to assemble the instrument. Demonstrate how to put the foot onto the body. Hold the body in the left hand with the bottom in the palm of your left hand. The bottom of the flute is the side opposite the row of keys (see Photo 2-9). The keys should be facing up. Wrap the fingers around the keys. Tell the students they can make a firm grip without damaging the keys. Hold the foot with the right hand below the keys and over the pads near the bottom of the foot. The two parts should come together in the same manner as the body and head joints (Photo 2-9). Adjust the E♭ key (baby finger) according to the length of the little finger. Have each student put his/her instrument together and adjust this for each student's hand size.

Photo 2-8

Photo 2-9

Turn your attention again to the beginning students. Have each student make a sound (with the head joint only), one at a time. If a student has a problem, take the time necessary to correct it. Usually if a student cannot make a sound, pushing the mouthpiece closer to his lips will produce a good sound. You may also need to shift the flute to the center of his lips. Move quickly and efficiently. Be careful not to spend too much time on one student. After students have made sounds separately, have them all play together. Act as if this is the most wonderful sound you have ever heard. The students are nervous and they need encouragement. Do not hesitate to give them more encouragement than you may think they need.

Now it is time to teach the advanced students how to play the entire instrument. Ask the first child to hand his instrument to you. He should hold out his left hand with the palm up. Bend the fingers slightly at the knuckles so you will be able to place the flute on the knuckle of the index finger (Photo 2-10). The finger should bend so the flute will rest on the knuckle while the first finger wraps around the flute so the first key can be depressed (Photo 2-11). Adjust the hand and flute positions to help bal-

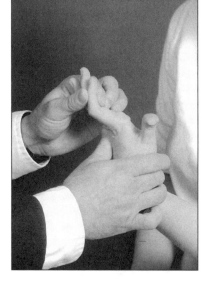

Photo 2-10

Photo 2-11

Photo 2-12

ance the flute. The left thumb should be placed on the long thumb key, which is just below the key that may be called the "golf club key." It may be a silly term, but it helps the students remember which key to push during the first weeks of study. Place the right thumb under the body between the F and E keys. Adjust the foot joint so the little finger can comfortably reach the E♭ key (Photo 2-12).

The first note the student will play is high B. This is an easy note for the student to play, and it is easy for the student to hold the flute while he plays it. Have the student hold the instrument properly, as you have just shown him. Gently put the flute up to the student's lips (Photo 2-13). You must place the instrument in the proper position so the student can produce a good sound. When the mouthpiece is in the proper position and the first finger, thumb, and baby finger (E♭ key) are depressed completely, ask the student to blow air out of his mouth into the flute just like playing the head joint only. The lips should start closed and the student should blow the air out by using the syllable "pu." Continue to hold the flute up to his lips. You may need to add more pressure against the lips or move the mouthpiece slightly to the right or left until a sound is produced. Make sure the student produces a high B. If a low B is played first, ask him to make it sound higher. Many times, this is all that is necessary to produce a higher sound. If that does not work, ask the student to put his lips tightly together and blow just as he did when playing the head joint only. Sometimes a student is not blowing enough air into the instrument. Ask him to blow a little harder. If he blows too hard, ask him to blow not so hard, but forcefully. Do not discuss air support at this time. Eventually, he will get the high B.

There are several reasons for starting with a high B as opposed to a low B. Producing a high note first makes the student start with a closed aperture, thus strengthening the lip muscles and producing a focused sound. Also, it is easier to start with a higher note and a tighter embouchure and move to a more relaxed position. If a student starts playing a lower note, the aperture is likely to be more open and the sound will be airy. After the first student has played the high B, tell him that note is B. Then ask him,

Photo 2-13

"What is that note?" He should answer B. If he cannot remember, tell him the name of it again and ask him to repeat it. Then have him play the note one more time. Have each beginning student play high B. This lesson should be done without the music. The student's concentration should be strictly on holding the instrument and producing a good sound. If you have a large group learning to play the entire flute, have the beginners play the head joint in between instructions for the advanced students. Keep the students involved. Do not allow anyone to sit without participating for more than five minutes.

Once all the advanced students have played B separately, have them all play it together. Compliment their sound. In the same manner as above, demonstrate how to play A. Next show the students how to play G and have them each play G. It will be difficult to accomplish all this in one half-hour lesson. You must move quickly and efficiently at all times. It is most important that all beginners get a clear sound on the head joint, and that the advanced students play at least the B as clearly as possible. It doesn't have to be perfect, but the better the sound, the better chances are for continued success. If you run out of time before the advanced students can play A and G, just show them the fingerings. Make sure they know to skip the key in between the index and middle fingers. If they can play the first three notes, then they have played their first song: "Three Blind Mice." Tell them they can also play "Mary Had a Little Lamb" by using only those notes. It is very unlikely that you will progress any further than this in the second lesson. However, no matter how well they do, do not show students how to play more than these three notes. They need to concentrate on producing a good sound, holding the flute properly, and playing high notes. You may also inform them that an easy way to remember the three notes they have just played is to spell the word "bag."

As always, give a specific assignment. Instruct the beginners to play with the head joint only, just as the advanced students did the previous week. It will be tempting, but they should not play the entire flute for the first week. Muscle development is essential for a good sound. They may make different sounds using the head joint only, just as you demonstrated to the advanced students the previous week.

The advanced students should practice first with the head joint only. After about five minutes, the entire instrument may be put together. Suggest that the students practice in front of a mirror so they can see when the mouthpiece is in the correct position. Also, the flute should not be pointing up in the air, but slightly down. The head or body should not be leaning down too far (see Photo 2-12). Advanced students should try to practice 30 minutes a day. You may want to suggest that the students practice in two 15-minute sessions if they feel lightheaded (some students may feel this way in the first weeks). But, regardless of how much time they practice, daily practice is essential.

As the students leave the room, compliment their playing. Be excited about their progress. Your excitement for their success will encourage them to practice and stick with the instrument. It is crucial to build enthusiasm every time you see them.

Flute Lesson 3 (Figs. 2-3 and 2-4)

The real art of teaching group lessons now comes into play. You will have students who have never played flute before, students who have played with the head joint only, and students who can now play the first three high notes with the entire flute assembled. You must be organized and very aware of the time in order to make sure everyone plays the instrument and learns something new in this lesson.

As the students enter the room, have the advanced students sit together. The students who played the head joint only should sit in one area, while the students who are receiving their instruments for the first time should sit next to each other in another area. While the advanced students are assembling their instruments, have the students who played the head joint only take out that part of the instrument. The new students, or beginners, should sit with their instruments in their laps. The cases should not be opened until you instruct them to do so.

Have each student who played with the head joint only the previous week try to make a good sustained sound on the head joint. You may tell them to hold it for four beats or just tell them to hold the note. As each student is doing this, start instructing the beginners on how to open the case. Remember, the handle is on the bottom half and the latches always open in an upward direction.

About this time, the advanced students should have their instruments assembled. Ask the first student to play the high B he learned the previous week. If he is having trouble producing a sound, look at the position of the mouthpiece. The opening should be lined up with the center of his mouth unless he has a teardrop lip, which makes the mouthpiece align slightly to the left or right of center. Gently move the flute into position so the flute will make a sound. You may also need to push the mouthpiece firmly against the lips. Once he feels how the sound comes out of the instrument with added pressure, he will do the same. The student can apply additional pressure by pushing out (or forward) with the right hand and in (or in the direction of the face) with the left hand. Have each advanced student play the high B. If there are problems and this process takes more than five minutes, then have the students who played with the mouthpiece only the prior week once again produce a sound on the head joint. During this time, make sure all beginners have opened the case properly, taken the head joint out of the case, and put the case on the floor under or to the side of their chairs. Follow the same procedure as in the previous lessons.

Figure 2-3
Music for Flute Lesson 3

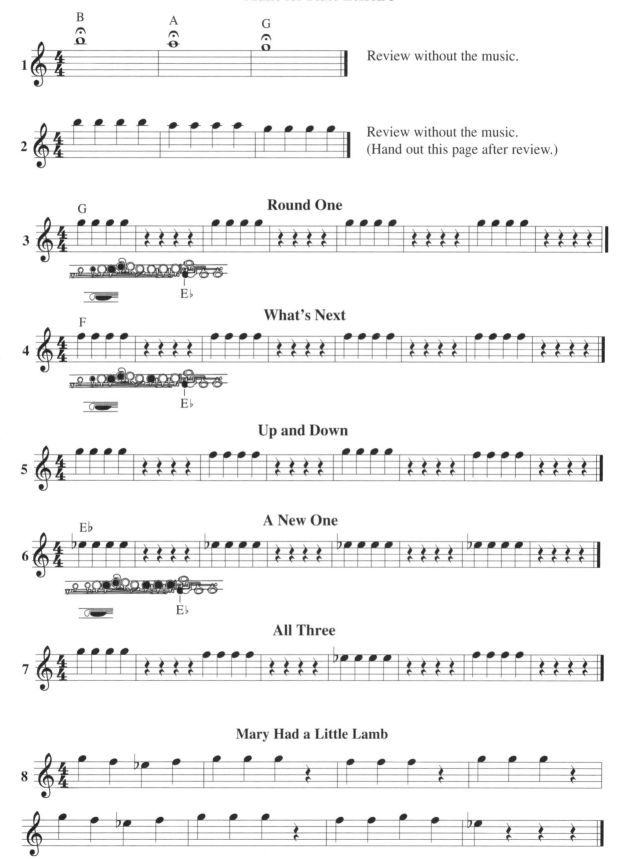

Review without the music.

Review without the music.
(Hand out this page after review.)

Round One

What's Next

Up and Down

A New One

All Three

Mary Had a Little Lamb

Figure 2-4
Music for Flute Lesson 3A
(for more high note practice)

Review without the music.

Review without the music.
(Hand out this page after review.)

Round One–A

What's Next, Doc?

Up and Down, Again

Gee Whiz

Three in One

Mary Had a Little Lamb–In the High Pastures!

Posture is very important for all instrumental students. It is critical for the flutes. Take a moment to ask all students to sit on the edge of their chairs with both feet flat on the floor. The students should sit at a slight angle so they can comfortably hold the flute and face the music and conductor at the same time (Photo 2-14).

Photo 2-14

Show the new students how to produce a sound using the head joint only. As in the previous lessons, take the head joint from the student, place it up to his lips, and have him close his mouth completely. Once the head joint is in position and the lips are closed, then have him blow air out of his mouth using the syllable "pu." As he blows air into the flute, you may have to adjust the head joint so a sound will be produced. It does not have to be perfect. If it is a clear sound, go on to the next student. Have each new student play a sound on the head joint.

Next you are going to do two things at once. You are going to review the notes A and G with the advanced students while showing the students who played the head joint only the previous week how to assemble the flute. The advanced students should play an A. How many students there are in the class and how much time has passed in the lesson will determine whether they play as a group or individually. Show the beginning students how to assemble the flute. Next, have the advanced students play a G. While reviewing these two notes with the advanced students, you will continue to help the other students assemble their flutes.

Now turn your attention to the students who have just assembled their instruments. As in the previous lessons, hand the flute to each student so the flute rests on the knuckle of his first finger, on his left hand. Once the flute is resting on his knuckle, have him put his thumb on the long thumb key, and the first finger should wrap around the flute and depress the first key. The thumb of the right hand goes under the flute between the F and E keys. The little finger presses against the E♭ key. Guide the mouthpiece to the lips of the student. Place the mouthpiece in the center (or the best position) of the lip so a sound will easily be played. Put enough pressure against the lip so the air will go into the flute. When the first finger, thumb, and baby finger are pressing the correct keys, and the mouth is closed, tell the student to blow the air out just as when he played the head joint only. Adjust the mouthpiece as necessary to help the student produce a sound. Once a sound is made, praise his sound and go to the next student. If you do not have too many students, you should be able to complete this process in about five minutes. You may wish to have the advanced students play G while you are showing these new students how to play the entire instrument. After they have played their first note, make sure they know they have played a high B. If a student does produce a low B, tell him to make the sound higher.

Have all students look at line 3 of Lesson 3 (Fig. 2-3, page 19). (If you feel you must use the heterogeneous band book, then show the students how to play an F. Instead of playing a G, teach the students how to read and play the line with an F in it. If the book is using lower notes, such as D, C, or B♭, start with the highest note.) Even though all the students are not going to play from Lesson 3 at this lesson, they may all look at the music and start learning to read the notes. Tell the students that G is placed just above the staff. Notes that are filled in and have a stem are called *quarter notes*. Quarter notes receive one beat each. Have the students play only the first measure of line 3. Explain that a *measure* is a space in between two bars. Watch their eyes as they play. Make sure they are looking at the music. Tell them that the four wiggly lines are *quarter rests* which receive one beat each. The first measure has four Gs and the second measure has four beats or foot taps of rest. Have the students play these two measures. Try to have the students tap their toes with the notes and rests. It is a good idea to get them tapping their toes from the very beginning—foot tapping is the basic measurement for note duration, and it helps the students feel the beat. After they have played the first two measures, have the students play the entire line. Watch their eyes. If they are looking at other students or their flute, or their eyes are wandering around, they are not reading music. This is common. Many students do not associate reading music with reading sentences, from left to right. Have the students play the line again. Walk up to a student who was not looking at the music and point to the notes with your baton as the notes progress. This will help the students see how to keep up with the notes as they are reading music. You may need to do this for several students. Repeat the line until everyone appears to be reading the music. A good test is to have everyone play the line again, and conduct. However, do not stop conducting at the end of the line. Pretend there is another note after the last four rests. If students play, you know they really do not understand about reading music. Make a game of this so it is fun. "Who will be the next person to play more notes than on the line?" The students enjoy this and it makes a very good point while having fun.

Have the students look at line 4. (You must move quickly because the class time is coming to an end.) Show them the difference between G and F (F is on the top line, G is above the staff). Play line 4 from Lesson 3 (Fig. 2-3, page 19). Follow the same procedure as above. If there is time, play line 5. If not, quickly show the students how to play E♭. You may not have time to go into the details of the line. Cover as much music as time allows.

By this point, you should be about out of time. Review with the beginners how to play a sound on the head joint only. If possible, have all beginners make a sound with the head joint. Review the three new notes with the students who just assembled the instrument for the first time, and review the new notes for the advanced students. It will be rare that you can accomplish this much if the class has more than six students in it. Try to never have flute classes in groups of more than six. Flute students need more attention in the first few lessons than students of most other instruments.

As with all instruments and all lessons, give students a specific assignment. Beginning students should play with the head joint only. Emphasize how important it is for them to develop the muscles in their lips before they start trying to hold the flute up to their lips. The next group should practice with the head joint only for about five to ten minutes a day and, only then, practice their three new notes: B, A, G. These students may practice Lesson 3 after they have played the three notes and they feel they have achieved a good sound. However, stress to them that obtaining a good sound is more important than learning as many notes as possible in the first few lessons. The advanced students should also practice with the head joint for five to ten minutes a day, then review B, A, G, and Lesson 3A. Lesson 3A is a continuation of the exercises playing high notes. They should practice as much of the page as possible. If they cannot remember everything they learned today, that is understandable. Be positive and tell them to keep trying, and to concentrate on developing a good embouchure and hand position. Early success for the flute is crucial. If the students develop a strong centered sound, they will become good flute players. Should you allow them to put the entire flute together on the first lesson, play low notes first, and not develop a good sound from the very start, they may have an airy, nondirected air flow. This habit may be very hard to correct once developed, and students may become discouraged and quit.

Be positive. Tell the class how pleased you are with their sound and how you look forward to teaching them next week. Make them feel good about their accomplishments today.

Flute Lesson 4 (Figs. 2-5 and 2-6)

If you have students attending a flute session for the first time, it is best to reschedule them to a separate group. This lesson will assume you cannot reschedule the classes, but you will be more successful if you do not have beginners in the group. It will slow the progress of the entire group, especially if more than one student is learning for the first time. Also, the new students will be so far behind, they may be discouraged and may eventually quit because of embarrassment or feeling as though they cannot play the flute very well.

As students enter the room, the advanced students should assemble their instruments immediately. As soon as everyone is seated, instruct the new students on how to tell the top of the case from the bottom

Figure 2-5
Music for Flute Lesson 4

Figure 2-6
Music for Flute Lesson 4A
(more high note practice)

A Fabulous Note

All the Way Up

Down the Tall Ladder

Over the Tall Hill

More High Notes to Play

Oops! Watch Out for That Rest!

Round and Round, Again

High Waves

of the case. Once that is accomplished, have them remove the head joint from the case and put the case out of the way.

Have the students who were beginners the previous week play a note using the head joint only. Assist anyone who needs help in producing a sound. Once these students have produced a good sound, ask the advanced students to play B, A, and G as a group. If a child is having a problem, try to correct it promptly. You do not have a lot of time to spend on each student individually, so move quickly.

If you are starting beginners for the first time this week, hopefully you will have only a few new students. As in previous lessons, take the head joint from the first beginning student. Place the mouthpiece in its proper position, instruct him to close his lips tightly, and blow using the syllable "pu." Adjust the position of the flute until the student produces a sound. Have each new student play the head joint. Praise each student as soon as he makes a sound, and then praise the entire group.

At this point you will be about 10 to 15 minutes into the lesson. Keep the class moving. The next group to which you must attend are the students who played the head joint only the prior week. Show the students how to put the head joint onto the body joint of the flute. Next, have them attach the foot joint to the body joint. Once the instrument is assembled, take the flute from the first student. Have the student hold out his left hand. Set the flute on the knuckle of his first finger between the first keys on the top of the flute and where the thumb will comfortably set on the thumb key. The student should press the thumb key and the first finger down completely. The right hand goes over the flute. The thumb is placed under the flute in between the F and E keys. Adjust the E♭ key so the little finger comfortably reaches this key. The little finger should press down the E♭ key. The teacher now places the mouthpiece against the student's lips. Adjust the mouthpiece to the center of the student's lips so he will have the best chance of obtaining a sound. Then check the angle of the flute; it should not be straight across or slanted up, but with a slight angle downward. Make sure the fingers are pressing the keys down completely. When everything is ready, tell the student to play. Adjust the head joint as necessary so the student will produce a sound. Notice whether the flute is too high on the lip or too low or far away from the aperture. Remember to press the mouthpiece firmly against the student's lips. Have each new student produce a sound this way. Tell him he has just played a B. Have everyone, advanced and beginners, play the B together (students with the head joint only obviously cannot do this). Show the students how to play A, and then play it together. Then show them how to play a G. Have all the students play B, A, G. They have thus played their first tune: "Three Blind Mice."

The advanced students should put Lesson 3 on their stands. Review some of the lines on the page or finish the page if you did not finish the previous week. Always keep an eye out for students not looking at the music. Point to the notes for students who do not appear to be reading the music. If a student is having trouble producing a sound, walk over to the student and apply pressure to the mouthpiece by pushing it closer to his or her lips with your finger. As you review Lesson 3, have all the students look at the notes on the page. The beginners will not know how to play the notes, but they will learn to read the notes, which will help their progress at home and in lessons.

Once you have finished reviewing Lesson 3, have everyone look at Lesson 4. Describe the difference between D and E♭. Point out the difference between the two notes on the staff, and the difference in playing the two notes. Have the advanced students play line 1. If there is time, have the students play more lines.

You must be careful not to spend the rest of the period with the advanced students. The students who just learned to put the instrument together must learn to play Lesson 3. At the top of the page are the three notes they just learned to play. Carefully explain to them how to read the three notes. Have all students play the B together. Then, have them play A and G. Do not yet have the students count the rhythms. They should hold the notes as long as you conduct them to do so. Then have everyone look at line 2. Discuss the quarter note rhythm with them. Have all of the students play the first four Bs together, then the As, and finally the Gs in the same manner. Normally this would be done without the music, but now you are trying to catch up with the advanced students, so they need to see the notes and begin to learn to read them. Now have all the students play line 3. This is a good review for the advanced students and it keeps them busy and practicing. As in the previous lesson (and all lessons), watch the students' eyes to make sure they are looking at the music. Show the students how to play F. Make sure they see the difference between G and F. Although it may seem obvious to you, many students do not see how the different notes are marked on a musical staff. In many cases, you must point this out.

The lesson should be coming to a close by this time. However, if you have time, instruct the beginners to make a sound on the head joint. Little time has been spent with the beginners in this lesson. You cannot afford to spend a lot of time with them at this point; if you hold the other students back, they may quit. The danger is, of course, that the beginners will not learn quickly enough, and they will also quit. However, since they need only play the head joint for the first week, you do not need to spend a lot of time with them. As mentioned earlier in this lesson, it is much better to reschedule beginners to other groups than to continue to add more students. Adding more students could cause your advanced students to become bored and drop out.

Give a very specific assignment to all students. The beginners should practice with the head joint only for the entire week. Students who just put the instrument together should practice with the head joint first for about five minutes. Then they should practice the three notes B, A, and G. First, they should play each note and sustain it, then play four tones on each note. Many beginner books have the students play whole notes first, but it is easier for a young student to play four notes and count to four in his or her head than to hold one note for four counts. That is an abstract thought and not an easy accomplishment for elementary students. After they have reviewed the first three notes, they may practice all of Lesson 3. They should not worry if they cannot play all of the page by the end of the week. What is important is daily practice. Advanced students should review Lesson 3 and play as much of Lesson 4 and 4A as possible. The students may always look ahead and play more than what is assigned. However, it is daily practice that will lead to strong muscle development and a good tone.

As the students leave, compliment their progress. Remember, your enthusiasm for their progress will keep them practicing.

Flute Lesson 5 (Figs. 2-7 and 2-8)

If any new students should ask to start the flute during this lesson, either reschedule the lesson with a group of new beginners or tell them it is too late in the school year to start an instrument. Anyone just learning to play is going to have a very difficult time catching up with this group. Allowing a new student to join will also greatly slow the progress of the students whose parents were responsible enough to obtain an instrument at the assigned time. If you must allow a new student to participate with this group, quickly show him or her how to make a sound on the head joint, but spend most of the class time with the other students.

When the students enter the room, they should assemble their instruments immediately. If anyone was a beginner the previous week, have him take out his head joint and play a note. Instruct him on flute assembly as the other students are assembling their instruments and starting to play their lesson.

Have all the students who have played the entire flute play "Mary Had a Little Lamb" from Lesson 3 together. After this review, start playing Lesson 4. Play the first three lines. Continue to watch for students who are not reading music. Point to the notes with your baton to help them keep up with the music.

Before playing line 4, finish your instructions on assembling the flute for the beginning students. Because of the amount of material to be covered in this lesson, you may decide to help assemble the instruments for these students. If this does not take very long, show them how to hold the flute and play B. Follow the same process as in the previous lessons.

Have the advanced students start with line 4 and continue a few more lines down the page (for about five minutes). Make sure they are learning to count the rhythms. The music in this resource is designed to make the students aware of rhythms and when to play and when to rest. If they are faking it, it will become very obvious. Make a game of this, and see who will play in the rest first. Students will laugh and have fun waiting to see who forgets to count, but you will be making a very important point: Count the

Figure 2-7
Music for Flute Lesson 5

Remember This One

An Old Friend

Twice as Long

Say It Again

Hot Cross Buns

Go Tell Aunt Rhodie

Skippin' Around

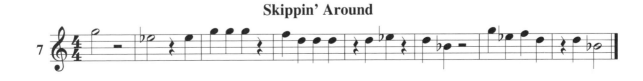

rhythms and notes at all times. I strongly encourage you to have your students tap their toes. It is very important that they learn to feel the beat. I am always very pleased to hear little feet tapping away at their first concert because this means the students are starting to feel the music. If they're tapping their toes, they're having fun.

Show the students who have just assembled their instruments for the first time how to play A and G (assuming they have already played B). If they progress quickly, have them put Lesson 3 on their stands. Have them look at line 3. Discuss the note placement on the staff and how rhythms are played. All the students should play line 3 together.

The advanced students should now continue playing Lesson 4. If possible, try to finish the page. Allow the students who just learned to play the notes A and G to follow and play along, but focus your attention on the advanced students. The tone quality of these students should begin to stabilize and to sound clear. If that is the case, make sure they are starting to use their tongues rather than their breath to separate the notes. At first, suggest that they say, "tu, tu, tu, tu," when playing notes. If that does not work, tell the student to put his or her tongue against the top teeth before starting the note with the syllable "tu." Have the student say the syllable without the flute up to her lips first. Then have the student try to play the notes using that technique.

Finally, Figure 2-8 provides one surefire way to get students to stop breathing before every note. This exercise works for all instruments. (Students should not see the exercise when playing it for the first time. You want them to concentrate on making the rhythm you are singing, not on trying to read a new rhythm.)

First, have the students play an easy note and hold the note for at least five beats. Then ask the students to play exactly the rhythm you sing. You will sing, on their pitch, four sixteenth notes and a whole note. The students might try to breathe before every note, but it is impossible to breathe and play the notes that fast. If they somehow manage to take a breath before every note, then sing the sixteenth notes faster. They will find out they cannot separate the notes with their breath or by making motions with their throats or lips. After the students can accomplish that rhythm, sing three eighth notes triplets and a whole note. Have the students play that pattern.

The next pattern to sing and have them play is four eighth notes and a whole note. Finally, sing four quarter notes. If at any time a student starts to breathe in between the notes, speed the rhythm to a tempo where he cannot fit in a breath. You may have to do this every week for a while with a student, but once he understands how to use the tongue to separate the notes, you will not have to worry about this again. If a student just cannot get the concept of using his or her tongue, go on to the next student. Sometimes, the student having a problem will see how to use her tongue by watching and hearing other students do this correctly. Be careful not to stay too long with one student. The student will become embarrassed, possibly humiliated, and will possibly want to quit the band. Whenever anything in music reaches a strong frustration point, continue to the next part of the lesson. Sometimes students need a few minutes (or days) to see how to perform a task. If a student can play repeated notes using her tongue but still breathes whenever she changes notes, use the same exercise as stated above. This time, make the last note you sing a different note. There must be no hesitation between the final two notes. Once the student sees how easy it is to tongue and play a different note, he or she will do it without thinking.

Be sure to save some time to have the students who just learned to play with the assembled flute play the remaining new notes from Lesson 3. Play at least two lines from this page, and more if at all possible. Tell these students not to worry. They will catch up with the other students in their class if they practice. Now that they can play notes on the flute, progress will come quickly.

You most likely will not be able to play all of Lesson 5 with the advanced class during this lesson. Discuss the half notes and half rests on this page. Also, make sure students see the repeat dots at the end of line 4. They should understand that when they see those dots at the end of the line, it means to play the line again. It is important that whenever you conduct lines with repeat dots, you insist that the students play the repeats. Otherwise they will ignore the dots, since you are demonstrating their lack of importance by not playing the line again.

Figure 2-8
Learning Not to Breathe Before Every Note

All on the Same Note

Huc– kle- ber– ry pie

(Students may think these words to play the rhythms quickly.)

pine– ap– ple pie

ap– ple ap– ple pie

pie   pie   pie   pie   pie

Changing the Last Note

If you started new students this week, you will have to show them how to play the head joint in between instructing the other students how to play the new lessons in this book. If you watch your time closely, you can make sure everyone plays his or her instrument. This is extremely important: Every student must play his or her instrument every lesson.

Give a specific assignment. The advanced students should practice all of Lesson 5. If they feel they are doing that well, they may start to look in the beginning band method book. Tell them what page would be best on which to start. The lessons included in this resource are designed to have the students continue in the beginning band method without having to go back to the first page in the beginning band method book. The students who just assembled the instrument today should play all of Lesson 3 and try to play as much of the other lessons as possible. It is still a good idea for every student to spend a few minutes a day playing only the head joint before assembling the entire flute and playing the new lessons out of the book. If you had new students this week, they should play with the head joint only.

Be positive. Be enthusiastic. In every lesson of the year, you must show the students how much you enjoy teaching music. This is what will keep them going when the going gets rough!

About Intonation

If the advanced students' tones are stabilizing, introduce tuning to them. The teacher should adjust the head joints for them, but help the students to hear high and low pitches. If they are not ready by Lesson 5 (which often will be the case), as soon as the students can produce a steady and clear sound, tune their flutes. You must work on good intonation from the very beginning or your band will never play in tune.

About Instrument Quality

It is extremely important that a beginning student have a good quality instrument in good playing condition. If you see a student come to a lesson with a brand you know to be of poor quality and/or the instrument is not in good playing condition, call the parents that day or evening. Let them know their child has little to no chance of success with that instrument in its current condition. Recommend a reputable dealer or repair person. The important issue is to let the parent know and understand that if the instrument is incapable of making a good sound, or any sound, neither will their child. Be diplomatic so they do not feel you are criticizing them personally. Many parents have no idea whether a musical instrument is in good playing condition, or if the brand is of poor quality. Be informative and helpful.

Troubleshooting the Flute

PROBLEM	CAUSE	SOLUTION
No sound	1. Instrument condition	Make sure the flute is in playing condition. Some brands will never play well. Check springs for trill keys and on stack. Check screws, especially on old flutes.
	2. Mouthpiece placement	(a) Center mouthpiece so air stream is blowing directly over the opening of the mouthpiece (directly under the aperture). If a teardrop lip is present, adjust so one of the streams is blowing over the mouthpiece opening.
		(b) Mouthpiece too high or too low on lip. Adjust the mouthpiece so the edge of the mouthpiece is at the edge of the lip.
	3. Aperture too open	Hole of the flute facing up, not toward the student. Have student start with mouth closed. Say syllable "pu" to start air stream. Do not say "who." (That starts with a wide open aperture.)
	4. Air direction	(a) The student may have the air stream blowing completely over the mouthpiece opening. Tell the student to direct the stream down a little more.
		(b) The student may have too much of the air stream going directly into the flute. Tell the student not to play into the flute like a soda bottle, but to blow the air over the hole saying "pu."
		(c) Directors: Please continue to check for the above as the students continue to progress, especially the position of the mouthpiece.
Unfocused sound	1. Embouchure	See Nos. 2, 3, and 4 above.
	2. Air support	(a) You should not discuss air support with an elementary student during the first few lessons. The student will not understand what you are saying, and you will only confuse him.
		(b) Tell the student to blow harder.
		(c) Put lips tightly together and blow the air out with more force.
		(d) Use this exercise to focus air stream (good for all instruments): Get a small sheet of paper about 3"× 5" or 6". Take the sheet of paper in one hand, holding it with the thumb and first finger. Point the paper directly toward the floor. Keep the other fingers parallel to the floor. These fingers should touch the wall, remaining straight, with the paper still pointing directly toward the floor. Now the paper will be about $2\frac{1}{2}$" to 3" from the wall. At arm's length, have the student try

to blow air out of his or her mouth and pin the paper against the wall with the air stream. At first the student will not be able to do this. The air will be moving up and down and out of control. But with a little practice, the student will learn to keep the air stream flowing in a constant direction. The air stream will have force and direction. This is how the air stream needs to flow out of the mouth to obtain the best possible sound.

(e) Practice with the head joint only for a few minutes every day.

Cannot play smoothly between two notes (especially C to D)	1. Lack of practice 2. Lack of coordination	Obviously, practice more. Practice down the scale first, regardless of the order in the music. It is easier to start with a lot of fingers on keys and remove them than to start with a few and add several fingers at one time. Do this several times in a row, slowly but with an even, steady tempo. Do not gradually speed up. Keep it very slow, but in good rhythm and tempo. Do it at least five times in a row without mistakes. Then have the student try it with music, slowly. (This is a good exercise for any instrument.)
Notes lose fullness as the student plays lower	Open aperture	A good exercise is to have the student play a B♭ above the staff for one beat, slurring to an A for three beats, repeat, and then A for one beat and G for three beats. Continue this pattern all the way down the scale to the lower notes of the flute (see Fig. 2-9). Daily practice of this will strengthen the lip muscles and the sound will stay focused at the lower octave.
Cannot play high notes	Open aperture	Basically same as the preceding exercise, but playing the scale up to the higher notes (see Fig. 2-10). This will also help the lower notes sound more focused.
Notes not starting on time	Not using tongue	(a) Start the note using the syllable "too" or "tee." (b) Make tongue touch the back of the teeth. (c) Be careful not to let the tongue stick out between the lips. (d) Put the tongue against the top teeth before blowing air. Start the air stream, then move tongue. The student should feel the tongue articulating the note. (e) Use the tonguing exercise in Fig. 2-8.
Airy sound or no sound	1. Puffy cheeks 2. Puckered lips 3. Lips shaped like a kiss	Have the student put lips tightly together and buzz like a trumpet player. This actually forms a perfect flute embouchure. Once the student can do this, have her play the flute in the same manner, but without buzzing her lips.

Figure 2-9
Developing a Closed Aperture
Focusing Sound and Tone Development
(Flute)

This lesson does not have to be learned all in one session. Practice the exercise until the lips get tired.

Do not continue after the notes sound bad. After the first note sounds poor, stop this exercise.

Continue to practice this much of the exercise until all of these notes sound good.

On the student's next day of practice, try to add one more note to the exercise.

Eventually the student will be able to play all the notes.

Adding one note at a time will develop a good embouchure.

Figure 2-10
Developing the High Notes

Follow the same pattern of practice as in the closed aperture exercise, Fig. 2-9.

Flute Fingering Chart

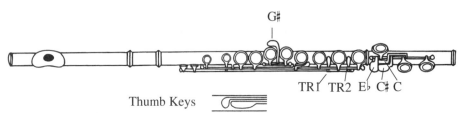

Thumb Keys

(continued)

Flute Fingering Chart, p. 2

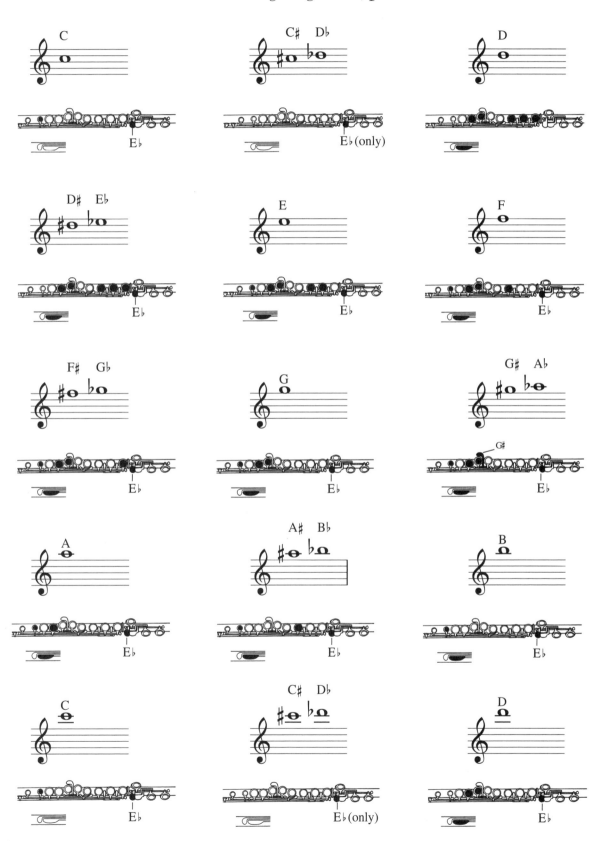

Flute Lesson Checklist

Lesson 1

- [ ] Chairs set up in advance
- [ ] Name tags on chairs (if applicable)
- [ ] Students with instruments in front row
- [ ] State rules
- [ ] Top of the case
- [ ] Check for instrument quality and repair
- [ ] Instruct: why head joint only
- [ ] Blow air out lips; no head joint
- [ ] Teacher puts head joint to student's lips
- [ ] Blow air with "pu" sound
- [ ] Student holds head joint
- [ ] Remove head joint and then have student put the head joint to lips and play again
- [ ] Everyone plays on head joint
- [ ] Make different sounds using the head joint only
- [ ] Contest: Who can hold the note the longest?
- [ ] Give practice assignment
- [ ] *Be Enthusiastic!*

Lesson 2

- [ ] Students who played before; take out head joint
- [ ] New students: Show top of the case
- [ ] Advanced students: Play head joint
- [ ] Assembly of the instrument
- [ ] Check instrument for packing corks, etc.
- [ ] Beginners make sound using the head joint only
- [ ] Advanced students: Hand position for holding flute
- [ ] Beginners continue to play head joint
- [ ] Advanced: Play first note: B (high)
- [ ] Start with closed lips
- [ ] Beginners continue to play head joint while advanced students are learning to play their first notes
- [ ] Advanced continue to learn to play A and G (high notes)
- [ ] Specific assignments to advanced and beginning students
- [ ] *Be Enthusiastic!*

Lesson 3

- [ ] Advanced students: Start assembling instrument
- [ ] Those who played head joint the previous week: Remove it from the case
- [ ] Beginners: Show top of case
- [ ] Advanced: Play high B
- [ ] Others: Play head joint only
- [ ] Beginners play head joint; take time to carefully instruct these students
- [ ] Remind all of good posture
- [ ] Advanced: Learn to play A and G, while instructing other students how to assemble the instrument

- [ ] Students who just learned to assemble instrument: show hand position
- [ ] Play high B
- [ ] New students: Play head joint if not played for too long
- [ ] Everyone look at Lesson 3 (or beginning method book)
- [ ] Everyone looks at notes
- [ ] Quick check for everyone playing instrument
- [ ] Specific assignment
- [ ] *Be Enthusiastic! Praise their achievement.*

Lesson 4

☐ If new students, you should reschedule them into new class

☐ Those who can assemble instrument should start immediately

☐ Others take out head joint: play

☐ New students: top of the case

☐ Advanced students: play B, A, and G

☐ New students: play head joint

☐ Students who played head joint only previous week: assembly instrument; hand position

☐ Advanced students start to play Lesson 3

☐ Watch out for students not reading

☐ Look at Lesson 4

☐ Everyone plays instrument

☐ Specific assignment

☐ *Enthusiasm!*

Lesson 5

☐ New students should be rescheduled

☐ If you must allow new students, spend minimal time with them; show them how to make a sound and move on quickly to others

☐ Students who just learned to play entire instrument previous week: play "Mary Had a Little Lamb"

☐ Instructions for instrument assembly

☐ Playing from book

☐ Tapping toes

☐ Counting rhythms—watch—make them all count

☐ Those who just learned to assemble instrument: learn to play B, A, and G

☐ Advanced: Continue to play Lesson 4

☐ Tonguing for those reading

☐ Everyone play from book according to where they are musically

☐ Quick discussion of Lesson 5

☐ Specific assignment

☐ *Always be enthusiastic. Compliment them on their accomplishments!*

BEGINNING CLARINET LESSONS

The lessons for clarinet are designed to help the instrumental music teacher start clarinet students in a group situation while maintaining good time management. They emphasize important elements of teaching while guiding the instructor through the first crucial lessons. The same techniques apply to private lessons, though the private instructor may cover more material per lesson.

Clarinet Lesson 1 (Fig. 2-11)

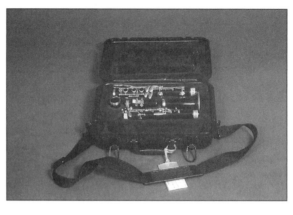

Photo 2-15

Before the students come into your room, be organized. Make sure the chairs and stands are in order. If you know who is attending the class, you may want to put their names on the chairs. Know what you intend to accomplish during each lesson. You may change your mind once the students enter the room. An intended goal for each lesson is important.

Photo 2-16

The first thing students must know is how to open the case. Have them put the instrument on the floor in front of them, with the bottom of the case on the ground. The bottom of the case is usually the part with the handle. On most cases, the latches will move up if the case is set properly. Many instrument manufacturers put the brand name on top of the case; however, do not rely on this. You may want to put a small piece of masking tape on the top of the case to prevent accidents (Photo 2-15).

Proper assembly is a very crucial procedure. Once students have placed the case properly on the floor, tell them to open the case but not take the instrument out. Show them where to apply the cork grease and explain that it is essential to apply cork grease so the cork does not dry up and fall off. Without the cork, the instrument will not play or stay together. Have them do this before you start to instruct them on assembling the instrument. Because of time constraints, you may want to do this for some of them to keep the lesson moving along.

Identify the lower and upper joints. The student should hold the lower joint, the longer one, at the bottom away from the keys, and twist the bell back and forth as the two parts are pushed together (Photo 2-16). If it is very difficult to push together, add more cork grease. The next step is very important. Putting the two joints together incorrectly can result in bent keys. Have each student hold the upper joint (the shorter piece) in the palm of his left hand with the holes up. In the right hand, have him hold the lower joint below the low key levers, with the bell already attached and the holes up (Photo 2-17). Make sure the left hand is covering the middle ring so the side lever will be raised when the instrument parts are pushed together (Photo 2-18). Have him twist the two parts together with his wrist using a back-and-forth motion.

Photo 2-17

Figure 2-11
Music for B♭ Clarinet Lesson 1

Teach this lesson without showing the music to the student. Students should concentrate on producing a good sound. Attempting to read music will distract from all that is needed to produce a good sound.

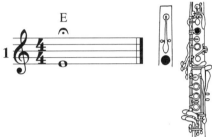

The note is sustained for a comfortable length of time. Counting is not necessary for the first note.

Students should play the note four times in a steady count. All students not playing should count out loud with the band director.

Follow the same procedure as above.

Follow the same procedure as above.

First song. Counting rhythms is not necessary the first time. A quick accomplishment is paramount.

	Three	blind	mice.
(or)	Hot	cross	buns.

Mary Had a Little Lamb

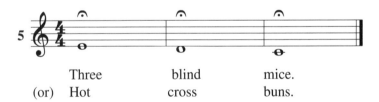

ASSIGNMENT: First, hold each note, then play each note four times.
Play "Three Blind Mice."
Challenge: Who can play "Mary Had a Little Lamb" using the three notes learned today? Be positive; wish everyone a nice day.
BE ENTHUSIASTIC!

Photo 2-18

The student must be careful not to turn the clarinet all the way around or he will bend or break the keys. After the parts are together, line up the two levers on the right side so the two pieces look and work as one instrument (Photo 2-19). Make sure every student has done this before you move on to the next step. Help any student who is having a problem.

Now, introduce the barrel to the students. Have each student set the bell of the instrument on his knee, hold the upper body at the top above the keys, and twist the barrel until the two parts are together (Photo 2-20).

The students should put the mouthpiece on the clarinet without the reed or ligature. This is done in the same way the barrel was attached to the body. Holding the clarinet at the barrel is an easy way to do this. The opening of the mouthpiece should line up with the side of the clarinet that has one long key and one hole below it, as shown in Photo 2-21.

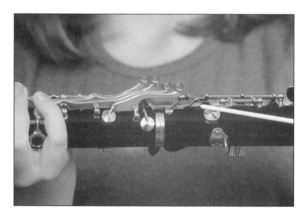

Photo 2-19

Photo 2-20

Photo 2-21

Mouthpiece/Reed Setting Demonstration
(This may be demonstrated to the entire group at one time.)

Photo 2-22

Photo 2-23

1. Hold the clarinet in front of you with the opening of the mouthpiece up.
2. Moisten the reed before putting it on the mouthpiece. You can do this by putting the reed into your mouth while assembling the instrument.
3. When the reed is moist, put the flat part of the reed (I recommend reed strength #2 for beginners and quickly move to #2$\frac{1}{2}$) onto the flat part of the mouthpiece (Photo 2-22).
4. Put your thumb on the bark of the reed to hold it in place. Very carefully, while looking at the reed, put the reed holder (ligature) over the reed. The wider end of the reed holder goes on first (Photo 2-23).
5. Line up the tip of the reed to the tip of the mouthpiece (Photo 2-24—tip of reed—tip of mouthpiece—thumb in place), **never touching the tip of the reed** with your finger (Photo 2-24). (After demonstrating, observe and help students accomplish this task.)
6. Put the thumb between the two screws of the reed holder (I do not use the word "ligature" until a few lessons later). Tighten the screws, the bottom first, until they stop turning. The screws do not need to be adjusted any tighter (Photo 2-25).

Photo 2-24

Photo 2-25

Many college professors and professional clarinet players suggest that the reed should be slightly below or above the tip of the mouthpiece. Here, we are discussing beginners who have never played an instrument before, and after more than 28 years of teaching and supervising teachers, I have found that students most easily produce a sound with the tip of the reed even with the tip of the mouthpiece. At this stage, I believe using the easiest way to produce a good sound provides the best possible chance for success and retention.

Teaching the students to properly assemble the instrument will take at least half of the first lesson, especially if there are several students in one class. As this is crucial, the time is well spent. Students without an instrument should be instructed to watch and listen carefully so they will be able to assemble the instrument at the next lesson.

Before instructing the students on how to play the instrument, make sure the instrument is properly put together and the reed is in the right position. It takes a very short time to inspect the instruments, even if you have many students in the class. Make sure the instrument can play easily. Inspect it for poor alignment, bent keys, dried pads, and warped or chipped mouthpieces. You may play the students' instruments; however, I would suggest you then use your own mouthpiece. Ronald Reuben, clarinetist of the Philadelphia Orchestra, insists that his student's instrument be in good playing condition. There is no point in trying to teach a student how to play an instrument when the instrument will not play.

Photo 2-26

Some parents will want to wait until the child performs well before they have the instrument repaired or put in good working order. Their children are most likely to become discouraged and quit. It is important to make parents understand their child will not be able to perform well until the instrument allows him to play well.

The First Note

The first note to teach the students is first line E as it is easy to play when holding the instrument as follows: Have them hold the thumb rest with the thumb and first finger of the right hand for the first few lessons. This helps them steady the instrument while they are concentrating on playing and establishing a good left-hand position. The left-hand thumb position is extremely important. The student should be able to easily rock the tip of the thumb on and off of the register key (Photo 2-26). If the student does not learn this in the first few lessons, the problem is extremely difficult to correct later. Also, make sure the student puts the left hand on top and the right hand on the bottom of the clarinet. Some students will want to put the right hand on top (Photo 2-27).

No sheet music is used during the first lesson. The student's attention should be focused on making a good sound. Have the student sit directly in front of you. Good posture is important. Tell him to sit on the edge of the chair with both feet flat on the floor and a straight back. (This is not the time to discuss air support. Good posture will help take care of this. Do not mention breathing.) Have the student put his first finger over the top hole and the thumb over the thumb hole. Sit or stand directly in front of the student and tell the student to look directly at you, and to refrain from doing anything until you ask

Photo 2-27

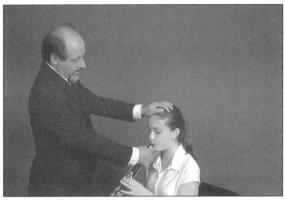

Photo 2-28

him to do so. As the student is holding the clarinet in front of him, tell him to open his mouth wide and cover the bottom teeth with the bottom lip. Watch carefully and tell him not to use too much lip, just enough to cover the bottom teeth. You can guide the clarinet into his mouth (the student should still be holding the clarinet): set it on the bottom lip and tell him to close his mouth, but not to blow. Make sure he keeps the bottom teeth covered, and the **top teeth on the mouthpiece.**

At this point, you are holding the clarinet with your right hand (the student is also holding the instrument) and your left hand is holding the top of his head (Photo 2-28). Hold the clarinet mouthpiece with your index finger between the ligature and the student's lips. With your left hand on the top of the student's head, you can make sure the top teeth are touching the mouthpiece by gently pushing or pulling the mouthpiece against the top teeth. Also, you can quickly move the mouthpiece in or out as needed. These two procedures will stop most squeaks in the first lesson.

Now, tell the student to blow using the syllable "tu." You may need to tell him to blow louder or softer. If no sound comes out, put more of the mouthpiece into the mouth. If the student squeaks, make sure the top teeth are touching the mouthpiece, and adjust the mouthpiece out of the mouth slightly. If a student is not putting enough air into the instrument, ask him to play louder (a fourth grader will not understand breath support, and you will take up too much valuable time trying to explain it). Notice the position of the clarinet. The bell should be at the knee, or at an angle where the clarinet passes between the legs at knee level (Photo 2-29). This may also prevent a squeak.

Photo 2-29

If the student is puffing out his cheeks, tell him to play the note you just showed him, and while holding the note tell him to bring in his checks. Say this over and over again while he is holding the note. This technique works because the student is starting with the cheeks puffed out, and the student can feel his muscles pulling in as he blows. You may have to do it for several lessons in a row for the student to remember, but it will work. Also, having the student suck air through the clarinet helps him form a better embouchure. If the note is unfocused, it is because he is bunching his lips up or puckering the lips forward. Tell the student to press his lips tightly against the teeth. This will focus the sound and aid in getting the student to bring in his cheeks (Photo 2-30). After the student has a good sound, I ask him the name of the note just played, and have him repeat its name out loud. Do this procedure with each student in the class. It is very important to be aware of time. By this time, you may have only five minutes left in a 30-minute lesson. You must move quickly.

In regard to tonguing, if a child plays the note correctly after you have told her to play the note using the syllable "tu," then say no

Photo 2-30

more. If a student does not start the note with the tongue, tell him to put his tongue up against the reed before releasing the air into the clarinet. After he has started to blow, he should then move his tongue. The first lesson is not the time to make a fuss over tonguing; however, that is not to say it is not important. If the child can play the note, but does not understand how to start the note with the tongue, and a very simple example like the one mentioned above does not work, go on to the next student. Often, just by seeing and hearing another student do it correctly, the student will correct the problem on his own. You may have to remind some students daily to use their tongues. The exercise on p. 55, Figure 2-16 is also very effective in getting a student to use his tongue to separate notes. However, I would not suggest using this exercise in the first lesson. Most students need to have a bit more control over the instrument before using the exercise.

The First Song

After everyone can play an E, have the whole class play it together. Give them a great compliment. Now have them tap their feet four times while playing four quarter notes. You should count out loud for them the first time, then see if they can stop after four counts without your help.

Show all the students how to play a D. After showing them where to place their fingers, have the students all play it individually and then together. The next note to learn is C. Then, have them play E, D, C. They have just played their first song, "Three Blind Mice" or "Hot Cross Buns." It is extremely important to play a song in the first lesson. At this point, tone is not so important as accomplishment. It will be very difficult to accomplish all this in one 30-minute lesson, but you can do it if you move quickly, even with six or more students in a class. Should you have more than eight in a class, I would suggest that you have an hour lesson. However, if that is not possible, keep track of time and move quickly. It can be done even with 15 or 20 in a class; however, you will probably only accomplish one or two notes in the first lesson. If you do not get so far as three notes, make sure everyone can play at least one note very well. A sense of accomplishment is very important. Also, keep the students playing. Do not let them sit too long without doing anything. As you teach a new student to play, continually have the students review and play the note with the new student.

It is also important to tell them not to worry if they go home and cannot remember the notes or how to get a sound on the instrument. What *is* important is to practice and try every day. If they keep trying they will remember more and more, and by the next lesson they will remember what they did in the first lesson. If they are still getting a squeak or no sound, tell them not to worry; you will show them how to make the sound again. Tell everyone they made a wonderful sound today. If you find you have done all this and you have extra time, work on sustaining notes longer. Have them tap their toes four times while holding a note, then five, and so on. However, do not add extra notes in this lesson—it will be tempting, but they will only remember so much, and it is better to work on those three notes the first week, and try to make a good sound. You may work on "Mary Had a Little Lamb" if everyone is doing extremely well.

At the end of the lesson, tell everyone to practice daily. Even if it is only for 10 minutes, a short time is better than no time at all. I do not demand 30 minutes for the first week. They do not have enough information or endurance to last that long, nor will their patience hold out.

Disassembly

To disassemble the instrument, students should proceed in the opposite order to which they put it together. I tell the students to take off the reed before removing the mouthpiece. The ligatures of beginning instruments are not of the best quality, and they will not hold up to twisting the mouthpiece back and forth. It is better to have them set the reed aside until the entire instrument is apart and in the case. Some teachers prefer the reed dry and put into a reed holder, and some prefer to put the reed back onto the mouthpiece. Watch the students carefully to make sure they hold the clarinet parts properly and do not twist the body completely around! Also, make sure the parts are put into the case properly. You may need to help them along so this process does not take too long. As they leave the room, remind them to practice every day.

Clarinet Lesson 2 (Fig. 2-12)

There is one common problem when teaching instrumental group lessons. As you advance the students from the previous lessons, there will be new students who will be receiving their instruments for the first

time. As you teach the new students, make sure you do not forget the students from the previous lesson. It is very important to keep both groups playing their instruments so they do not feel they are wasting their time. To avoid discipline problems, keep students busy—student participation is very important in every lesson.

As students enter, have those who played the previous week put their instruments together. While they are assembling their instruments, have the new students put their cases on the floor. You will follow the procedure from the first lesson. However, you will work much faster than the first session. Hopefully, the students paid attention and will remember some of what they witnessed from the previous session. While

Photo 2-31

the new students are putting their instruments together, keep an eye on the other students (Photo 2-31). When the students who started the prior week finish putting their instruments together, check their reeds. If the reeds are in good shape and in proper position, ask them to play E for four counts, then D, and finally C. As you are doing this, you may continue to instruct and help the new students assemble their instruments. Hopefully, by the time E, D, and C are reviewed, everyone's clarinet is together, and you can start to teach the new students how to play E. Then have everyone play E together (old students included), holding the note for approximately four counts. Follow the same procedure for the other notes. As you do this, look at their hand positions and embouchures. Correct any problems immediately. Posture is extremely important—remind them of good posture each week until it is no longer necessary. They should look straight ahead, not at the floor or the clarinet. After everyone has played each note, have a contest to see who can hold the note the longest. This will help keep the excitement. The class should now be about half over, and you may have everyone playing the same notes. Now have them all play the first three notes of "Three Blind Mice" together. By having the students from the previous week help the new students, you are keeping everyone playing. No one feels left out.

The Beginning Book

Introduce Figure 2-12 or the first lesson reading notes in the method book to all students, even those who have just started. Quickly explain to the students what a *staff* is: five lines and four spaces. That is all you need to say. In many beginning band books, the first note in the book is E. If the first line uses a different note, I skip to the line with E (you do not have to follow the book in order). I tell everyone to look at the line, see the goose egg (if it is a whole note) or the note on the bottom line of the staff. "That is an E. Anytime you see a note on the bottom line it is an E." Now have everyone say it: "E." "Now we will all play it together while looking at the note. All right, play." (Conduct—and hold the note.) Using the rhythmic value used in the book, tell them how the shape of the note determines duration. Then, tell them the name of the rhythmic value and how many times to pat their feet. Explain to the students what type of rest is in the following measure, assuming there will be a rest, and how many beats to hold each rest. "Now that everyone knows what the first note is, what it looks like, and how long to play each note and rest, let us play the line together."

Figure 2-12
Music for B♭ Clarinet Lesson 2

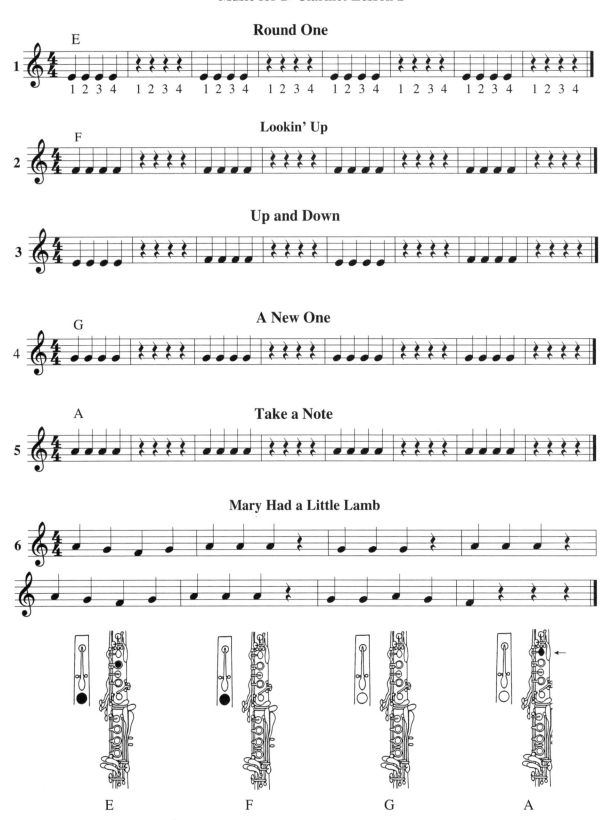

Tap toes: one foot tap per beat. Start with toes up; heels anchored on floor. Practice tapping toes while playing every line.

I suggest that you use a baton to conduct the students, even in small group lessons. It will make the students feel like they are in a band and part of something special. Your hands will also help them to keep count. Make sure they are looking at the notes while they play. Do not let them fake it. Some students will have a hard time keeping their eyes on the music. When that happens, use the tip of the baton to point to the notes as everyone is playing the line (Photo 2-32). Making a game of naming the notes may be helpful and fun. Also, make sure they tap their toes and count in their heads while they are playing. You should

count out loud to help them at first, then do not count out loud. Make sure your students learn to count while reading notes. It is also very important to learn to read notes by the second lesson. I do not recommend rote learning. The next note in line 2 is F. If you must use a band book, skip to the line with F. Have your students play that line, following the same procedure as above. Point out the differences between the notes: One is on a line, the other on a space. Make sure they see the difference. The rhythms are usually the same as the first, so this should be fairly easy. Play lines 1, 2, and 3 on the music page (Fig. 2-12). After they play each line, praise them. This is the time for positive reinforcement. If you are negative, you may discourage them and they will want to quit. Keep it fun and pleasant.

Photo 2-32

Line 4 introduces G to the students. Show the students how to play the note. Then, follow the same procedure as above. If you must use a heterogeneous book, teach the students how to play the line with G in it. If the book uses lower notes, the note will probably be a D or C. Keep your eye out for bad posture, puffing out of the cheeks, and wrong hand positions. Keep reminding them to sit up straight and not to lean back in the chair. Emphasize the difference between the three notes. Make sure they see and understand the difference.

Have the students play as far down the first page as they can. However, do not push too hard in the first few lessons. It is unlikely that you will finish the first page during the second lesson. Assign the students to practice all lines on the first page every day. They may look and play ahead, but I do not recommend assigning them too much in the first few lessons. If the next page has several new notes, do not introduce them until next week. Students may be doing fine in class, but you will not be going home with them to remind them of what they learned that day. They are receiving an incredible amount of information in this half-hour lesson. They will absorb only so much. As they are leaving, remind them to practice daily and give them a positive statement. Tell them you are proud of them and they sound great. Show your enthusiasm.

Clarinet Lesson 3 (Fig. 2-13)

Now, the real juggling act begins. This lesson must cover students who have never held a clarinet before and students who can play all the first page in the book and more. If you cannot reschedule students to a more appropriate group, you must move quickly and efficiently. Keep track of each student to make sure everyone is learning.

As the students are walking in, instruct the students from the previous weeks to put their instruments together immediately. While they are doing this, as quickly as possible show the new students how to put their instruments together. To save time, you may help them assemble some of the parts. Once the advanced students have their instruments assembled, ask them to play E four times one beat each. The new students may still be assembling their instruments. That is okay; however, make sure that no one is sitting too long without playing his or her instrument.

Figure 2-13
Music for B♭ Clarinet Lesson 3

Steppin' Up

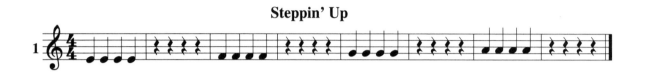

Down the Ladder

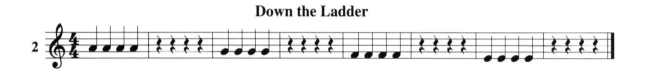

Over the Hill

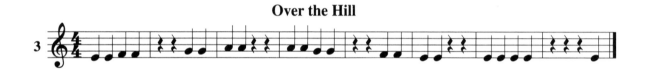

More to Play

Watch Out for That Rest!

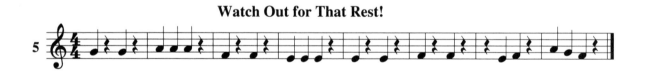

Round and Round

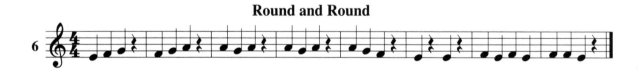

Waves

While you are reviewing the notes learned from the previous week, show the new students how to play their first notes, just as in the previous week. After the new students can play E, have everyone play E, including last week's students. Have the more advanced players play something from last week's lesson (a line from the book). Show the new students how to play D. Now, everyone plays D together for four beats (or plays four quarter notes on D). The advanced students can play another line from their lesson book, followed by the new students learning to play C. Everyone plays C together. Have the whole class play "Three Blind Mice." Next, have the advanced students play another line from their assignment. The new students are now ready to play the first line in the book that contains E, so have everyone review this together. All the students are reviewing and learning together—with skill, a close eye on time, and a little luck, you will have the students playing together, and you are only halfway through the third lesson.

Intonation

It is in the third lesson (fourth at the latest) that I like to introduce tuning to the students. If the third lesson is more than half over, teach tuning in the fourth lesson. It is extremely important that students learn to listen to their sound and tune from the very beginning. You cannot tune the students for the first time just before a concert and expect the band to play in tune for the entire concert—they will sound terrible because they have not learned to listen. They must learn to listen to their pitches from the earliest stages of playing.

The first time you teach tuning to the class, it will take up a good portion of the period. It is worth it. In addition to teaching intonation, you will be teaching your students to listen to tone, balance, and each other. I recommend that you use your ear to tune your students and not a mechanical tuner. You cannot teach your students to use their ears if you are not using your own. New teachers are often apprehensive of this procedure; however, the students know less than you. Do not tune the clarinets to A440 or the best student. The pitch will be too high for the weakest student. I like to pick the student whose pitch is about in the middle of the class. The better students can pull out their barrel to tune, and the weaker students will have to lip up and improve their embouchure in order to match the pitch. Do not tune to the lowest pitched player. The weaker students will never improve if they do not learn to listen and tighten their embouchure. As time passes, you might be able to have everyone play at A440, but it is not necessary during the first few weeks of playing. I recommend this same technique for the whole band, not just for clarinet section rehearsals. It is better for the whole band to play at A430 than to have the pitch vary from player to player. No one in the audience will be aware of a high or low pitch as long as everyone in the band is fairly close to the same pitch. However, do not stay below pitch too long. Move up to A440 as soon as possible. It will foster better embouchure on all instruments. Once your students are used to playing in tune, they will demand good intonation.

I like to tune the whole band to concert B♭. This is especially good for the clarinets. I have seen many directors tune clarinets to open G. That is one of the most inconsistent pitches on the clarinet. C is easy to play, has good tone quality, and the students can easily hear this pitch. Have everyone play C together. Make sure they notice the sound quality. After you have picked your tuning person (someone with good tone quality), have another student play the note together with the tuning person and then separately. Ask the students if the second person's pitch is higher or lower than the tuning person. You will probably get both answers; that is fine. Do not correct them. Let them hear for themselves. You might even ask them to sing the notes. If they can sing and match the pitch of the notes being played, it will be easier for them to hear if the note is higher or lower (do not use the words *sharp* and *flat* in the first lesson). Have the second student pull the barrel out. Now, let everyone hear the pitch being played too low. Gradually move the barrel in until the pitches match. All of the students will hear what you are talking about. Do not worry if you cannot always tell whether the pitch is sharp or flat. Just move the mouthpiece to an extreme degree and adjust it until the pitches match. Both you and the students will learn something, and the students will never know you could not hear whether the pitch was low or high. Tune each student in the class. After everyone is in tune, have them all play together. Have them notice the difference from the first time they all played together. Make sure they understand they must listen at all times. You can tune the first note, but they must listen to make sure the other notes are in tune by tightening or loosening their lips. Tune the students in every lesson of the school year. Only the first tuning lesson will take long—after the initial instructions, tuning will take only a few minutes.

If you are still in your third lesson, the period will be nearly over after tuning. Have everyone play a song from Lesson 3 (Fig. 2-13) in this resource or something out of the book together. Make sure they are aware of the difference in sound from the first time they played and the sound after tuning. Give everyone an assignment before they leave. Be specific. Tell them what lines on what page to play. It is not necessary to assign every line, but make sure you assign enough to keep them practicing all week. If they forget how to play something at home, tell them to keep trying every day. It may come back to them before the week is over, and, if not, it will be easier for you to teach them again if they keep trying.

Clarinet Lesson 4 (Fig. 2-14)

By this time, you would hope all the new students have already started. However, do not be surprised if you have one more student walk in with an instrument. If you cannot reschedule, work with this student very quickly as the other students are putting their instruments together. You will follow the same basic procedure as in Lesson 3; however, the learning process should be faster. Review with the advanced students while you show the new student how to hold and play the instrument.

As soon as everyone has played a few notes or a line from this resource or the method book, tune the group. Do this first, so they realize the priority of tuning. Even though tones are not well developed, it is not too early to start listening. This will help tone production as well as intonation. If you did not tune during Lesson 3, take your time now to teach them to listen to their pitches. Tune them quickly if intonation was taught at the last lesson. You may adjust the barrel for them if it is necessary to hurry the process along. However, do not allow them to depend on you to do all the listening. Have them listen and assist you every time you tune the band.

After tuning, review the first couple of lessons by playing at least one line from each of the first two pages. Teach the new students the first three notes as you work with the other students. After playing a couple of lines on page one, go to page two even if the new students cannot play with everyone. After a couple of lines, have everyone play something in which the new and advanced students may participate. Go on to the next page or to the new assignment. Play a line or two, then go back to the students who cannot play that page. Keep doing this until everyone can play the same line together. Do not worry if every student cannot do it perfectly—right now they need to see progress.

It is extremely important that you be very excited by what the students are accomplishing. Let them feel and hear your enthusiasm for their success. No matter what these first sounds are like, let the students think they are wonderful. (You are not being dishonest. It is wonderful to be able to make a sound on the first day.) Note their improvement. Every time they progress to the next level, praise them and let them feel your pride in their accomplishment. This is the fuel that will keep them going when they get discouraged. Let the students know you love what you are doing, and you love what they are doing.

As the lessons progress, there are some points of which to be aware. Make sure everyone is reading the music. Look at their eyes and see if they are following the music or just faking it. Use your baton to point to the notes while they are playing; sometimes their eyes need a little help to follow the notes in time.

Make sure the students are tapping their toes. Tapping our feet is the basic tool of measurement of rhythmic value. Make sure they do this while the rhythms are easy. Continue to demand that they tap their toes and count their rhythms. Help them by counting out loud while they play. You may also play rhythm charts, clap, and sing, but make sure they play more than sing. They did not sign up for the clarinet to sing and stomp their feet. The more they play the clarinet, the better the chances are they will not drop out.

Figure 2-14
Music for B♭ Clarinet Lesson 4

Keep your eyes on their embouchure. Make sure their top teeth are touching the mouthpiece. If their cheeks are puffed out, tell them to bring them in. It may take a lot of coaching, but they will start to bring in their cheeks. The bottom lip must cover the bottom teeth.

Good posture is essential. Make sure they are sitting on the edge of their chairs, both feet flat on the floor, looking straight ahead and not at the clarinet or their feet. The bell of the clarinet should be about knee level or passing between the legs at knee level. The clarinet should not be against their chests or sticking straight out. This is an easy area to neglect, but it will have a definite effect on tone quality and concentration on what they are trying to accomplish.

At the end of the lesson, show the class any new notes or rhythms on the next page. If you have time, try playing a line or two. Most likely, you will barely have time to discuss the new notes. Give them a specific assignment. You may assign them the whole page, or choose certain lines that are fun and include the new notes and rhythms. Make sure you assign enough to keep them busy all week without over-whelming them. If you assign them two lines, that is all they will practice. If you assign students too much, they will not practice at all. I like to assign a little more than I think is easy for them to do. That usually challenges them, but does not discourage them. It is important they feel they are accomplishing something each week. You must use your judgment based on what you are hearing. You have to learn when to be very demanding and when to let things go.

It is usually during the fourth lesson that practice slips are distributed. Emphasize that practice slips affect their band grades and must be filled out completely and signed by the parent (this encourages parent involvement and participation in the student's new activity). Beginners should be required to practice a minimum of one half hour a day, five days per week.

Clarinet Lesson 5 (Fig. 2-15)

When the students come in for their fifth lesson, the first order of business is tuning. Have students play a couple of notes for review and warm up, but tune before beginning any real work for this week's lesson.

If you have any more new students, teach them in the same manner as in Lesson 4. It is time, how-ever, to give serious consideration to not accepting new students. From the very beginning, make sure everyone knows the cut-off date for having their instruments. When that day comes, you must follow your own rule. Once students see you mean what you say, next year they will take care of business more quickly.

In this lesson the goal is to have everyone on the same page of the book. Begin by reviewing some-thing for everyone to play. Select lines from the book or lessons for review that add the next level of difficulty until reaching the previous lesson. Following the review, begin working on the new assignment. As the students play, closely observe embouchure, posture, rhythm, and tonguing, and make sure the students are reading the music. Watch their eyes. Make sure they are following the notes on the page. As in the previous lesson, point out the notes on the page with your baton.

Beginning teachers often go into long discussions about breathing. This is a waste of time. Do not worry during the first several lessons if students are not breathing properly. They are doing something very unnatural. They are trying to hold the clarinet in their mouth, while putting their fingers over spe-cific holes in order to play the correct note. At the same time, they are going to exhale air into this instru-ment with their lips curled over their bottom teeth, and they are scared to death that nothing will happen or they will squeak. Not only that, they are trying to tap their toes and count in their head. They are nerv-ous and frightened. After several years of teaching, I have learned that if you just do not say anything about it, students will breathe correctly after a few lessons. Do not add one more thing to their long list of items to accomplish or even think about breathing when they are first learning to play the instrument. If breathing is a problem several months from the beginning, then you may consider talking about it. Usually, telling them to play louder or blow harder will correct this problem.

Figure 2-15
Music for B♭ Clarinet Lesson 5

The Whole Time

Jingle Bells

Ode to Joy

A Little Bit Longer

London Bridge

Duet

I also like to tell students about chair positions during this lesson. Let them know that first chair is not only the best player, but section leader. This is the person who sets a good example by knowing how to play the music and having good conduct, posture, and attitude. I do not necessarily have the challenge for chairs on the fifth lesson. Most likely, I tell them about this event and inform them in a couple of weeks that they will receive notice of what music they must play. I also tell them they will get a grade according to how well they play the music. This should be encouraged as a friendly competition in which everyone learns and becomes a better player.

At the end of the lesson, give a specific assignment. If the class is ready, let the students know the date of challenges for first chair. I will usually tell them it will be a line from a particular page, but I do not tell them which line. Experience has taught me that if you give them a specific line, that is all they will practice. Let them know challenges will take place often so they may not be first or last chair all year. Make this a fun event to encourage practice and leadership. Do not let this get into a bitter battle among the students.

Final Suggestions

This is a basic guide for teaching the first five lessons for beginning clarinet class. You will need to alter your procedure to fit the individual situation and your personality.

Progress the class as quickly as you can. The more they learn, the more they will want to learn. Keep the pace moving quickly so it will be fun.

You will notice some students breathing before every note. Following is a simple exercise to show a student how to use his tongue instead of his breath to separate the notes: First, pick a very easy note to play (E). Have the student hold the note for at least five beats. Ask him to play back the rhythm that you sing on the same note. The first rhythm you will sing is four sixteenth notes and a whole note. Sing the sixteenth notes as quickly as possible, but clearly; then have him play it for you. The point of this exercise is that he cannot possibly breathe before every note, so he must use his tongue. Sometimes a student will not be able to produce the rhythm of fast sixteenth notes. If the rhythm he plays comes out in triplets, that is fine. Do not insist on the faster rhythm unless the student is breathing between the notes. Next, sing a set of eighth note triplets and a whole note. (It is important to make the last note long, so the student is thinking beyond the last note.) After the student can play that without breathing to separate the notes, sing four eighth notes and a whole note. If at any point he starts breathing between the notes again, speed up the rhythm. Finally, sing four quarter notes and a whole note. Once the student has done that, tell him that he has now played without breathing before every note and that is how to do it while playing a song. You may have to repeat this exercise again next week, but very soon, the students will know how to use their tongues instead of their breath to separate the notes (see Fig. 2-16, "Learning Not to Breathe Before Every Note"). If a student is still having trouble understanding where to put her tongue, here are a few suggestions. First, I will have another student try the exercise. If that student does it well, that will often show the other student how to perform it and will work better than a teacher demonstration. Another way to show a student how to tongue a note is to tell the student to put the mouthpiece into his mouth and put the tongue firmly up against the reed. Next, the student should blow air before releasing his tongue from the reed. When the student removes his tongue, he will feel and hear what his tongue is doing and how to use his tongue to separate notes. Sometimes just asking a student to sing the syllable "tu, tu, tu, tu" will help him feel where to place the tongue.

As soon as possible, try to get your students to play with better equipment. A good ligature with a good quality reed will make a tremendous difference in sound. These two items are not necessarily expensive. Good student-level mouthpieces are very affordable. If you can persuade the parents to purchase the items, your clarinet section will sound better. If the parents are reluctant to purchase these items, buy one and have the students play it. (Make sure you sterilize the mouthpiece before students play it.) Once they hear the difference, they will persuade their parents to buy new mouthpieces. Perhaps you can make an arrangement with your dealer to give you a special discount if you buy a larger number at one time. This may further encourage the parents to buy the mouthpieces.

Figure 2-16
Learning Not to Breathe Before Every Note

(All on the same note)

(Students may think these words to play the rhythms quickly.)

(Changing the Last Note)

Within a few weeks, if not right away, have the students play a $2^1/_2$ strength reed. The stronger reed will improve their sound immediately and encourage better air support. The stronger reed will also help the students as they begin to play over the break. Certainly, you do not want the clarinet students playing anything less than a $2^1/_2$ or a medium reed by mid-year.

In order to keep the students in the band, they must sound good. Tune them every day. If you do not tune them, they will sound bad, and they will quit the band because they are discouraged. This is something you must take care of from the very beginning. If they learn to listen to tuning, they will listen to each other and play better together.

The students always feel a great deal of accomplishment when you hand out folders in which to put their books and sheet music. I usually wait until the first full band rehearsal to do this. This is their reward for becoming band members. They are no longer beginning clarinet players—they are members of a band!

The students are very excited when they receive their first sheet of music. This feeling of accomplishment cannot be underestimated. Hand out music and plan for your first concert as soon as possible. (Find music that is fun, but easy enough to play after the first four or five pages in the book. You may need to go to your local store, but do your homework. A great way to see what new music is available is to go to your state Music Educators Association convention; the publishers are there to display all their newest publications. The representatives will help you find the music you need and you can study the scores. Most publishers have websites, and often the music may be viewed on site.)

Perform often. Do not limit yourself to one or two concerts a year. Ask your principal if the band can play at least one song to start assemblies. Use any excuse for playing. Performing will increase your students' retention rate more effectively than anything else you do for your band.

Let the students know you can tell when they are not practicing. Do it in a positive way, but when a student has not been practicing, let him know it. Students will ask how you can tell. Explain that there are tell-tale signs of practicing, such as sound quality and the manner in which they learn and improve during the lesson. Tell them you care, but they must practice because you cannot keep the other students from progressing just because one or two people are not practicing. Do not yell or raise your voice. Let them feel your concern. And then, continue with the lesson. They will practice when they see you will not wait for them. You do not want to have the students who are practicing lose interest because you are spending too much time with the students who are not putting their best effort toward learning.

As you continue to teach the students, it is important to keep their excitement and interest at a very high level. Show your enthusiasm daily. Be excited at every little accomplishment they make. Let them see how you are sharing something with them that is extremely important to you. Your dedication is inspiring. Enthusiasm is very contagious.

Crossing the Break

Crossing the break (playing into the upper register) is one of the major problems clarinet students experience. This section focuses on that problem and suggests ways to eliminate or at least ease it.

Band directors sometimes make too big a deal about this problem. Do not start out by telling the students that they are about to reach a very difficult part of clarinet playing; if you do, your prediction will come true. Do not scare them before they have even tried to play over the break. The exercises in Fig. 2-17, "Clarinet Studies—Crossing the Break," will better prepare them for high notes, and you do not have to warn them of difficulties that may not exist for them.

Some students have very small fingers, and have a hard time covering the holes completely. If that is the case, work with them by showing them where to put their fingers and by moving their fingers over the holes (Photo 2-33 on page 64). As they grow physically, of course, this problem will disappear.

The following exercises require that students cover the holes completely. If they do not, they will hear an unfocused, poor quality sound. Fortunately, they will get a sound even if they are not covering the holes properly. This will give them a chance to notice the "fuzzy" sound, and adjust their fingers until the

Figure 2-17
Clarinet Studies—Crossing the Break
(Speed is not important. It is extremely important to maintain a constant tempo.)

Figure 2-17
Clarinet Studies—Crossing the Break (cont.)

Figure 2-17
Crossing the Break—Clarinet (cont.)

sound is better. It is important that, at this time, you observe and make sure that the left thumb is in the proper position (Photo 2-26 on page 42). If they develop a good habit now, it will be much easier for them to play the high notes. It is a good idea to continually remind them from the very beginning to put their thumbs in the proper position.

By this time, the students should be playing a strength $2^1/_2$ or 3 reed. A better quality mouthpiece and reed will also be very helpful.

Pay attention to good posture and embouchure. Sitting up straight and holding the clarinet with the bell around knee level with a good tight-lipped embouchure around the mouthpiece will be very helpful.

Playing low notes is the key to playing above the break. Some of the beginning band method books published in recent years have included exercises with songs written in the lower registers. However, many of the older books spend little time preparing the students for playing above the break. I suggest that when reviewing a method book, give priority to a book that has the clarinets playing in the low register for at least three pages before they start to play above the break. Never choose a book that has a clarinet player playing up the break. Playing down the break is easier, and it will help the students get the correct hand position. Later, going up the break will be easy. If the students start with a very negative experience, they will want to quit. Playing above the break does not have to be difficult, but it must be approached properly.

When you reach the section where the clarinets cross the break, you may wish to copy the exercises in Figure 2-17 and have the clarinet players practice these pages before continuing in the band method book. It is extremely important that they play the exercises in the exact rhythms, and keep a steady tempo at all times. Speed is not important. Rhythmic motion will help ensure a good hand position. Going slowly is far more important and helpful than trying to play quickly. Again, do not make this a big deal—just tell students that these songs are for fun and will help them to learn more songs later.

Troubleshooting the Clarinet

PROBLEM	CAUSE	SOLUTIONS
Squeaking	1. Equipment	(a) Make sure the clarinet is in good playing condition. (b) Pads covering the holes. (c) Pads in good condition. (d) Springs in place. (e) Levers working. (f) (See minor repairs at end of troubleshooting.) (g) Make sure it is a **quality** instrument.
	2. Mouthpiece	(a) Good quality. (b) No chips in tip of mouthpiece. (c) Table not warped.
	3. Ligature	(a) Ligature should be past the curve or slant (top). (b) Notice whether the screws should be on the top or bottom of the mouthpiece. If the screws are on top, but it is a "regular" ligature (screws on bottom), the reed may not seal along the table. (c) Quality: The ligature must hold the reed on the mouthpiece without slipping off. It must create a seal across the flat part of the reed and mouthpiece.
	4. Position of reed	(a) Tip of the reed to the tip of the mouthpiece. (b) Make sure the reed placement is not crooked.
	5. Mouth position	(a) Too much mouthpiece in mouth; less in mouth. (b) Too little mouthpiece in mouth; more in mouth. (c) The correct position may vary slightly from student to student. Have the student move the mouthpiece slightly in or out until the best sound is produced.
	6. Teeth position	(a) Top teeth **must** be on the mouthpiece. Often, it will appear that the top teeth are touching, but they are not. If squeaks continue, but embouchure looks good, lightly tap mouthpiece with a finger. If the top teeth are touching, the mouthpiece will not move. (b) Bottom teeth must be covered with lower lip. (c) Bottom teeth touching the reed. Cover teeth.
	7. Cheeks puffed out	(a) Tell student to bring in cheeks. (b) Tighten corners of lips. (c) Flatten chin against jawbone. (d) If all this fails, tell the student to hold a note (an easy note). While the student is sustaining the note, tell the student over and over again, very quickly, to bring the cheeks in. Usually, just as the student is running out of air, he or she will bring the cheeks in. Thus, the student

will feel the muscles working. You may have to do this one or two more times with the student, but this technique works because the student can feel how to use the muscles in his or her cheeks.

(e) Pretend to suck the air out of the clarinet. That will produce a perfect clarinet embouchure.

8. Blowing too hard

Tell the student to relax and not blow so hard.

9. Clarinet angle

The clarinet is pointing too high and away from the student. The bell of the clarinet should be at about a 45-degree angle or the clarinet should be just above the knees of the student (see p. 43).

Unfocused sound

1. Clarinet

(a) Quality of instrument: good brand (with the advent of the Internet, parents are obtaining cheap, poor quality instruments.) Try to warn them of this danger at the parent meeting or by sending letters to interested parents during the recruiting season.

(b) Condition of instrument: pads seating, poor quality pads, springs out of place, keys out of alignment, bent keys, etc.

2. Mouthpiece

(a) Poor quality.
(b) Warped table.
(c) Chipped in the tip—though it usually will not play at all if chipped.
(d) The only solution is to get a new one.
(e) Clean the inside. Dried saliva can build up to a point that air cannot pass through the mouthpiece into the clarinet!

3. Reed

(a) Quality: Some brands are much better than others. Try to have reeds that do not have the heart or center of cut section all scraped away.
(b) Reed too soft: Obtain a stronger reed.
(c) Reed too old: Get a new reed!

4. Bunched up lips (lips puckering)

(a) Tighten lips against the teeth.
(b) Lips should not be pointing forward.
(c) Lips flat against the teeth.
(d) Chin flat against jawbone.

5. Mouth position

The student should have the correct amount of mouthpiece in the mouth. Too little will cause an unfocused sound. Adjust until the sound is better.

6. A key

(a) Make sure the screw at the top of the A key is all the way in. If not, the pad will not seat, allowing a leak.

		(b) Bent A key. If the A key is bent too much, it will remain slightly open, thus creating just a small enough leak to sound bad but still play.
		(c) The key may be bent so it will not open to its proper height. See minor repairs (p. 65).
	7. Angle of clarinet	If the clarinet is too close to the body, the sound will be stuffy and unfocused. The bell should be just above the knees.
Unable to play over the break	1. Clarinet	(a) Make sure the pads are sealing; separate the two body joints. Take one piece at a time. Cover the tone holes by pressing the keys to close all the pads. With the other hand, place the bottom of the body joint against the palm of the hand. Create a vacuum by sucking the opposite end of the body joint. If the instrument holds suction, the pads are seating. You will hear and feel a leak if the pads are poor or out of adjustment. If this is the case, the instrument will need to be taken to a qualified repair person.
		(b) Follow the same procedure with the remaining body part.
	2. Mouthpiece	Must be in good condition. See previous comments about mouthpiece.
	3. Reed	(a) Reed too soft. Use at least a strength of $2^1/_2$. The better the brand, the better the tone quality. If using a brand that does not use numbers for strength measurement, have the student play a medium strength reed.
		(b) Reed too hard. If the reed is too hard, the student will not be able to blow enough air into the instrument. Change to a slightly softer reed.
		(c) Warped reed. If the tip is warped, the student can place the tip of the reed on the table of the mouthpiece and push the tip down with the thumb. The reed should be moist before this is done.
		(d) If the reed is warped at the table of the reed, then the reed is useless. Throw it away. You can tell if the reed is warped at the table by placing the reed on a flat surface. If there is a bow in the reed, it is warped toward the back of the reed and little can be done to make the reed play effectively.
	4. Covering the holes	Make sure the fingers are completely covering the holes. The teacher may push the fingers 3 down, 4 up, and 6 down to help the student feel the correct hand position to cover the holes (Photo 2-33).
	5. Biting	Squeezing the reed with mouth: Tell the student not to push the chin or bottom teeth (covered by lips) into the reed. The reed must have room to vibrate.

Photo 2-33

	6. Not enough air	Blow louder.
	7. Thumb position	Make sure the thumb is in correct position so the tip of the thumb can be rocked back and forth without lifting the thumb off the tone hole.
	8. Cannot play up the break	Have the student practice the pattern in reverse order, going down the break. This exercise may be practiced in a slower rhythm, such as quarter notes, but the tempo must remain constant. After several times of playing down the break correctly, the student should then practice playing the passage as written.
Clarinet will not make a sound	1. Clarinet	Back to step 1: Check the quality and condition of the instrument.
	2. Mouthpiece	Same as step 2: quality and condition of equipment.
	3. Reed	(a) Check quality and condition of reed. (b) Reed too soft or too hard.
	4. Embouchure	(a) Top teeth touching the mouthpiece. (b) Bottom teeth covered with bottom lip. (c) Make sure the mouthpiece is far enough in the mouth. (d) Be careful that the student is not putting so much pressure against the reed that air cannot pass into the clarinet.
	5. Air not going into instrument	(a) All of the above. (b) Clarinet too close to body. Bell should be just above the knees.

	6. Covering holes	Make sure the students are completely covering the holes.

Instrument problems — Minor repairs

(a) Check all springs, especially along the stack. The low E is notorious for coming off its hook. Most springs are an easy fix: simply attach the string back onto its hook (Photo 2-34).

(b) Cannot hear a difference between G and A. The A key is bent. Pull or push the lever up where the student plays the key. Do this only a very little bit at a time until the A key lifts off the tone hole. BE CAREFUL. You do not want to pop the key off the instrument or break the key.

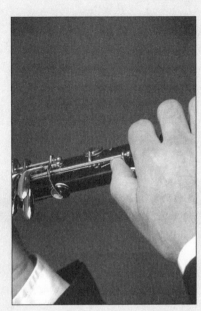

Photo 2-34

(c) The side B♭ key will often get jammed against the key next to it. Bend it back to its original position.

(d) If the student cannot play above the break and the low notes sound "fuzzy," often the top bridge (or lever) key is pushed too much against the bottom key. When the top key is jammed against the bottom key, it will cause the ring on the second hole to rise just enough to allow a leak, even if the student has a good hand position. Usually high notes will not play. Take the two body joints apart. Take the top body joint and push the lever up slightly so the key will not strike the lower lever bridge key when assembled (Photo 2-35).

Caution: When bending keys, bend only a little at a time. Some instrument keys may break very easily. Once a key is broken, the clarinet must go to the shop. Bend keys only in very small steps at a time. Stop the moment you feel uncomfortable about bending the keys. If you have a feeling you are about to go too far, you probably are!

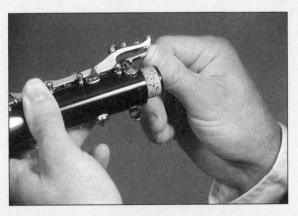

Photo 2-35

B♭ Clarinet Fingering Chart

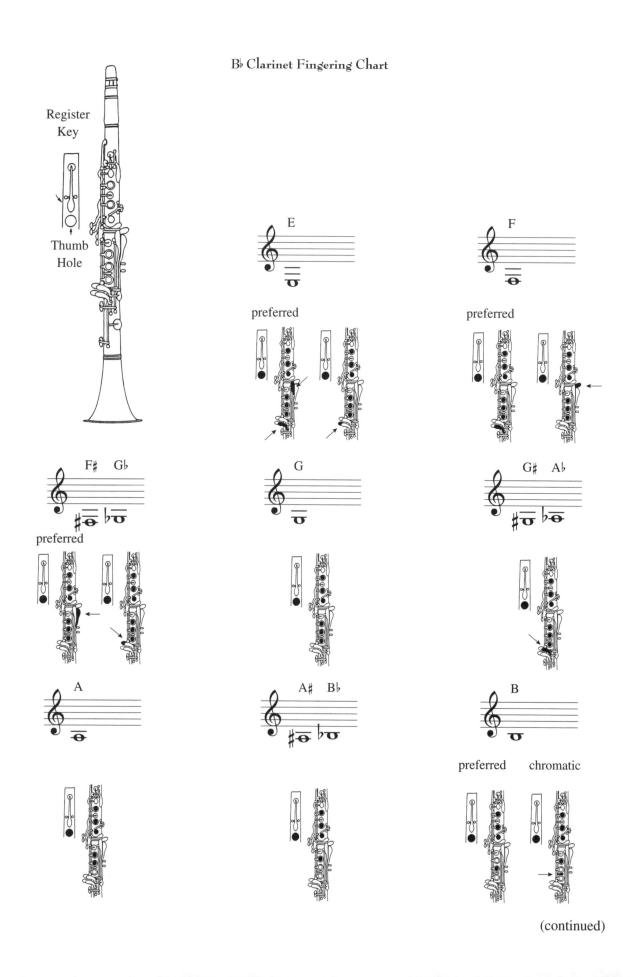

(continued)

B♭ Clarinet Fingering Chart, p. 2

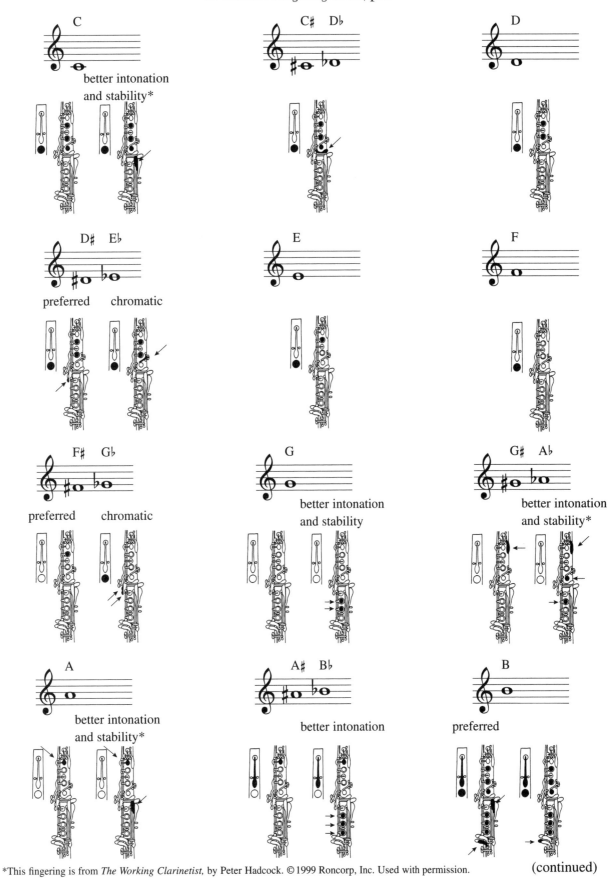

*This fingering is from *The Working Clarinetist*, by Peter Hadcock. © 1999 Roncorp, Inc. Used with permission.

(continued)

B♭ Clarinet Fingering Chart, p. 3

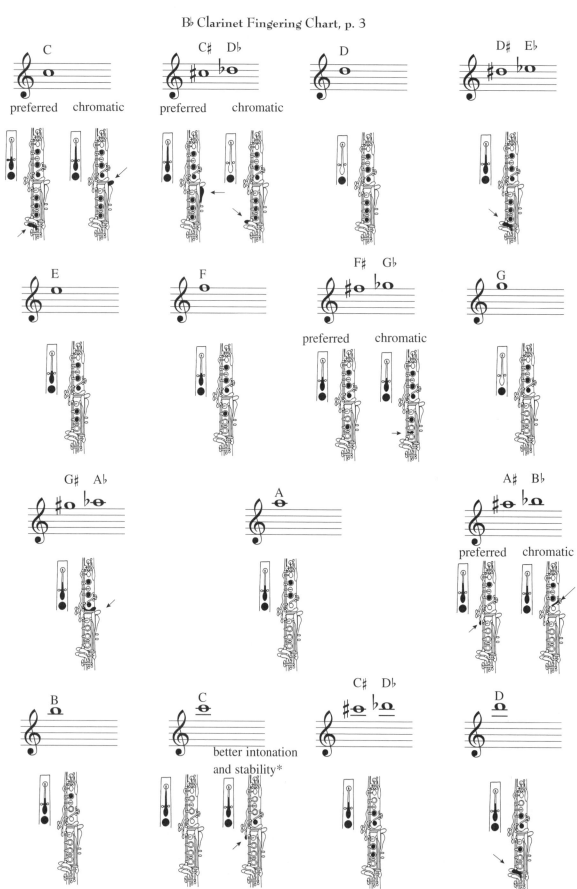

*This fingering is from *The Working Clarinetist,* by Peter Hadcock. ©1999 Roncorp, Inc. Used with permission.

Clarinet Lessons Checklist

Lesson 1

- [ ] Chairs and stands in order
- [ ] Name tags on chairs
- [ ] Top of case
- [ ] How to open
- [ ] Cork grease
- [ ] Assembly
- [ ] Moisten reed
- [ ] Reed to mouthpiece
- [ ] Tip of reed to tip of mouthpiece
- [ ] Inspect instrument for quality/repair
- [ ] Hand position
- [ ] First note: E
- [ ] Embouchure
- [ ] Bottom teeth covered with lip
- [ ] Top teeth on mouthpiece
- [ ] Adjust mouthpiece to mouth
- [ ] Angle of clarinet/posture
- [ ] Tongue the note
- [ ] Play notes D and C
- [ ] First song: "Three Blind Mice"
- [ ] Instructions on how to practice
- [ ] Disassemble the instrument
- [ ] Specific assignment
- [ ] *Be Enthusiastic!*

Lesson 2

- [ ] Advanced students: Assemble instruments immediately
- [ ] While advanced are assembling instrument, show new students top of case
- [ ] Reed check for advanced students
- [ ] Review notes with advanced students
- [ ] Continue to show new students how to assemble their instruments
- [ ] Posture
- [ ] Advanced: Play "Three Blind Mice"
- [ ] New students: E
- [ ] Advanced students: Start to play book, beginners follow along
- [ ] Show beginners D
- [ ] Advanced: Continue with book
- [ ] Show beginners C
- [ ] No book for beginners while playing
- [ ] Make sure advanced understand how to read the notes—no faking
- [ ] Only first page for advanced
- [ ] Beginners work on first three notes only
- [ ] Specific assignment
- [ ] *Be Enthusiastic!*

Lesson 3

- [ ] Advanced: Start assembling instrument
- [ ] New students: Start showing top of case and assembly while advanced students are assembling instruments, reviewing, and playing their first notes
- [ ] Most advanced: Play lesson-reading notes
- [ ] Students who just played for the first time last week: Review notes
- [ ] Continue with beginners, as other students are playing their notes
- [ ] Keep reviewing all lessons

- [ ] Use baton/conduct
- [ ] Point to notes if students are not reading
- [ ] Have everyone follow along even when not playing
- [ ] Posture
- [ ] Tonguing
- [ ] If the students are ready, start discussing intonation
- [ ] Specific assignment
- [ ] Notice their accomplishments and tell them how they have improved
- [ ] *Be Enthusiastic!*

Lesson 4

- [ ] If possible, reschedule new students
- [ ] Advanced students start assembling instrument as they enter the room
- [ ] Start showing the new students top of case and assembly
- [ ] As soon as tones are stabilized, start tuning the instruments
- [ ] Continue to instruct beginners as you teach the advanced
- [ ] Counting/toe tapping
- [ ] Playing the notes (advanced—reading the notes)
- [ ] Embouchure—start to be more particular about skin tight against the chin
- [ ] Posture
- [ ] Show new notes and rhythms for next lesson
- [ ] Insist on practice
- [ ] Give specific assignment
- [ ] ***Enthusiasm!***

Lesson 5

- [ ] New students should be rescheduled
- [ ] Assemble instruments immediately
- [ ] If you must have new students, teach instrument assembly while teaching the other students
- [ ] Advanced students: intonation
- [ ] As advanced play, watch eyes to make sure they are reading
- [ ] Posture
- [ ] Tonguing
- [ ] Breathing between notes
- [ ] Discuss chair positions
- [ ] Embouchure
- [ ] Try to move as many students as possible to the same page
- [ ] Keep everyone playing—no more than a 5-minute break for anyone at any time
- [ ] Specific assignment
- [ ] ***Enthusiasm!***

BEGINNING SAXOPHONE LESSONS

Saxophone Lesson 1 (Fig. 2-18)

Prepare the classroom before the students enter the room. Have the chairs ready, and put name tags on the chairs if possible. Often on the first day you will have no idea how many students are interested in playing the saxophone. Be prepared for a large group. When they enter the room, have the students sit or stand where you assign them. Do not let them have control of the room on the first day. Now is the time to state any rules you have about class conduct, being on time for lessons, and promptly returning back to class (if this is a program where you take the students out of another class). Have pen and paper ready for a sign-in list. Ask the students to write their names, grade, and homeroom on the paper so you will be able to find them in the future.

On the first day there may be many students without instruments. Have the students with instruments sit in the front of the class. Ask the other students to sit next to a student with an instrument, or stand where they can see and hear what is happening. This is a good time to instruct the students without instruments that they should listen, learn, and not cause a distraction or they will be asked to return to their classrooms, or be separated from the group. Tell the students they will receive their instruments soon, and if they listen they will know what to do.

Proper assembly is essential for any instrument. Woodwind instruments can easily be damaged if not taken out of the case and put together properly. As simple as it may seem, students must be instructed in the proper procedure to open the instrument case. Make sure the students know the top of the case from the bottom of the case. On most cases, the handle is on the bottom section. The brand name is often on the top, but not always, and on most cases the latches will go up in order to open the case. Instruct the students to set the instruments on the floor in front of them with the bottom of the case on the floor and the instrument handle facing them. Check to make sure they have done this. Do not assume they can do anything without your help and supervision. Tell them to open the case, but not to take the instrument out until you instruct them to do so (Photo 2-36). If the instrument is new, have them unwrap the neck and other parts that are packaged for travel. If their saxophone's keys are still tightly wrapped and corked, you may want to unwrap the instrument yourself. It is very easy for keys to become bent and pads to be accidentally pushed off or for the saxophone to lose its proper adjustment. Inspect the new instruments for corks that are placed between the keys and braces to prevent

Photo 2-36

movement during shipment. Remove these corks and other devices for the students. Show the students the neck strap and have them put it on. Then, show them which saxophone part is the neck and where the cork is on the neck. Take one student's saxophone neck piece and show how to put cork grease on the cork. The other students should do the same.

As you assemble the instruments, check the quality and condition of each student's instrument. It must be in good working order for the students to produce a good sound. If an instrument is in disrepair, write a note to the parents informing them of the situation. Inform them in no uncertain terms that their child will not be able to succeed in playing the saxophone if it is not in good working order. Many parents may say they do not want to spend the money on a repair unless they first see success and progress on the instrument; do your best to help them understand there will be no progress or success, because the unrepaired instrument will not allow the student to be successful. It is unfair to the student to ask him or her to play a poor quality instrument. Give parents the names of reasonably priced repair people in the

Figure 2-18
Music for Saxophone Lesson 1

Teach this lesson without showing the music to the students. Students should concentrate on producing a good sound. Attempting to read music will distract from all that is needed to produce a good sound.

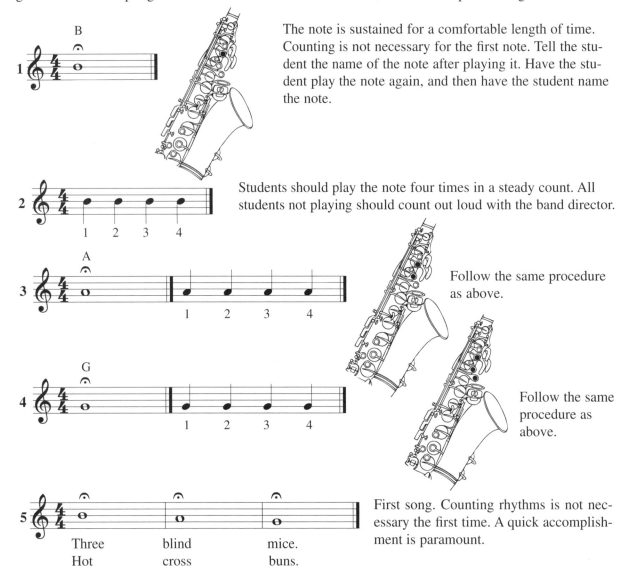

The note is sustained for a comfortable length of time. Counting is not necessary for the first note. Tell the student the name of the note after playing it. Have the student play the note again, and then have the student name the note.

Students should play the note four times in a steady count. All students not playing should count out loud with the band director.

Follow the same procedure as above.

Follow the same procedure as above.

First song. Counting rhythms is not necessary the first time. A quick accomplishment is paramount.

Three   blind   mice.
Hot   cross   buns.

Mary Had a Little Lamb

ASSIGNMENT: First, hold each note, then play each note four times.
Play "Three Blind Mice."
Challenge: Who can play "Mary Had a Little Lamb" using the three notes learned today? Be positive; wish everyone a nice day.
BE ENTHUSIASTIC!

area. Sometimes new instruments are very poorly built. Inform parents of this in a very nice, diplomatic way. Do not be insulting, but suggest that they return the instrument immediately, and receive a

Photo 2-37

refund, or credit toward a good quality instrument. I cannot stress this enough. If the instrument does not play easily, the student will become discouraged and quit. He will not practice, the parents will be miserable, and you stand to lose a client.

Demonstrate how to put the neck on the body of the saxophone (Photo 2-37). Instruct the students to loosen the screw on the body first. Then put the neck onto the body. The neck should be turned back and forth, not turned around in circles, while pushing the neck down into the saxophone body. When that task is completed, the neck should be pointing in the opposite direction

Photo 2-38

of the bell of the saxophone. Tighten the screw so the neck will not slip around or off the saxophone.

After everyone has the neck and body assembled properly, take a mouthpiece out of one of the student's cases. Do not put on the reed. Show the students how to put the mouthpiece on the neck. The mouthpiece should be twisted back and forth and pushed onto the neck at the same time. If it is very difficult to push the mouthpiece onto the neck, have the student apply more cork grease (Photo 2-38). (Too much will not hurt the instrument. Too little cork grease may cause the cork to crack and break.)

Photo 2-39

The instrument will not play without cork on the neck to create a good seal. The flat part of the mouthpiece with the opening should be facing the floor if the instrument is being held vertically.

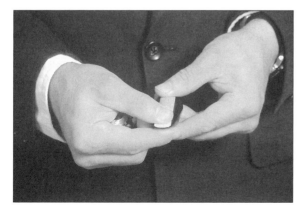

Photo 2-40

Before you put the reed on the mouthpiece, have the students put the reeds into their mouths and start to wet the reeds with their saliva. Tell them to be careful with the tip of the reed. The tip is very thin and very easy to break. A broken reed will not play easily, if at all. They can continue to moisten the reeds while you demonstrate how to put the reed on the mouthpiece. Take one of the student's instruments and lay the bell across your lap with the mouthpiece opening facing you. The flat part of the reed should be put on the flat part of the mouthpiece (Photos 2-39 and 2-40). Put the ligature over the reed. Do not call the ligature by its name at this time. The students are absorbing a tremendous amount of information during this first

Photo 2-41

lesson. Using a name they have never heard before may confuse them, and they probably won't remember the name anyway. Instruct them to carefully watch what they are doing while putting the "reed holder" over the reed. It is very easy to split the reed while looking away and talking to a neighbor. Adjust the reed so the tip of the reed is even with the tip of the mouthpiece as shown in Photo 2-41. There are different schools of thought about where the best sound will occur with the placement of the reed. However, at this time, you should be more concerned with the student getting any sound rather than a special sound. The students may be scared that they may make a terrible sound, but they are more worried that nothing will come out at all and thus of being seen as a failure. If the reed plays, but it is difficult to blow

into the instrument, the student may be discouraged and may want to quit. The goal at the first lesson is to produce a sound as easily and as quickly as possible. Once the reed is in place, put your thumb between the two screws (Photo 2-42). Tighten the screws until they do not turn. Do not tighten them as much as your strength allows—the vibration of the reed may be restricted and/or the screws may break. Before you completely tighten the reed, you may need to adjust the reed again. Hand the saxophone back to the student and have him attach the neck strap to the saxophone. Have the remaining students do this (Photo 2-43). Watch them carefully, and help them as needed. You must move quickly and encourage the students to move carefully and quickly. Also, remember there

Photo 2-42

may be other students in the class without instruments. Keep an eye on them. Do not allow them to talk among themselves. Make sure they pay attention to you and to how the saxophone is being assembled.

Many instrument manufacturers and music stores put a $1\frac{1}{2}$ strength reed in the case. That strength is too soft. A #2 strength or medium soft reed is the proper strength for a beginner. If the reed is too weak,

Photo 2-43

it may close up against the mouthpiece and prevent air from entering into the saxophone. It may also cause the instrument to squeak. Have a box of reeds ready to give a student a #2 strength if the reed in his case is too weak. Remember to keep moving. You have a lot to teach in one half hour. Try not to get behind in time. Everyone should have the instrument assembled and play at least one note before the end of the first lesson. This will help them to feel they have accomplished something.

The First Note

Do not use the book or sheet music for the first lesson. The student's concentration should be on holding the instrument and making a sound.

Posture is very important and now is the time to introduce it; do not wait until a later lesson. Instruct the students to sit on the front edge of the chair on the right-hand side. The saxophone should be coming down on the right side of their leg (Photo 2-44). Do not allow them to lean back in the chair—their backs should be straight. Often professionals will play the saxophone between their legs; however, they are much bigger than most young students 9 to 12 years of age. When the students are older and taller, they may then sit in that posture. Adjust the neck strap so the instrument hangs down with the mouthpiece at mouth level.

Photo 2-44

The first note they will play is B, third line of the staff. This is the best note to start with because it helps the students hold the saxophone, does not involve too many fingers, and the note responds very easily.

Show each student, one at a time, how to hold the instrument and play the note. Correct posture and adjust the mouthpiece to the right height. Tell the first student to place her/his left thumb on the thumb rest in the back of the saxophone (Photos 2-45 and 2-46). Then the first finger goes around the saxophone to the B key. The B key is not the very top key on the saxophone, but it is the first big key. The uppermost key is for very advanced notes and will not be used for several years. As the student reaches for the B key on the front of the saxophone, make sure her/his thumb does not slip off the thumb rest and the hand and fin-

Photo 2-45

gers do not depress the side keys. This is an easy mistake to make, especially since the student's hands at this age are not very big. Once she/he sees how to hold the saxophone properly with the B finger ready for playing, it is time to demonstrate the proper embouchure.

Tell the student to cover her/his bottom teeth with the bottom lip. All that is needed is the top of the lip over the teeth. Too much lip is unnecessary. Have the student put the top teeth on top of the mouthpiece. It should feel as though the weight of the head is resting on the saxophone (Photo 2-47). Once the top teeth are in place, about a half inch from the tip, and the bottom lip is covered, have the student close her/his mouth around the mouthpiece. If the instructor holds the saxophone in such a manner that his index finger is between the ligature and the student's mouth, it will be a good measure for distance between mouth and mouthpiece. This will also make it easier for the instructor to quickly move the mouthpiece in and out of the student's mouth. It may be necessary to hold the student's head to make sure she/he keeps her/his top teeth on the mouthpiece (Photo 2-48).

Photo 2-46

Photo 2-47

Before you allow the student to blow, quickly check posture, saxophone height, finger position, and embouchure. Once everything is ready, instruct her to blow air into the saxophone. Whatever sound she gets, compliment her! She may puff out her cheeks, blow so loud it startles you, or produce a very soft sound, but it is a sound, and it should be praised. If there is no sound, check the reed. Make sure it is straight and the tip of the reed is adjusted to the tip of the mouthpiece. Ask her to try again. If there is still no sound, tell her to relax. She may be nervous and squeezing her mouth too tightly around the mouthpiece. The saxophone is easy to blow, and it does not take a lot of pressure to produce a sound. Show her how the reed closes shut against the mouthpiece when too much pressure is applied. Use your thumb on the reed to demonstrate this. Then have her play again. If she is still squeezing too tightly, then have her put more mouthpiece into her mouth. You may need to have her put so much mouthpiece into her mouth that the sound becomes bad, but at least it is a sound. Gradually pull the mouthpiece out until the sound is a good centered and focused sound, or at least a good sound for the first day.

If you are in a group lesson, do not get stuck on one student. You must move quickly. Even if a problem persists, move on. Chances are the student is getting nervous and needs a chance to relax. By going to the next student, you take the pressure off the student with the problem, and many times he or she sees exactly what to do by watching another student performing the procedure correctly. In addition to spending too much time with the problem student and not enough with everyone else, there is a good chance you could have a child crying, and it is very hard to turn that into a positive situation. Keep track of time and be pleasant at all times.

Here are some solutions for noisy-blatty sounds:

1. Too much mouthpiece: Put less mouthpiece into the mouth.

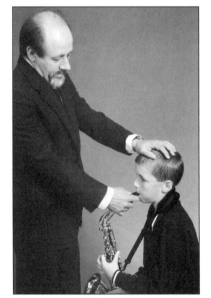

Photo 2-48

2. Puffing out cheeks:

   • Tell her not to do this; sometimes that is all that is needed.

   • Tell her to pretend she is eating a lemon. The student can then feel the muscles tighten up.

   • Suck the air out of the instrument. When the student does this, she can feel the muscles in the cheeks tighten up.

   • Tell the student to hold an easy note to play (B at this time). While she is holding the note, tell her to bring her cheeks in. Keep repeating this phrase over and over again until she brings her cheeks in. This procedure often works. It takes a minute or two to do, but it works because the student starts with the cheeks puffed out and she can feel the process of the muscles in her cheeks working for the first time.

3. Playing too loud:

   • Tell her to play more softly.

   • Adjust the mouthpiece in her mouth where she has better control of the air supply.

The sound does not have to be perfect. A student is more afraid that no sound will come out than he is of making a bad sound. Praise him for his sound and go on to the next person.

As the student plays, watch for fingers lifting. Even when playing a B, it is very easy for a student to lift the first finger slightly without realizing it. Just push her finger all the way down and she will understand what you mean when you tell her that her finger is floating up.

If the first finger is all the way down but she still is making a flat or incorrect sound, look at the side keys. Young saxophonists often depress the side keys in both hands without realizing it. You may need to adjust her hand position so she is not touching the side keys (Photos 2-49 and 2-50). Once she sees what you are talking about, she will be more conscious of the side keys and try not to press them

Photo 2-49

while playing. You may suggest that students have their hands make the shape of the letter C while playing and holding the instrument (Photos 2-49 and 2-50).

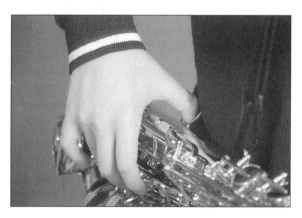

Photo 2-50

Once everyone has played a B, have the students all play it together. Gesture to hold the note and then cut it off. Praise them. Students who were having a problem getting the correct sound will often play better with the whole group. It does not matter if it is not done perfectly; it is great to just get the first sound out of the instrument. Have the students all say the note out loud: B. Next, have them play the note four times, one beat apiece. Sing the rhythm for them. Then, count off the beats and conduct while they play. It is important to start conducting immediately. It helps the students keep the beat and play together. You should not explain conducting to them on the first lesson—it is too much to remember. After they have played the note four times, have them hold the note for four beats. Make sure they are tapping their feet. Counting is extremely important and they must start immediately. And praise them again (this cannot be done too much).

The second note to teach is A. Demonstrate the fingering to them. You may need to place the finger in position for a student. Make sure she does not press the *bis key,* the little key between B and A keys (see diagram). Watch the side keys. The more keys she has to finger, the more likely it is she is going to depress the side keys by accident. Make sure the top teeth are on the mouthpiece. When the embouchure is correct and the fingers are in position, tell her to blow. Repeat the name of the note and ask her to say its name out loud. Have her play the note again, and check for the same problems she may have experienced on the first note. Praise her sound and go to the next student. Move quickly as you are running out of time. When you look at your watch you will notice you have only a few minutes left. Don't panic. Just move quickly from one student to the next. Use the same procedures as you did to teach the note B. This part of the lesson should progress more quickly because students have all made a sound and they are not so nervous as before.

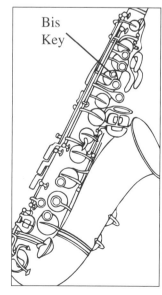

Bis
Key

Quickly show the students how to play G:

1. Show the fingering.
2. Place fingers in correct place if necessary.
3. Watch for side keys.
4. Tell the student to blow (you may have them do it all together if you are out of time).
5. Tell them the name of the note and have them say it out loud.
6. Check for the same problems as with the previous note.
7. Praise their sound.
8. All play the note four times (conduct).
9. All play the note for four beats.
10. Praise them again.

Now they are ready for their first song. Have them play B, A, G slowly one note after another (one beat each). The students have just played their first song, "Three Blind Mice." Tell them that these are the first three notes of "Mary Had a Little Lamb." Challenge them. See who will come to their next lesson and play all of "Mary Had a Little Lamb" without your help. Some students will figure it out. Ask the students what B-A-G spells. It will help them to remember the notes learned today.

You are out of time by now, especially if you have a large class. Disassemble the instrument in the opposite order it was assembled. While the students are putting their instruments in the cases, tell them to go home and practice. If no sound comes out when they practice at home, tell them to stay relaxed and keep trying. Most of the time when a sound does not come out, it is because they are trying too hard and squeezing the reed against the mouthpiece. Even if they do not get a sound the whole week, they should keep trying. They all obtained a sound today so they will all make one again. Stress that it is important to practice every day even if they are not getting the same good sound they obtained in school. It will happen again, even if they have to wait until their next lesson. As they leave the room, remind them to practice daily and to have a nice day/weekend/holiday or whatever is appropriate.

Be pleasant. Be enthusiastic. What happens today may determine whether they stay in the program or drop out quickly.

Saxophone Lesson 2 (Fig. 2-19)

The success of this lesson depends on your organizational skills, as well as your ability to keep track of time and to teach quickly and efficiently. You have to deal with students who have played their instruments for one week, students who are receiving their instruments for the first time, and students who intend to sign up, but have not received their instruments.

As the students come through the door, instruct the students who received their instruments at the previous lesson to put their instruments together and sit next to each other. Students who are receiving their instruments for the first time should sit together, and the remaining students should sit where they can see what the other students are doing. While the students with instruments from the previous week are assembling their instruments, start instructing the new students on how to assemble their instruments. Follow the same procedure used the previous week, starting with putting the bottom of the instrument case on the floor.

The advanced students will finish assembling their instruments before the new students. Start to review the previous lesson with them as you continue to help the new students assemble their instruments. Have the advanced students play a B all together. From this lesson forward, students who have played before will be referred to as "advanced" and those who are receiving their instruments for the first time are the "new" or "beginning" students. If the note sounds good and no one had a problem, then you may proceed to A. However, if some did not play the note well or had difficulty producing a sound, have them all play B individually. All the while you are doing this, you are continuing to help the new students assemble their instruments. Reminders for a good sound are:

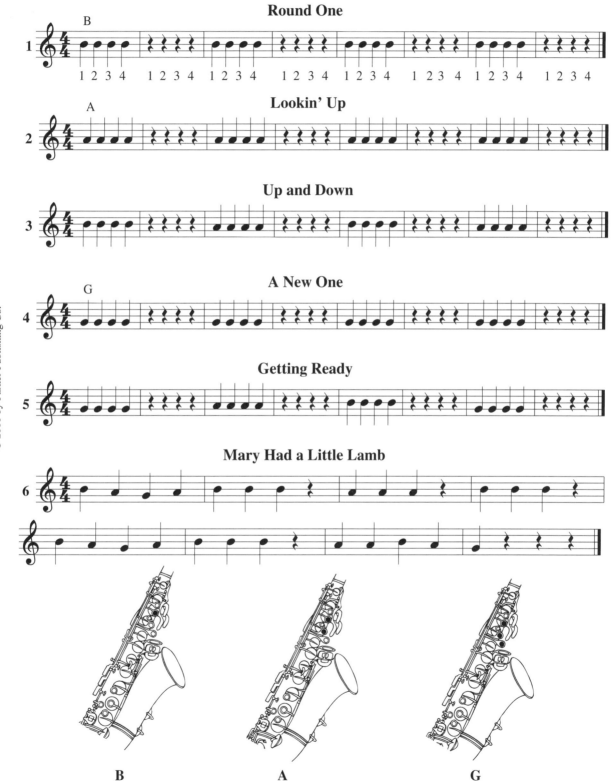

Figure 2-19
Music for Saxophone Lesson 2

Tap toes: one foot tap per beat. Start with toes up; heels anchored on floor. Practice tapping toes while playing every line.

1. Keep the bottom teeth covered with the bottom lip.

2. Top teeth should be firmly resting on the mouthpiece.

3. If no sound is coming out, relax and put more mouthpiece into the mouth.

4. If a blatty sound is being made, put less mouthpiece into the mouth.

5. Do not puff out cheeks. Use the same exercises or examples used in the first lesson.

The new students should be ready to play a note by the time the students with instruments from the previous week have played B, A, G. You will teach the new students one at a time, just as in the previous lessons. Make sure the saxophone is hanging down on the right side of the leg. The strap should be adjusted so the mouthpiece is at the student's mouth when the saxophone is hanging down from the student's neck. Tell the first student to cover her bottom teeth with her bottom lip and to put her top teeth on the mouthpiece, and when the embouchure looks right and the first finger is on the first key, instruct her to blow. You may need to hold her head down with your hand to keep her from lifting her head and teeth away from the mouthpiece. Once the sound is fairly good, go on to the next student. You do not have time for perfection; this is not a private lesson. If you do not move quickly, there will be students at the end of the lesson who have not played a note. They may be upset and, therefore, more likely to drop out early.

After you have taught the new students to play B, have all the students play B together four times, one beat each, then one note for four beats. Continue with the new students, teaching them to play A. Follow the same procedure as before.

Be mindful of students in class without instruments. Speak to them occasionally. Remind them to watch closely so they will learn quickly. If you pay no attention to them, they may become a discipline problem. However, do not allow them to detract from your main objective of teaching the students with instruments. If anyone becomes a conduct problem, send her back to the regular class, if this is a program where you take children out of another class, or back to her parents, if this is a summer lesson.

Once all the new students have played A, have everyone play A together. Have them play four quarter notes, praise them, and then ask them to play one whole note for four beats. Make sure everyone is tapping their toes, even students without instruments.

Review A with the students with instruments from the previous week, and then instruct the students to play G. Then have them play B, A, G on your cue. Next assign a rhythm—two counts each.

Now it should be fairly easy to teach G to the new students. They have already played B and A, and have seen the older students play A and G. Show the students, one at a time, how to play G. Watch for the side keys and check that fingers are all the way down on both keys. When all the new students have played A, have the older students join in.

Ask the advanced students if anyone can play "Mary Had a Little Lamb." Allow volunteers to try. Do not spend a lot of time trying to show a student how to do this. They're going to learn the song on the first page of the book.

Have the students look at Lesson 2 in this resource. If you must use a commercial band method for the lesson, then locate the line that has B in it. Not all books have the first note as B. There is no rule that requires you to start each group with the first line in the method book. Many books have their first note in line one as a D, but that is too hard for the first note, regardless of the students' age. Start easily and they should not become discouraged. Indicate to the students that the first note is on the third line of the staff. Explain that the staff is the chart that tells us what our notes are when we read music. The third line will always indicate B. The first note is a quarter note; explain to them that a quarter note is filled in solid with a stem. The direction of the stem does not change the note or the duration of the note. Because it is filled in and has a stem, it is called a quarter note and receives one beat or one foot tap. Have everyone play the first note only. Then have them play all four quarter notes. Make sure they are tapping their toes. Counting out loud for them may help. If you are using a band method book that starts with whole notes, have everyone play the whole note first. Make sure you explain that the shape of the whole note indicates the note should be played for four beats, and has nothing to do with the name of the note. Remind students that the note on the third line of the staff is always B. Have everyone play the first measure together. The second measure of line 1 is four quarter rests. Explain that rests are a certain number of beats of silence. Remind them that this is not a time to stop counting and start daydreaming. Now have everyone play the entire line together.

While students are playing the notes on the page, watch their eyes carefully. If someone is looking at other students' fingers or around the room in confusion, she does not understand how to read the music. The easiest way to get a student to read music is to point to the notes with your baton as the group plays. Have everyone play the line again. This time, use your baton to point to the notes on the page of the student who is having trouble reading the music. By seeing the notes as everyone plays, she can see the progression from one note to another. You may have to do this more than once and for more than one student, but this should help them to understand how to read the music. Also point out that they should continue to look ahead to the next note.

Once they have all played this line, continue to line 2. Play the line with an A if you are using a heterogeneous band method. Follow the same procedure as that in the previous paragraph. However, take a moment to point out the difference between the two notes on the staff. Instruct everyone to point to the A on the second space. Ask them to look at the previous line they played and have everyone point to the B on the third line. Make sure they can see the difference between the two notes.

Show the new students how to play a G. It should be an easy process, but once again, watch for the side keys. Instruct the new students to practice without the book before they practice reading the notes on the page. Concentrate on putting the mouth in the proper place on the mouthpiece (introduce the word *embouchure* later), and concentrate on not touching the side keys.

During this time, do not forget about the students without instruments. Ask them to sit where they can see the book. Tell them to pay attention and learn where the notes are on the page. Ask some of them to name the notes as you point to them. There are only two notes learned so far so it should not be too difficult.

For those using a hetereogeneous method, if the book does not have an A or G on the first page but does have a C, go to that line. Show the students the difference between the notes. Note that B is on the third line and C is on the third space. Tell them to "see the difference." Point to the two notes with your baton. Focus your attention on rhythm. When they play, make sure they are all tapping their toes, playing the right notes, and looking at the page. Remind all students not to puff out their cheeks.

Many beginning method books will include D on the first page. D is not an easy note for a beginning saxophonist. The problem with this note is that the fingers on both hands must depress the six major keys and octave key while not depressing the side keys. For a fourth-grader with small hands, that can be difficult. Before looking at the book, have each student, one at a time, play the note. Before they play the note, make sure the fingers are on the correct keys and they are not touching the side keys. Quite often, a student will not be aware that a finger is not all the way down. Look closely, and gently push down any fingers that are raised. When the fingers are in proper position, have the student play the note. Watch closely, because many students will lift a finger or two without realizing it. Again, gently push down the fingers while they are playing the note. Have each student play the note, and then have everyone play the note together.

Next, have the students play line 3 on the music page (Fig. 2-19). This will reinforce the difference between the notes B and A. After this line has been played correctly, have the students continue to line 4. Point out the difference between B and G. Make sure they can see that the G is on the second line of the staff and the B is on the third line of the staff. By the time they are reading and playing line 4, they should begin to understand how the staff works to indicate which notes to play.

As in the previous lines, have the students play the first measure alone and then play the whole line. All the while, keep an eye out for a good embouchure. Make sure the top teeth are touching the mouthpiece. They should not cover both top and bottom teeth, only the top. If a student complains about the vibration, you may suggest a rubber pad for the top. These are very easy to make: From a rubber glove purchased in a supermarket, cut a small piece in the shape of the top of the mouthpiece. (Do not buy a thick rubber glove—a very thin layer is all that is needed.) With nontoxic glue, attach it to the top of the mouthpiece. This will cushion the mouthpiece to stop vibrations. Continue to remind the students not to puff out their cheeks. Do not forget posture. Constantly remind them to sit up with their backs straight. (Most likely you will be doing this for your entire career.) If you do not remind them daily, they will forget.

Play as many lines as possible on this page. Do not worry if you do not play the entire page—most likely, you will not. But at least the students will have enough information to play the entire page at home. Do not worry if the students who just received their instruments at this lesson did not progress so far as the students who started with instruments at the previous lesson. Having played the same notes, or at least most of them, they can practice the first page over the next week.

Give the students a specific assignment. Tell the advanced students to practice the entire page. The new students should practice without the book at first. They should start with the B: Play it four times, one beat each, then hold it for four counts. They should do that with each note: B, A, G. Instruct them to try to play "Mary Had a Little Lamb" using those notes. After they feel comfortable about playing these notes, they should start on the assignment in this resource or in the book. Remind the students that if no sound comes out of the saxophone when they practice at home, it is probably because they are squeezing the reed too tight with their lips. Just tell them to relax and put more mouthpiece into the mouth. Encourage the students to look ahead. It is always okay to play more than what is assigned. Be positive, encouraging, and enthusiastic. Make sure you reserve enough time for them to put their instruments back into their cases.

Saxophone Lesson 3 (Fig. 2-20)

The third lesson becomes even more complicated than the previous lesson because there will be students in the room who have received two lessons, some with one lesson, some who will be receiving their instruments for the first time, and students who still have not obtained their instruments but intend to play. Time management is a major concern. If you can reschedule the new students into a different group, you will be able to spend more time with the others and increase their chances for success.

It is advisable to set a deadline from the first lesson as to the last date a student can obtain an instrument and still participate in the band program for the current school year. That deadline will vary according to your school situation. You want to be fair and give the parents ample time to obtain instruments, but you do not want to give them so much time that it becomes unfair to students who received their instruments from the first lesson. Consider all the factors in your situation and give the parents a week longer than really necessary, but once you set the deadline, stick to it. This is the time to give a stern reminder about the deadline. By the third lesson, you may want to tell students without instruments that they will have to stop attending the music class. Establish that only students with instruments may continue to report to lessons. When students are sent back to the regular, nonmusical class, the parents will usually make arrangements to obtain instruments or inform you that their children will not participate this year.

As students enter the room, give the following instructions: Students who have learned to assemble the instrument should do so immediately; students receiving their instruments today or learning to assemble the instrument for the first time should sit in the assigned chairs. The chairs should be in a row so you can work with these newer students while listening to the other students play their assignments from previous lessons.

As the more advanced students are assembling their instruments, have the new students place their cases on the floor in front of them with the bottom of the case flat on the floor. Instruct them to open the case. Have the students put cork grease on the neck.

Keep an eye on the other students. If their instruments are assembled by this time, have them all sit with good posture and play a B for four counts on your cue. Always conduct. It helps the students feel that they are important, that they are part of a band, and that you are giving them the exact moment in which to play. They are not secure enough to know when to play. The more you do for them, the easier it will be for them to perform.

Figure 2-20
Music for Saxophone Lesson 3

Show the new students how to put the neck onto the body of the saxophone. As they are doing that, have the other students play A. Keep an eye and ear out for students striking the side keys with their hands. Always watch for good embouchure and posture.

Now the new students are ready to be shown how to put the reed on the mouthpiece. Follow the same procedure as in Lesson 1.

As the remaining new students are doing this, have the advanced saxophonists play a G. Have the students look at the music for Lesson 2. Tell them to silently review this page while you show the new students how to play their first note.

Before you have a new student play the first note, make sure the ligature is on properly, the reed is not chipped or split, and the tip of the reed is adjusted to the tip of the mouthpiece. Tell her to sit with good posture, and press the first finger all the way down on the first key. Watch for good hand positions and the proper way of holding the saxophone. Tell her to cover the bottom teeth with the bottom lip, and to put the top teeth firmly on the mouthpiece with the weight of her head on the mouthpiece. Once everything is ready, tell her to blow. No matter what the sound is, tell her it is wonderful! Also, correct problems. If cheeks are puffed out, instruct the student how to correct this. Some students may touch the side keys after they start to play the note. Correct these and any other problems immediately. Remember to move fast. The process described here should go faster than in the first two lessons because these students should have been paying attention in previous classes and should catch on more quickly.

As soon as the new students have played their first note, turn your attention to the advanced students. Have them play line 1. Make any corrections and then go to line 2. Make corrections and play line 3. This is a quick review of Lesson 2.

Have the new students play a B four times for one beat each, and then one time for four beats. Instruct them to pay attention as you have the other students play. The advanced students should play the next couple of lines in the book. (Most books put "Mary Had a Little Lamb" on this page. Stop before that song.)

Have the beginners play their notes one more time, but this time, have the advanced students play along. Show the beginners how to play A. After all the beginners have played A, have everyone play all together. Finally, show the beginners how to play G. All beginners should play G individually, and then all students play G together.

The advanced students should play the last song on the page, which is "Mary Had a Little Lamb." Work on rhythm and playing together. They should observe all rests accurately. Always conduct the students and use your baton. This will help the students keep a steady beat and get used to watching a conductor.

Introduce the new students to the line with B. Make sure everyone understands that the B is the note on the third line of the staff. Explain the rhythm to them. When you are ready for them to play, have everyone play along, including the advanced students. It is a good review, and it keeps them playing.

Keep track of time throughout the lesson. If you have more than five minutes left, show the new students how to play C. After all beginners have played C, have advanced and beginners play the line together. Play as many lines of Lesson 3 as possible. All the while, make sure no one is silent for more than five minutes. Everyone must keep playing his or her instrument.

As the students are playing and reading music from the book, keep your eyes and ears open for the following:

1. Puffing cheeks.

2. Top teeth on the mouthpiece.

3. Breathing before every note. (Do not overdo this yet. Just mention to them not to breathe before every note.)

4. Bottom lip covering the bottom teeth.

5. Too much or too little mouthpiece in mouth.

6. Tapping toes. (This is extremely important. Students must count from the very beginning. Tapping their toes is the only means by which they can keep count at this time. Counting in their heads only is too abstract.)

7. Reading the notes. (Watch their eyes. If they are not following the notes, use your baton to point to the notes.)

8. Pressing the side keys accidentally.

9. Hand position.

10. Posture. (Always remind them of this.)

Before the lesson is over, reserve enough time to show them how to play the notes on the next page. You may not have time to have everyone play them individually, but show them how to read the fingering chart. Also explain to them any new rhythms, the duration, and how to tell the difference from rhythms they learned on the first page.

Give a specific assignment. The entire class does not have to receive the same assignment. Perhaps the students who are on their third lesson with an instrument can be assigned to review the first three lessons. Tell the students who have just received their second lesson with an instrument to practice Lesson 2 until they can play very well. Have the new students first practice playing the notes they learned today without the book. Concentrate on a good tone and all of the things discussed in class today. Then if they feel they are doing a good job, they may start to work on Lesson 2. Instruct the students that it is always okay for them to move ahead of the class assignment. Encourage it, but tell them they must at least try to do all that is assigned to them. They learn from trying even when they are not playing it perfectly. Encourage them to establish a habit of practicing daily.

As they leave the classroom, tell them to have a good day and to practice daily. Also, praise them one more time. You cannot do this too often.

Saxophone Lesson 4 (Fig. 2-21)

As students enter the room, you will be faced with musicians who have played for three lessons, two lessons, and one lesson, and students who will be attending their first lesson with an instrument. If at all possible, try to reschedule the last students into a new group. However, since that is often not an option, you must be more mindful of your time and manage it carefully.

Students who have played the instrument before should immediately start assembling their instruments. Have the new students sit next to each other so you can work with them while the other students play assignments in the book.

Follow the same procedure as in previous lessons, and teach the new students how to assemble their instruments. As soon as the other students are ready to play, start them off with a review of the first page. They should be ready before the new group has their saxophones completely assembled. That will, of course, depend on the number of students receiving their instruments for the first time. Have the students who played last week start with line 1 of Lesson 2 or the first page of music in the band method book. This may seem too redundant for the students who started the first week, but if you do not dwell on it, they will not mind the review. They are still nervous about playing the instrument, and they want to sound good. The students will be glad to keep it easy if you keep the lesson moving.

While the students are playing, continue to keep an eye and ear out for:

1. Posture.
2. Tapping feet.
3. Correct rhythm.
4. Faking reading.

5. Puffing cheeks.
6. Embouchure.
7. Side keys.

If the students' tones are stabilizing and becoming fairly well in control, this is the lesson to introduce tuning. You should teach the students to listen from a very early stage of development. If you show them how to listen to each other and adjust their pitch to match each other, your band will sound better, the students will feel good about themselves, and your retention rate should improve dramatically. If the majority of the students' sounds are still out of control or some are playing with a blatty sound, then you may

Figure 2-21
Music for Saxophone Lesson 4

want to wait until Lesson 5 to introduce tuning. However, do not wait until the day of the concert to tune the band. If they have not learned to listen by then, tuning them will only accomplish having the tuning note on pitch. Within the first few measures, they will sound as terrible as every rehearsal leading to the concert. The students may feel discouraged and be more inclined to quit.

The best note for tuning the band is Concert B♭, which is a stable note for every instrument. Some teachers use Concert F as the tuning note. Concert F is a D, fourth space for the alto saxophone, one of the most out-of-tune notes on the saxophone. If you tune to D, all the other notes they play will be flat, since D is the sharpest note on the instrument.

Have the students help you tune. Make all of the students listen. Have one saxophonist play G, then have a second student play G. Ask the class whether the second note was higher or lower. You will probably get both higher and lower for your answer. Do not tell them that they are wrong. Ask them to listen again. Inform them that you are referring to pitch, not volume. This time, acknowledge whether the pitch was higher or lower when the students tell you the direction of the second player's pitch. Tell the students that if the pitch is lower, they should push the mouthpiece in. If the pitch is higher, they should pull it out. Explain that as the two students' pitches come closer together they will hear the sound waves hitting each other making a "wawa-wawa" sound. Tell them, "We need to match the pitch so we can get rid of the wawa-wawas." This sounds funny, but it is a description to which the children can relate. When the pitches match, they will hear the difference in sound. Take the time to tune every student, even if it requires the entire period. It is worth it. Your band will never sound good without good intonation. Do not wait too long to start teaching this very important aspect of playing. If they are not ready at this lesson, start tuning by Lesson 5 even if everyone is not ready or cannot hold a steady tone. Students should learn to listen to each other and understand good intonation from the very beginning.

The students do not need to play every line on the first page. Select two or three lines and then have them turn to the next page. By this point, the new students should have their instruments completely assembled.

Remind the students that the saxophone should go to the side of their right leg, not between their legs. Let the strap do the work. Adjust the strap so the mouthpiece meets the mouth without the student having to raise or lower her head. Describe the embouchure as in previous lessons. Make sure the top teeth are touching the mouthpiece. Let the weight of the head rest on the mouthpiece. The student should be relaxed and not put so much pressure on the reed that she closes the opening into the mouthpiece and no air is allowed into the saxophone.

Show the new students how to play a B. Again, watch for side keys being accidentally struck. I call this the "sick cow" sound. Once all the new students can play this note, have all the students play a B together. Remember to move fast. If that did not take very long, show the new students how to play A. Once the new students can play A, have everyone play it together. Depending on how long that takes (usually less than five minutes), have the new students play G, and everyone join in for the last time.

Next, turn your attention to the advanced students. Have them play the first line on the second page (Lesson 3). Review any new notes and rhythms. Starting with this lesson, you want to be more particular about rhythm. Make sure they are stopping the notes as the rhythm indicates. All students should be tapping their toes together. You might need to help them with this. There is nothing wrong with the band teacher reaching down and helping the students tap their toes. Sometimes this is necessary for the student to understand how to tap her toes and keep count of the beat.

If the line has quarter notes, notice if the students are breathing before every note. If they are not breathing before every note, do not say anything. You do not want to create a problem that does not exist. Most likely some students will be breathing before every note. Simply tell the students not to, and to use their tongues to separate the notes using the syllable: ta, ta, ta, ta. If a student does not understand what tonguing is or how to do it, tell her to put her tongue against the reed, and when you tell her to blow, she should remove the tongue after she has started the airflow. By doing this, the student can often feel the use of the tongue and how to use it. You may also tell the student to pretend she is spitting using the "t" sound. Do not make too big a deal about this yet; there are other exercises to help tonguing which will be discussed shortly. Try not to make a student too self-conscious about playing the instrument. This is not the time to embarrass them or allow them to feel they cannot play the instrument properly. If they continue to breathe before every note, go on. A lot of material must be covered during the lesson and at this point the lesson is more than half over.

Have the beginners open their books to Lesson 2. Find the line with B. Explain to them as in previous lessons how the B is marked on the staff and what the rhythm of the note is. Have everyone, advanced and new, play that line together. Continue to the next line. Discuss the difference between the notes and again have everyone play along. Make sure all students are tapping their toes. Start rhythm counting early. You want this to become second nature as soon as possible.

Pay attention to the advanced students. Have them play Lesson 3, line 1. Discuss any new problems that may occur in this line. If it was performed smoothly and the students understood what they were doing, play one more line.

Have the new students play as much of Lesson 3 as possible. Show them any new notes and/or rhythms. Have everyone play along. If possible, start playing the music in Lesson 4.

Continue in this manner until the end of the lesson. Leave enough time to give a complete assignment. Show the new students how to play the new notes and rhythms in Lesson 2. Instruct them to practice the notes without the book and concentrate on making a good sound. After they feel comfortable with their sound, they should then open the book and start playing the first lesson. Once they can play all of that page, they should go ahead to the next. The advanced students should be instructed to review Lessons 2 and 3 and start Lesson 4. Be sure to show them how to play any new notes and how to recognize and count new rhythms. Both groups should realize that it is okay to move ahead in the book. Remind each student to practice every day, even if the student is unable to accomplish playing the song in a manner that suits her. She will get better only if she practices daily.

Saxophone Lesson 5 (Fig. 2-22)

This lesson is a real juggling act. Students will run the gamut from four lessons with an instrument through the first lesson with an instrument. I would recommend that anyone without an instrument should be sent back to the regular class. Inform the students that they must have instruments in order to receive any more lessons. If you allow students to start after this lesson, you will risk delaying the other students so much they may lose interest and quit. In addition, students starting this late may feel embarrassed and discouraged and are likely to drop out early. If you cannot reschedule them into groups of all beginners, it is better to tell them to wait until next year or next semester.

As in previous lessons, have the students who played their instruments before start assembling their instruments as soon as they enter the room. Immediately start instructing the new students on how to assemble their instruments. The students who played before should have their instruments assembled before you have completed the instructions to the new students on how to put their instruments together. Have the advanced students review by playing the first line in Lesson 1 and then "Mary Had a Little Lamb."

Tune the advanced students. It will not take so long this week as it did the first time. If you have not introduced tuning to the students, start now. Follow the procedures in Lesson 4.

If the new students have the instruments assembled, show them how to play B. Follow the same procedures as in the previous lessons. Continue to watch for:

1. Top teeth on the mouthpiece.   4. Posture.
2. Cover bottom teeth.   5. Puffing out cheeks.
3. Touching side keys.

When each new student has played B, have everyone play B together. Hold the note for four beats and then play four quarter notes. Show the new students A. Follow the same procedure as when playing the B. If they are learning quickly, show the new students how to play G.

Figure 2-22
Music for Saxophone Lesson 5

The Whole Time

Jingle Bells

Ode to Joy

A Little Bit Longer

London Bridge

Duet

Turn to the music for Lesson 4 (Fig. 2-21) and have the more advanced students play the first line on the page. Make sure they are tapping their toes. Counting rhythms is important. Continue to watch their eyes. If they are looking at their neighbors' hands or looking around, they are not reading the notes. Go over to their stand and point to the notes with your baton as everyone is playing. Do not draw attention to the student; simply walk over and point to the notes without comment. Most students will follow your baton. Do not embarrass the student.

Once the first line has been played well, continue to the next line. Have all the advanced students play this page. Even though some of the students did not practice this page, show them the notes and fingerings, and have them play along. They may do just as well as the other students. The idea, however, is to try to pull everyone together as quickly as possible.

Turn your attention to the beginning students. Show them B on the staff. Explain to them how the note is marked on the staff and how the time value is indicated. When everyone understands, have all students play the line. Continue to the next line with A, and then G. Make sure the students understand how to play the notes, how they are marked on the staff, and their rhythmic indication. Again, everyone (advanced and new) should play the line together. If the students are moving along quickly, play the line with D. Show the students how to play D. Be very careful that they are not pushing the side keys down while attempting to play D. Once the new students can play D, have everyone play this line together. Keep an eye and ear out for any of the students pressing the side keys. It will take a couple of weeks before all the students can play the notes with the proper hand position without depressing side keys.

Work with advanced students. Play several lines in a row if you can. Have the new students follow along in the book. They do not have to play along unless they can play the notes and understand the rhythms. Some students will be able to jump ahead. Never discourage a student's progress.

Many students may be breathing before every note. First ask the students to tongue the notes and not to breathe before every note. Sometimes this is all that is needed. Here is an exercise that works for all instruments: Choose an easy note to play on the saxophone. Have the student play four sixteenth notes and one whole note all on the same note. It is important to play a long note last. This should be done at a tempo at which the student cannot possibly breathe before every note. Do not name the rhythms to her, but sing the rhythm and ask her to imitate it. After she can play that pattern, play eighth note triplets and a whole note. Follow that with four eighth notes and a whole note, and finally four quarter notes and a whole note. You may need to do this a few more times, but very soon the students should all realize how to use their tongues to separate the notes. (See the clarinet and flute exercises in Fig. 2-8.)

Continue in this manner until the end of the period. Never leave a child or a group of children without playing for more than five minutes. By the end of this lesson, the students should start to pull together and play on the same page. Start playing the music for Lesson 5 with the advanced students. If you run out of time, at least discuss any new notes and rhythms on this page.

Give a specific assignment. Do not give only one or two lines; if you do, that is all they will practice. But do not assign too much. If you assign the students three or four pages, you will overwhelm them and they will not practice at all. I recommend that you assign one full page. For the beginners, assign the first page but recommend that they try to play the pages assigned to the more advanced students. Within two weeks, all saxophone players should be reading off the same page.

Troubleshooting the Saxophone

The teacher should check the instrument for quality and state of repair. If the instrument is of poor quality, even if the instrument is in good repair, it will not play well. Some brands of instruments do not play well. If the instrument is not in good repair, it will not play. Check the pads for leaks, and make sure the springs are in place. Parents must understand that their child will not be successful on any instrument if the instrument is not made by a quality manufacturer and in good playing condition. The quality of the mouthpiece is also essential. There are many very inexpensive and poor quality mouthpieces. Convince your student's parents that a good mouthpiece is a worthwhile investment in their child's musical future and enjoyment.

PROBLEM	CAUSE	SOLUTIONS
Squeaking	1. Reed crooked	Adjust the tip of the reed to the tip of the mouthpiece. The reed should line up directly over the rails.
	2. Chipped reed	Replace the reed.
	3. Bottom teeth on the reed	Cover the bottom teeth with bottom lip.
	4. Top teeth not on mouthpiece	Instruct the student to anchor the top teeth on the mouthpiece as if the weight of the head is on the mouthpiece.
	5. Warped mouthpiece	Replace mouthpiece. It cannot be repaired.
	6. Too much mouthpiece into mouth	Gradually have the student put less mouthpiece into mouth until it stops squeaking.
	7. Not enough mouthpiece into mouth	Usually this is not the problem, but have the student put more mouthpiece into mouth until the squeaking stops.
	8. Warped reed (tip)	If the tip is warped, have the student wet the reed with saliva or water. Put the tip of the reed over the table (flat part) of the mouthpiece. Place the thumb over the tip of the reed and press down. Gently move the reed back and forth with very little distance. This does not need to be done for long.
	9. Warped reed (table)	Place the reed on a flat surface, such as a plate of glass. If the back of the reed is flat against the surface, the reed is not warped. If the reed rises in the middle, the reed is warped. If the warp is very slight, place the flat side of the reed over a sheet of very fine sandpaper which is over the glass or a perfectly flat surface. Sand the reed down until the reed is no longer bowed. This will only be effective if the warp is very slight. If the student has to sand the reed down too much, it will take out too much of the heart of the reed and the sound will not be full. If the bow is deep, throw the reed away. It will never blow easily.

	10. Puffing out cheeks	Tell the student not to puff out cheeks. Sometimes that works. If not, tell her to play a note. As she sustains the note, tell her over and over to bring in cheeks. Usually by the end of her breath, she will bring in her cheeks. Tell the student to suck the air out of the mouthpiece. The shape of the lips and the shape of the muscles are the same as needed to blow air into the mouthpiece without puffing out cheeks. The saxophone embouchure is more relaxed than the clarinet embouchure, but still firm enough to keep cheeks from puffing.
Unfocused sound	1. Too much mouthpiece	Have the student put less and less mouthpiece into her mouth until the sound improves.
	2. Depressing side keys	Students often push the side keys of the saxophone down without realizing it. Show the student where she is touching the side keys with the insides or palms of her hands. The student must arch her hand around the saxophone in order to avoid striking keys unintentionally.
	3. Puffing out cheeks	See number 10 in **Squeaking.**
	4. Top teeth not on mouthpiece	Students at the beginning level must keep top teeth on the mouthpiece. Though some professionals use different embouchures for different reasons, at this level the basic fundamentals are essential. Tell the students to let the weight of the head rest on the mouthpiece.
	5. Blowing too hard	Tell them not to blow with their entire strength. Playing the saxophone is natural. It would not be natural to scream all day long, so neither would it be natural or wise to scream through a musical instrument all day long.
Thin sound	1. Too little mouthpiece	Have the student put a little more in at a time until the sound is full.
	2. Weak reed	Never start anyone with a $1^1/_2$ strength reed. Start beginners with a strength 2 reed and move to $2^1/_2$ as soon as the student is ready. You do not have to be so quick to move a student to a strength 3. When the sound becomes thin on a new $2^1/_2$ reed, it is time to try the next strongest reed.
	3. Too hard a reed	Use a softer reed.
	4. Pinching the mouthpiece	Tell the student to relax. Only put enough pressure on the reed to seal the air from coming out the sides of her mouth. You may need to add a little more mouthpiece into the student's mouth. Again, do this in small steps.

	5. Not enough air	Students should not blow air out with all their might. The student needs to push the air out with enough force to fill the saxophone.
	6. Posture	Sit on the edge of the chair, back straight, both feet flat on the floor. The neck should be straight and not hanging the head down. Adjust the strap so this is not a problem. (You will be surprised how many students will never think to shorten the strap to make the saxophone easier to play.)
Wobbling sound	Embouchure	Too much pressure from lower lip: loosen embouchure or drop lower jaw. This usually happens in lower register.
Poor intonation	1. Instrument	The instrument must be in good playing order with pads sealing and height adjustment correct for every key. This is usually the job of a professional repair person.
	2. Embouchure	All of the above items apply.
	3. Not listening	It is up to the teacher to instruct each student how to listen to his or her playing and notice when he or she is not in tune and how to fix it.

T = Press
octave key
with thumb

Saxophone Fingering Chart

If more than one fingering is given, always use the Preferred example,
except for the playing situation indicated.

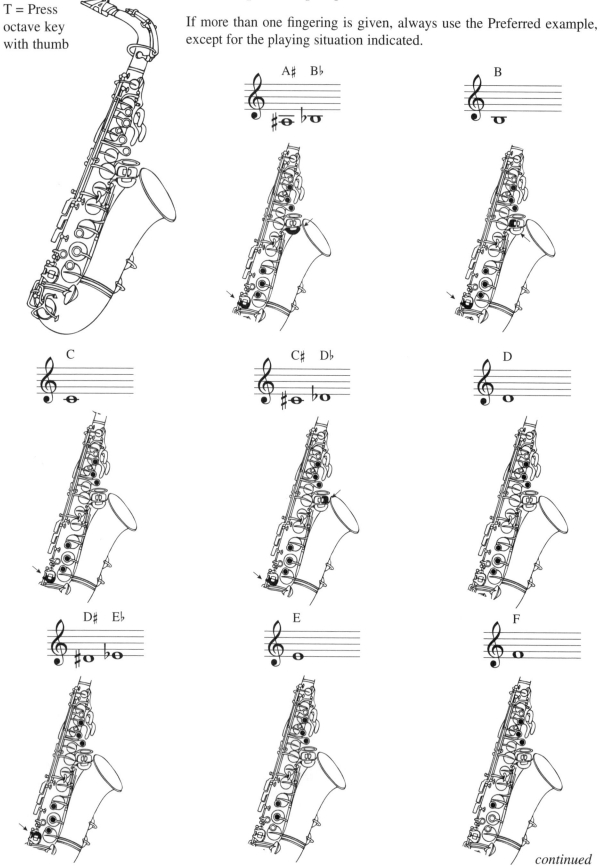

continued

Saxophone Fingering Chart, p. 2

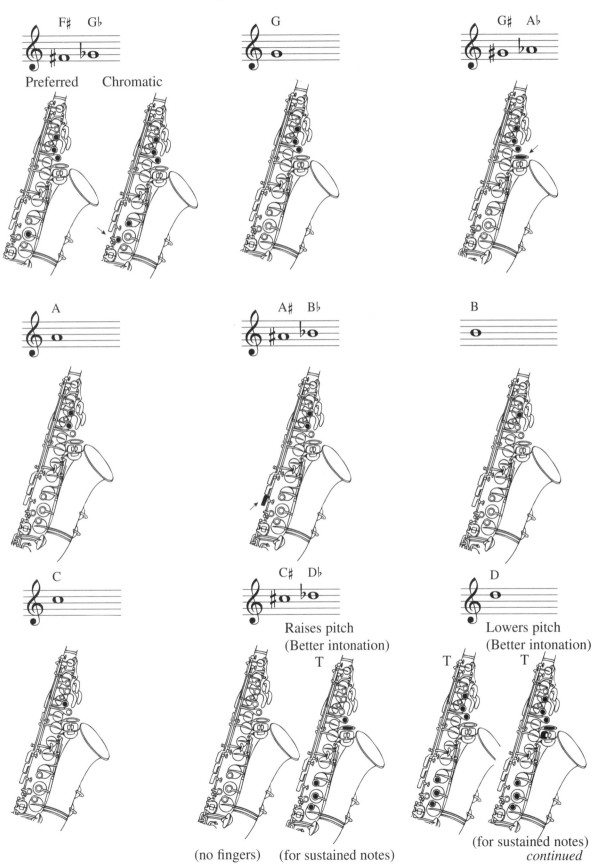

continued

Saxophone Fingering Chart, p. 3

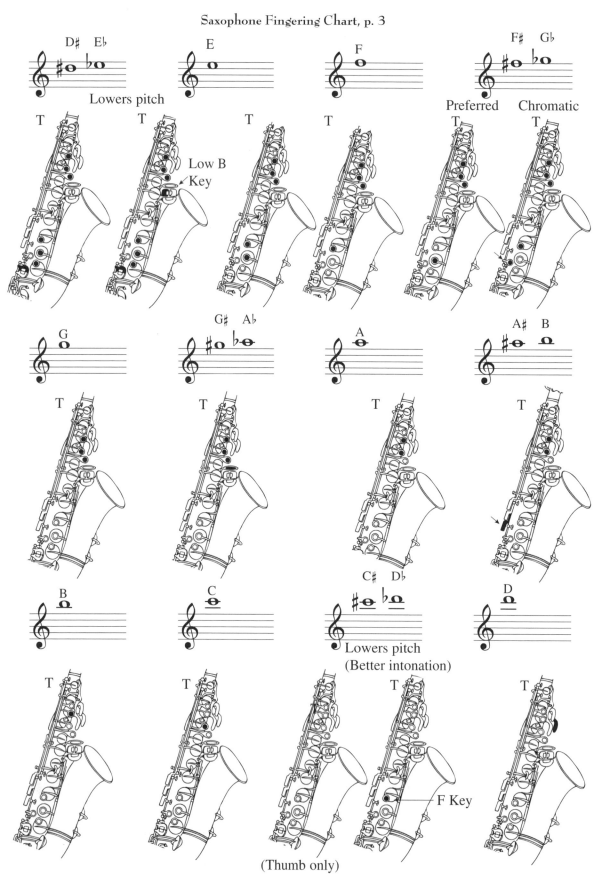

(Thumb only)

Saxophone Lessons Checklist

Lesson 1

- [ ] Chairs and stands in order
- [ ] Name tags on chairs
- [ ] Top of case
- [ ] How to open
- [ ] Cork grease
- [ ] Assembly
- [ ] Moisten reed
- [ ] Reed to mouthpiece
- [ ] Tip of reed to tip of mouthpiece
- [ ] Inspect instrument for quality/repair
- [ ] Neck strap adjustment
- [ ] Hand position
- [ ] Posture
- [ ] First note: B
- [ ] Embouchure
- [ ] Bottom teeth covered with lip
- [ ] Top teeth on mouthpiece
- [ ] Adjust mouthpiece to mouth
- [ ] Sax on right side/posture
- [ ] Tongue the note
- [ ] Play notes A and G
- [ ] Watch out for hand position—hitting side keys
- [ ] First song: "Three Blind Mice"
- [ ] Instructions on how to practice
- [ ] Disassemble the instrument
- [ ] Specific assignment
- [ ] ***Be Enthusiastic!***

Lesson 2

- [ ] Advanced students assemble instruments immediately
- [ ] While advanced are assembling instrument, show new students top of case
- [ ] Reed check for advanced students
- [ ] Review notes with advanced students
- [ ] Continue to show new students how to assemble their instruments
- [ ] Posture
- [ ] Advanced: Play "Three Blind Mice"
- [ ] New students: B
- [ ] Advanced students start to play book, beginners follow along (without playing)
- [ ] Show beginners A
- [ ] Advanced continue with lessons or book
- [ ] Show beginners G
- [ ] Keep watch for hand position
- [ ] Neck strap—sax hanging down on right side—not bending neck down to reach mouthpiece
- [ ] No book for beginners while playing
- [ ] Make sure advanced understand how to read the notes; no faking allowed
- [ ] Only first page for advanced
- [ ] Beginners: Work on first three notes only
- [ ] Students without instruments: Warn to obtain instruments immediately—watch throughout for conduct problems
- [ ] Specific assignment
- [ ] ***Be Enthusiastic!***

Lesson 3

- [ ] Advanced: Start assembling instrument
- [ ] New students: Start showing top of case and assembly while advanced students are assembling instruments, reviewing and playing their first notes
- [ ] Remind deadline for obtaining instruments; send students without instruments back to class
- [ ] Most advanced: Play lesson—read notes
- [ ] Students who just played for the first time last week, review notes
- [ ] Continue with beginners, as other students are playing their notes
- [ ] Keep reviewing all lessons
- [ ] Use baton/conduct
- [ ] Point to notes if students are not reading
- [ ] Have everyone follow along, even when not playing
- [ ] Posture
- [ ] Tonguing
- [ ] Tapping toes
- [ ] If the students are ready, start discussing intonation
- [ ] Specific assignment
- [ ] Notice their accomplishments and tell them how they have improved
- [ ] ***Be Enthusiastic!***

Lesson 4

☐ If possible, reschedule new students
☐ Advanced students start assembling instruments as they enter the room
☐ Start showing the new students top of case and assembly
☐ As soon as tones are stabilized, start tuning the instruments
☐ Continue to instruct beginners as you teach the advanced
☐ Counting/toe tapping
☐ Playing the notes (advanced: reading the notes)
☐ Embouchure—start to be more particular about skin tight against the chin
☐ Posture
☐ Neck strap position
☐ Show new notes and rhythms for next lesson
☐ Insist on practice
☐ Give specific assignment
☐ *Enthusiasm!*

Lesson 5

☐ New students should be rescheduled
☐ Assemble instruments immediately
☐ If you must have new students, teach instrument assembly while teaching the other students
☐ Intonation for advanced students and all but the students who just learned their first notes today
☐ As advanced play, watch eyes to make sure they are reading
☐ Posture
☐ Side keys
☐ Tonguing
☐ Breathing in between notes
☐ *Discuss chair positions
☐ Embouchure
☐ Try to move as many students as possible to the same page
☐ Keep everyone playing, no more than a 5-minute break for anyone at any time
☐ Specific assignment
☐ *ENTHUSIASM!!*

*Though not discussed in text, it is important to inform students about chair positions and the responsibility of the first chair player: the best player in the section.

The first chair, or section leader, helps to keep his/her section together. Other students hear this person playing the music correctly and follow the section leader. Though chair auditions may still be a few weeks away, it is a good idea to introduce this concept by the fifth lesson.

BEGINNING TRUMPET LESSONS

Trumpet Lesson 1 (Fig. 2-23)

Be prepared. Before the students enter the room, have the chairs in position. If you know who is coming into the room put name tags on the chairs. If not, designate where students with instruments should sit and where students without instruments should sit. Paper and pen or pencil should be ready. Have each student write his or her name, grade, section or homeroom. If you have more than one brass instrument in the class, use a different sheet with the name of the instrument at the top of each page. This will enable you to find students when they do not show up for a lesson. (This section assumes that there are only trumpets in the class.) The first lesson is the time to state the rules about discipline and general classroom procedures. If this is a program where you have to take the students out of another class, inform them that at the end of the lesson, they must return to the regular class quickly and quietly.

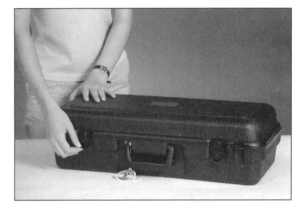

Proper assembly of any instrument is essential. Instruct the students to follow your directions as you give them and not to get ahead of you. Though assembling the trumpet is easy, it must be done properly. The students with instruments should place the case flat on the floor with the bottom side on the floor, top side up. The top is usually the side with the brand name. On most instrument cases, the handle is on the bottom (Photo 2-51). In almost all cases, the latches move up to release the two case parts. All other students should watch carefully in order to remember what to do when they receive their instruments. Once all the cases are sitting on the floor right side up with the handles facing

Photo 2-51

the students, the students may open the case, but not pick up the instrument. After the oohs and ahs, they may pick up the mouthpiece and the trumpet.

Instruct them to gently put the mouthpiece into the trumpet. Do not push, shove, twist, or force the mouthpiece into the instrument. Simply putting the mouthpiece into the trumpet until it stops is appropriate (Photo 2-52). If the student pushes too hard or twists it in, it will not come out except with a special tool. Instruct the students not to slap the palm of the hand over the mouthpiece to make a popping sound. It sounds funny, but it will also jam the mouthpiece into the instrument. You may demonstrate this noise on the trumpet by holding the mouthpiece just slightly out of the instrument and slapping the mouthpiece with your palm. If the teacher makes the sound first, it may stop some experimenting on the student's part. You should not make light of this. Do not allow the students to *pop* the trumpet mouthpiece in your presence. If you make this rule clear from the very beginning, you will have few, if any, problems with mouthpieces becoming stuck in the instruments. Tell the students that if the mouthpiece gets stuck, their parents will have to take the instrument to a music shop and have it pulled with a special mouthpiece puller. This will cost their parents money. If students know it will cost their parents money (and possibly them also), they may be more likely to take better care of the instrument. Tell the students not to try to pull out the mouthpiece with a pair of pliers—that will only damage the instrument. Some teachers carry their own mouthpiece pullers. The teachers who have

Photo 2-52

Figure 2-23
Music for Trumpet Lesson 1

Teach this lesson without showing the music to the student. Students should concentrate on producing a good sound. Attempting to read music will distract from all that is needed to produce a good sound.

The note is sustained for a comfortable length of time. Counting is not necessary for the first note.

Students should play the note four times in a steady count. All students not playing should count out loud with the band director. Before playing line 3, have the students play G and then C, or high and low. This is a good exercise for strengthening the lips.

Follow the same procedure as above.

Follow the same procedure as above.

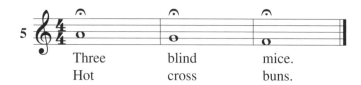

First song. Counting rhythms is not necessary the first time. A quick accomplishment is paramount.

Mary Had a Little Lamb

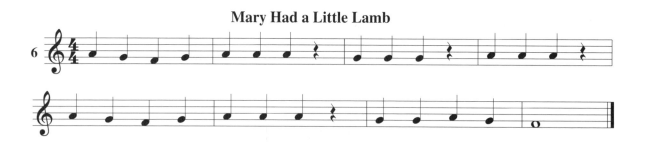

ASSIGNMENT: First, hold each note, then play each note four times.
Play "Three Blind Mice."
Challenge: Who can play "Mary Had a Little Lamb" using the three notes learned today? Be positive; wish everyone a nice day.
BE ENTHUSIASTIC!

Photo 2-53

such a tool are always using it. Students understand that if the mouthpiece becomes stuck, the case will not close with the instrument in it. The instrument is no longer protected and is likely to become damaged. Thus, the instrument may need more extensive repair than just having the mouthpiece pulled, causing more expense to the parents. This is an easy repair to avoid.

Once the mouthpiece is attached, assembly is complete. Have the students remove the cases from directly in front of them. If the cases will fit under the chairs, allow students to put them there. If not, placing the cases on the side or in back of them will be acceptable for today.

Proper hand position is next. The left hand holds the trumpet. The thumb goes on the side of the cylinders that is closer to the player and all the fingers go on the opposite side of the cylinders, called valves. The ring finger may go into the third valve ring. The teacher may need to adjust the position of the ring so it is comfortable for the student to place his finger in the ring (Photo 2-53). The thumb of the right hand is placed under the tube leading from the mouthpiece and between valves one and two (Photo 2-54). The first three fingers go over each valve with an arch and the ends of the fingers directly over each valve (Photo 2-55). The little finger should not be in the hook at the end of valve three. Tell the students the hook is used when they are more advanced and need to turn a page while playing a song or using mutes. However, within the next lesson or two, they will forget and have the little finger back in the hook. Make quick reminders, but do not spend too much time on this. Check every student's hand position to make sure he understands how to hold the trumpet. You will have to remind students constantly about arching the fingers in the right hand. Do not give up on this. It is extremely hard to break the habit of playing trumpet with stiff fingers.

Photo 2-54

Though you are spending all of your time with the students with instruments, do not forget the students who have not received instruments. Remind them to pay attention. It will save time in the next lesson when they receive their instruments. Plus, it helps to avoid discipline problems.

Photo 2-55

The students are ready to play their first note. Before anyone tries to play the instrument, first give the instructions on making a sound. The sound of a trumpet is made by putting the lips together and blowing air out making a buzzing sound (Photo 2-56). A sound will not come out by just blowing air directly into the mouthpiece. The students should put their lips together as if making the sound "mmmmmm." Instruct them to wet their lips before playing the instrument or attempting to buzz their lips. With the lips shut tight, have the students blow. They may all do this at the same time. It will sound funny to the students, but a little fun and humor is acceptable as long as the teacher maintains control of the class. Once the students can make a buzzing sound, start with individual students. Tell the first student to make the buzzing sound one more time. If he makes one, then it is time to try it with the mouthpiece (not the entire trumpet) (Photo 2-57). The trumpet must be played during this lesson, but it is extremely important to buzz the lips, play with the mouthpiece, make a siren sound with the

Photo 2-56

mouthpiece, and then play the assembled instrument. If the buzz was good, I let him try to make a siren sound. The siren sound is made by tightening and loosening the lips while buzzing. The teacher should demonstrate this first. Then, instruct the student to buzz the mouthpiece and make the siren sound a couple of times before he puts his instrument together each day. This is a fun exercise and stu-

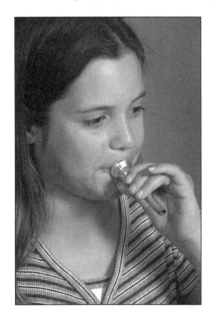

Photo 2-57

dents should practice this daily. Doing this will get the muscles in the lips and cheeks working properly, and the student's practice will be more successful. You will not spend the entire class buzzing the lips and mouthpiece. Proper buzzing is important and may take up to one-fourth of the class time. However, make sure you manage the time so every student plays the trumpet in the first lesson.

Once everyone has buzzed the mouthpiece and made the siren sound (if you have a large class, you may want to have the class do this together), then have the students put the mouthpiece back into the trumpet. Allow each student to try and make a sound (Photo 2-58). Do this individually if you have time. If a student does not make a sound on the first try, notice what was done wrong. (Many times, students just forget to buzz their lips.) Tell him to buzz hard. Play loud. Air support is extremely important with all instruments, but especially with brass instruments. A young child will not understand your descriptions of good air support, but he will understand the instructions to play loud. If the student is not getting a sound because he is not buzzing, but instead blowing air, try the "eat a lemon technique": Tell him to put his lips together and ask him, "What do you do when you eat a lemon?" He will say "eeeeww." That is the perfect embouchure for trumpet. Now, just buzz with that shape of the lips. If the sound is low and blat-ty, make sure the top lip is buzzing or vibrating. Sometimes a beginner

Photo 2-58

will push out the bottom lip to make a buzz. There will be a sound, but not a very good one. Tell the student to roll his bottom lip in and put the top lip slightly over the bottom lip (Photo 2-59). If the student puts too much top lip over the bottom he will hit a very high note. Have him gradually put less lip over the bottom until the sound is a G in the staff or a C below the staff. Do not worry which note it is at this time. The object is to get a sound fast. Most students will play either a middle C, G second line, or C third space. Praise whatever note comes out. Then have him try a lower or higher note. If he plays a G or C third space, ask him to play lower. If the student plays a low C, ask him to play higher. Don't mention the name of the notes yet. Praise the sound. You are not looking for perfection. The student is scared that nothing will come out. If you try too hard to make him play with a perfect sound from the very first note, he may become confused and frustrated and not be able to make any sound. Obtain a sound first, then work on improvement as you hear everyone play again. After the first person plays a note, then a higher or lower note, go to the next person quickly. Once everyone has played a note individually, have everyone play together. Praise them again. They will not be playing the same note, or with great tones, but getting a sound is the most important goal at this time. The students made a sound, and they are relieved. Let them know your pleasure with their first success.

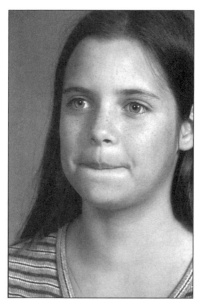

Photo 2-59

Now is the time to gain more control of the instrument. Have the first student play a note. At first, do not name the note, or ask for high or low. Let him play whatever note comes out. This allows his effort to be a success. Little successes are very important at this stage. If he played a G, second line, ask him to play lower. If he played a low C, ask him to play higher. Once he can play higher and lower notes, tell him what note he is playing. "The higher note is G, the lower note is C." If he is playing a C, third space, ask him to play lower. Before you get into any long explanations of how to play higher and lower, just ask for lower. You might get lucky. Even if a student plays what you want correctly, do not confuse him with unnecessary explanations. You do not want to give a student information overload, which is very easy in the first lesson. Try to help the student understand when he is playing lower and higher. That will be a significant step in the first lesson. A good exercise for the entire class is to ask the students to identify the high and low notes. This will get the students listening from the very beginning.

After the first student can play C and G at your command, go to the next student. If one student cannot play C and G, do not stay too long with that student; you could very quickly end up with a crying child on your hands. That can be traumatic. They may learn just by listening and watching other students play the trumpet.

When the students can play a C and G, they can play a part of the "2001, A Space Odyssey" movie theme music, "Also sprach Zarathustra." Some of the students may be able to play C, G, and third space C. It is important not to push the students too far on the first lesson. Even if they are learning quickly and making good sounds, do not add too many notes. If you give them more information than they can absorb, they may forget most of what you taught them. Review and practice. Work on controlling the pitch. If the students have learned all three notes before adding more notes, make sure they can distinguish the difference between notes. Also, ask the students who are without instruments to identify the notes. When a student plays a note, ask a listening student to name the note. Work on ear development, pitch, and rhythm control.

At the end of the lesson, you may show them how to play an F, G, and/or A. Do this only as an assignment and encouragement for further practice. The emphasis should not be on playing the specific notes, but instead on controlling the sound. If there is time, have the students play "Three Blind Mice" (Fig. 2-23, line 5).

Do not read the music in Fig. 2-23 or use the book in the first lesson, even if the students are progressing quickly. Encourage the students to listen to their sounds so they can hear their tone and pitch. If they can control high and low, regardless on which notes, by the next lesson the students will be on their way to becoming very good trumpet players.

Give a specific assignment. First, they should practice buzzing their lips and making the siren sound. Then, tell them to first work on holding all notes with a good and steady sound for four beats. They should also practice playing each note four times, one beat each. It is important to work on foot patting and counting rhythms. The students should practice playing both quarter and whole notes. Also, practice playing the song they learned in class today. Practice should be daily, even if for only ten minutes. This is good for muscle development which is important. Suggest that they practice holding each note as long as they can with a good sound. At the next lesson, you may have a contest to see who can hold the notes the longest.

As the students leave the room, you should remind them to practice and encourage them. Show your enthusiasm. It is important that the students feel that you are happy with their progress.

Trumpet Lesson 2 (Figs. 2-24 and 2-25)

When the students enter the room, have the students who played last week assemble their instruments. Students who are receiving their instruments for the first time should sit together. Since the procedure for assembling the trumpet is so easy and fast, the students who played last week will have their instruments ready to play very quickly. Have these students put their cases away from their chairs and out of the way. The new students should place the case in front of them with the bottom of the case flat on the floor. While the new students are assembling their instruments, have the other students play a G or the higher note. Students who played their instruments at the last lesson will be referred to as advanced students. Students just receiving instruments will be called beginners or new students. The new students should open the case and put the mouthpiece into the trumpet. Remind the students never to push, force, or "pop" the mouthpiece into the trumpet. Have the advanced students play C. Then, play the G. Before this session is over, have a contest to see who can hold a note the longest. Usually, I use a G because it is easy to play. The teacher should do the counting using a slow steady beat. Be consistent and use the same tempo for every student.

It is now time for the new students to play their first note. Demonstrate how to hold the trumpet. Next, demonstrate how to buzz their lips. One at a time, have each student buzz his lips and play the first note. After each student has played his note, ask him whether the note was high or low. This is a good exercise to help develop the ear. Ask the students without instruments to help identify high and low notes. Keep them involved by asking them questions that require listening to the students who are playing. Encouraging them to identify high and low as well as specific notes will help them when they finally receive their instruments. They are also less likely to become disciplinary problems.

All students should put the music for Lesson 2 on the stand or open the book to the first page on which there are notes to play. The first note to read and play is a G. It is strongly recommended that you use the music in this resource. If you must use a book, find the line that has an E. Do not start students lower than E. Most students will play a G easily in the beginning. It is easier to go from a position of tensed to relaxed muscles than to play low, such as a C, and then go higher. You do not have to start with line 1 in the book. If the first line does not start with G, find the line that has G. (If G is not on the first page, start with the line with E.) Make a point to show that G is marked with the note on the second line. If you are using this resource, explain to them that the quarter note is played for one beat because it is marked with a circle that is filled in with a stem on it. Since there are four in a row, there are four notes to be played. Have everyone sing the first measure using the syllable "tah." It is not important for students to sing the correct pitch, but the teacher should sing the correct pitch. Singing the correct rhythm is the objective. Everyone in the class, with and without instruments, should participate. After the first measure has been sung correctly, then have the students who started in the first week play the first measure only. The second measure will be four quarter rests. Explain to them the rhythm of the rests. Have them count the rests. It is important that all the students tap their toes while counting both the notes and the rests. Students need to feel the beat. Tapping their toes is the first step in getting the students to feel the beat and understand the rhythm. Students must use their bodies to play music. The advanced students should now play the first two measures. Even though it is only one measure of notes, this will be just enough for them to understand what you are talking about. Then have them play the entire line. Use your baton and conduct. It will help make the students feel like they are in the band, and it will also give them a visual perception of the beat. Watch the students' eyes—if they are looking at the other students' hands, or just looking around, they do not understand how to read music. Reading music can be very confusing. Have everyone play the line again. Stand in front of the student not reading. This time use your baton to point to the notes as they

Figure 2-24
Music for Trumpet Lesson 2

Round One

valves: 1 2 OPEN

Lookin' Up

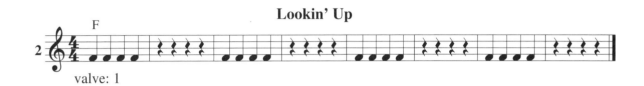

valve: 1

Up and Down

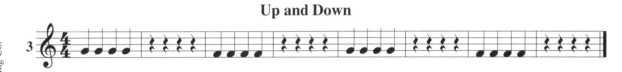

A New One

valves: 1 2

Take a Note

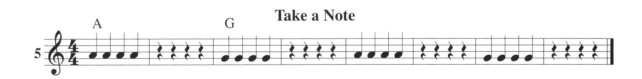

Mary Had a Little Lamb

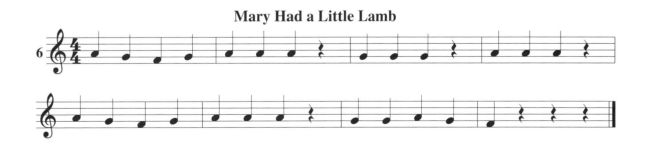

Tap toes: one foot tap per beat. Start with toes up; heels anchored on floor. Practice tapping toes while playing every line.

Figure 2-25
Music for Trumpet Lesson 2A
(Use only with students who cannot play the notes in Lesson 2.)

Round One

Lookin' Down

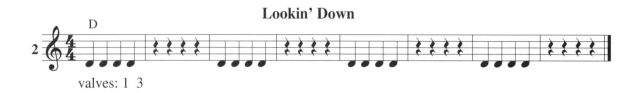

Up and Down

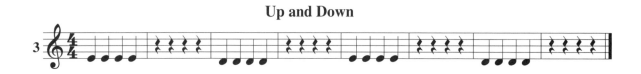

A New One

All the Notes

Mary Had a Little Lamb

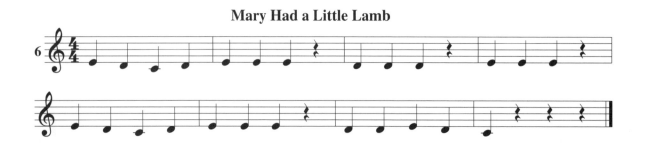

Tap toes: one foot tap per beat. Start with toes up; heels anchored on floor. Practice tapping toes while playing every line.

play the line. Have everyone play and do not mention that the student is not reading. Just point to the notes on the student's page (Photo 2-60). Pointing to the notes as everyone is playing will allow them to see how to follow the notes and the music while playing.

Photo 2-60

Turn your attention again to the new students. Ask them to play a high note, G, then a low note, C. Have the students play four Gs, then four Cs in quarter note rhythms. If a student can play a G but cannot lower the pitch, suggest that he lower his jaw or pull his teeth apart without opening his mouth. If the student can play a C but cannot raise the pitch, then make the following suggestion: Tell the student to pretend he is eating a lemon. As in the previous lesson, this will make him tighten his lips. Have each student play both the high and low notes at least once. Make sure students are buzzing predominantly with their top lips, not their bottom lips.

Have the advanced students look at line 2. Follow the same procedure as with line 1. Make sure everyone is paying attention, even the students without instruments. Point out to the students the difference between G and F. Note that G is on the second line and F is on the first space. Remember to watch the students' eyes. Point to the notes with your baton. (Some books will have E, D, and C on the first page. In that case, play the page, but quickly move to the next page with the higher notes. It is best to have the lip muscles get used to tightening up as soon as possible.)

Review the first line again. Have all the students play this line, including the new students. Remind them about G being on the second line of the staff, and watch their eyes as they play. Use your baton to point to the notes whenever necessary. Play as many lines on the page as possible.

By this time the end of lesson has come or is rapidly approaching. If you only have time to show the students A, make sure that everyone understands that A is on the second space and G is on the second line. If you have time, have everyone play the line together.

Give a specific assignment. Have the beginners practice the high and the low notes first. The low to high notes comprise their first song, "2001, A Space Odyssey." Before they practice playing the first page in the book, they should learn to control the C and G. They should be able to hear the difference between high and low. Then they may start playing out of the book. Advanced students should review the high and low notes and then practice Lesson 2. The goal is to be able to play the entire page by the next lesson.

Tell the students you are pleased with their progress. Be enthusiastic. Tell them to have a good week, have fun, and practice.

Trumpet Lesson 3 (Fig. 2-26)

Before the students enter the room, have the chairs arranged in order as you wish the room to be designed. As in the previous lessons, the students with instruments should assemble them as soon as they enter the room. Have the students who are receiving instruments for the first time sit together.

Immediately begin instructing the new students on how to assemble the instruments. The bottom of the case should be placed on the floor. If advanced students are ready, have them play a G and then a C (or high and low if they do not remember the names of the notes). While doing this, have the new students open the case.

The advanced students should open the book to Lesson 2. Have them play the first line. Remember, this will be a review for some students, but it is part of the assignment for the students who learned to play on the second lesson. Playing this line together will strengthen their ability to play and hear the notes. Show the new students how to hold the trumpet with their left hands, where to put their fingers, and the hand position of the right hand. Review and have the experienced students play line 2. Continue with the

Figure 2-26
Music for Trumpet Lesson 3

Steppin' Up

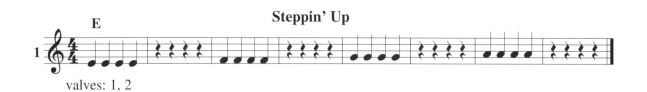

valves: 1, 2

Down the Ladder

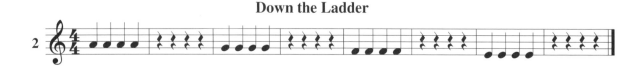

Over the Hill

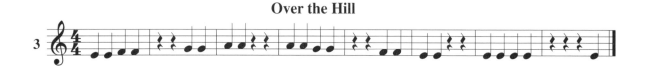

More to Play

Watch Out for That Rest!

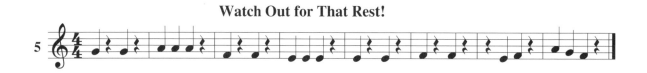

Round and Round

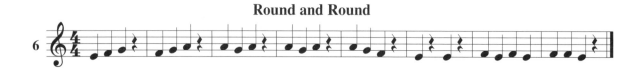

Waves

advanced students for at least two more lines down the page. If the students are playing well, continue to the end of the page.

Be careful that you do not keep the new students idle too long. Five minutes should be the maximum length of time without instruction for any group of students. Never spend too much time with any one group of students, even if there is a problem developing. Do not ignore problems: Be ready to return and correct a problem, but keep everyone involved in learning music for the entire period.

The new students should play one at a time. Ask the first student to play a high note. If he plays a G, praise him and tell him it was a G. If a low or high C comes out, tell him to play lower or higher depending on the note. If he accomplishes that pitch, praise him. If the student is playing too low and cannot bring the pitch up, try telling him to pretend he is eating a lemon. The "eeeeew" sound will make him stretch and tighten his lips. Many students who have trouble playing and controlling pitches are using the bottom lip to vibrate or buzz rather than the top lip. Tell the student to put his top lip over his bottom lip and buzz. At first this may cause a very high note to sound. Do not criticize him; instead tell him that was great. To lower that pitch, just put less top lip over the bottom lip. Very quickly the pitch will come down. If the student is playing G easily, but cannot play lower, instruct him to loosen his lips, lower his jaw, or pull his teeth apart without separating his lips. Do not make too much of an issue about notes being too high. It is much easier to relax the muscles and lower notes than to try and make them tighten up and play higher. Once they can play and control high and low notes to some degree, turn your attention to the advanced students. Complete the first page if you did not do so in the previous session. If this does not take more than five minutes, start on the next page. Review any new notes, and then play the first line. Play as many lines as you can, but again, do not leave any group of students idle for more than five minutes. If there are students sitting in class without instruments, keep them involved by asking them questions or reminding them to pay attention so they will remember what to do when they receive their instruments. This will also be a good time to remind them to obtain their instruments by the next lesson, if at all possible. If you have enrollment and/or rental forms, hand out the forms again. If you have set a deadline for receiving instruments, remind them of that deadline and warn them time is running out. The longer they wait to receive instruments, the more work will be involved in catching up with the other students. Also, these students are more likely to become discouraged and quit.

The most important accomplishment you want to stress with the new students is controlling high and low notes. However, since the new students started late, you will need to show them how to play Lesson 2. Have everyone turn to this lesson, even the advanced students. This will be a good review, and they will not be sitting in their seats doing nothing, or worse, talking and creating a disturbance. Start with line 1. Show them the fingering, and where the note is placed on the staff. Ask if anyone can identify the rhythm of the notes. Do not allow this to become a long discussion. A quick answer will do. Keep the students involved, but do not allow this to be an excuse to waste time. Once this is established, have everyone play the first measure. If they play it well, play the entire line. Ask any student who cannot play the correct pitch to play individually. Help them acquire the pitch with some of the techniques mentioned above, or by any other means that will work. However, do not dwell too long on any one student. You do not want to humiliate him, nor to make him feel that he cannot play the trumpet.

Once you have played that line, and it does not have to be perfect, proceed to the next line or a line that has F in it. Follow the same procedure as before. Watch their eyes. Make sure they are reading the music and not just playing along. Use your baton to point to the notes as they play if their eyes are wandering.

If there is time, play the line with the final new note on the page. You may have no more time than to simply show them the note and ask them whether it is high or low. Do not spend so much time with the beginning group that you do not have time to take at least a quick look at the music in the next lesson for the more advanced students. If you can, play a line or two. Most likely you will only have time to talk about new notes and possibly the new rhythm that is on the page.

Give everyone a specific assignment. First, the new students should practice playing high and low. They should know when they are playing G and low C. After they can accomplish that task, then they should start playing the first lesson. The advanced students should review the second lesson and practice Lesson 3. Be sure to give them a specific assignment every lesson. They will not know what to practice if you do not tell them. Let them know they may go ahead in the book, but they should always try to play the entire assignment by the next lesson. It is not important that they do the entire lesson perfectly by the end of the week, but it is important that they try to play all of the lesson. If they do, it will be easier for you to show them how to play the music correctly.

Tell them to be patient. They are doing a great job, and you are looking forward to hearing their progress at the next lesson.

Trumpet Lesson 4 (Fig. 2-27)

As in previous lessons, advanced students should assemble the instruments as they enter the room. Cases should be put out of the way so the teacher does not have to step over them. Students who are receiving their instruments for the first time should sit together.

Students who do not have instruments should be sent back to class (if this is a program where students are taken out of a classroom situation). You do not have time to pay attention to students who want to get out of class, but do not really want to join the program. Or it may be that they want to play, but their parents cannot afford an instrument. At any rate, it is time to end the procrastination. This gesture will either cause the parents to obtain an instrument or admit that the child will not participate in the program. If this is a summer program, inform the parents through a note or phone call that their child will not be admitted to the lesson without an instrument. If you have not set a deadline for obtaining an instrument, Lesson 5 should be the last time you will accept students without instruments. You must not continue to slow the progress of the other students while you are starting new beginners. That action could cost you several good students just to gain one or two more.

As the advanced students are assembling their instruments, instruct the new students to put the bottom of the case on the floor with the handle facing them. Once that is accomplished, have them open the case. Instruct the advanced students to turn to Lesson 3. Carefully show the new students how to put the mouthpiece into the trumpet. Remind all students not to "pop" the mouthpiece into the trumpet. The new students should then put their cases under their chairs or someplace out of the way. Ask the advanced students to play the first line on the page. Use your baton, count them off, and conduct. It is important that they hear you count the beat, and see your baton giving them a beat. Do not try to explain to the students what each direction of your baton means—simply give them a good steady beat to follow. As before, stay on the lookout for nonreaders. If you see wandering eyes, walk over to the stand and start pointing to the notes he should be playing. Do not call attention to him any more than this. The student will catch on to what you are doing. After the line is played, praise them and make any necessary corrections.

Show the new students how to hold the trumpet. Remind all students that the little finger should not be placed in the hook at this time.

If the advanced students' notes are starting to become stable in pitch, now is a good time to introduce tuning to them. Have the first student play C. Then have the second student play C. Ask the class if one student's note is higher than the other. It is very likely that someone will say the pitch is higher when it is only louder. Make a point to the class that you are to listen to pitch, not volume. When a student tells you correctly when the pitch is high or low, acknowledge him. Point out the difference in sound between the two pitches. Tell the students that pitches can be made lower by making the instrument longer, or higher by making the instrument shorter by adjusting the tuning slide. Show the class the tuning slide. Adjust the second student's pitch to match the first student's pitch. As the pitch comes closer to the pitch of the first, the sound will improve and the students will hear fewer beats in the sound wave. The objective is to eliminate the sound waves hitting each other and have a smooth matching sound. I do not recommend using a tuner at this time. Use your ears and make the students use their ears. Playing at A440 is not necessary at this time. Learning to match each other's pitch is a major accomplishment at this time. Do this with each advanced student. This will take a major portion of the lesson, but it is worth it. Do not

Figure 2-27
Music for Trumpet Lesson 4

Remember This One

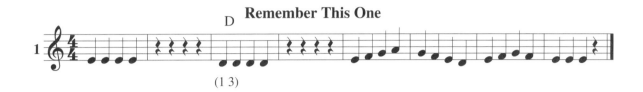

An Old Friend

Twice as Long

Say It Again

Hot Cross Buns

Go Tell Aunt Rhodie

Skippin' Around

wait until the concert to tune the students. They will not play in tune if you do not teach them to listen to themselves and each other from the very beginning. If you do not tune them soon, they may realize that they sound bad, begin to think they are poor students, and quit. The object is to sound good and have fun. Good intonation is essential to having a good band. If you do not feel there is time or the students are not ready, start tuning the students in the fifth lesson. Add tuning for the beginners as soon as their sounds begin to stabilize.

Show the new students how to buzz their lips. Have each new student play a note individually first with the mouthpiece, and then with the assembled instrument. Ask the first student to play a G. Do not mention the name of the note before he plays the pitch. Ask him to play higher or lower until the student plays a G. Praise him and tell him he has just played a G. Once the student can play G, then have him play lower at C. Students may not have much control yet, but try to have each student at least play a sound that is higher or lower than the other. By this lesson, you should not have more than two or three new students, so this process should not take too long.

Have the advanced students play two or three more lines from the third lesson. Make any corrections necessary. Rhythm is extremely important at this stage, so correct improper rhythms immediately. Make sure all students are tapping their toes. It is not only the way to measure the length of a note, but also the way the body can feel the pulse of the song (it is not necessary to explain this to them). Continue to watch for wandering eyes.

Everyone should turn to Lesson 1. Start with line 1. Show the new students where the note is on the staff. Explain to them that the note is on either a particular line or a particular space. As you are doing this, make sure all students are paying attention to you. It is during this explanation that perhaps one of the students who was having trouble reading the notes will catch on to reading notes on a page. Then discuss the rhythm. Even though you have done this three times before, chances are the new students were not giving you their full attention. Once all explanations are completed, have everyone play the line, advanced and new students. Quickly try to correct pitches. However, do not stay too long with one child.

Play the remainder of Lesson 3 with the advanced students. If you finish this page, discuss any new rhythms or notes, and play the first line of music for Lesson 4 (Fig. 2-27). Do not skip lines. Drill and reinforcement is important. Most likely you will not complete the entire page in this lesson. That is acceptable. Try to cover the new rhythms and notes.

The new students should play at least the three notes on the first page even if they do not play all the lines on the page. Playing and controlling the pitches as much as possible are the most important objectives for their first lesson. Tell the new students not to worry if they get home and cannot play the trumpet in the way they played it at their lesson. However, it is important that they try every day, even if they are not getting as good a sound as they did in class. It is important that the muscles in their lips and jaws strengthen so they can control the pitches. Since they all were able to play the note to some degree today, they will do well. Tell them to keep trying and don't give up! Remember, praise and encouragement are your best tools for their success.

As in the previous lessons, give very specific assignments to everyone. The beginners should first play high and low notes at the beginning of every practice session. Then start practicing the lesson. Tell all the students that if they can accomplish at least two new lines a day, they will be preparing themselves to become very good trumpet players.

Instruct the advanced students to practice all of the music for Lesson 3 again, concentrating on rhythms as well as pitches, then proceed to the music for Lesson 4 (Fig. 2-27) and practice the entire page if at all possible. The assignment for all students, always, should be: *You can always look ahead and play as much of the book and extra music as possible; just don't get behind. Always practice and try to play at least what was assigned.*

As the students are putting their instruments into their cases and heading back to class, praise them for their efforts, let them know they are doing well, and tell them to have a nice day! Never let down your enthusiasm.

Trumpet Lesson 5 (Fig. 2-28)

This should be the last lesson with students playing for the first time. It is better to start a new group if that is possible, or inform students who do not have instruments that they will have to wait until the next school year.

Students who have played before should know by this time to assemble their instruments and take their seats and get ready to play. Students receiving their instruments should sit together and put their instruments on the floor with the bottom of the case on the floor.

Tune the advanced students. If this is the first lesson in which you are discussing intonation, follow the procedure from the previous lesson. Do not worry that the first time you tune the students it takes a long time. Good intonation is essential to having a good band and building a quality program with a great number of students. This cannot be overemphasized. You may want to start the new students' instructions while tuning the advanced students.

Have the advanced students open their books to Lesson 4. Have the students play line 1 together. As always, count off, conduct, and be ready to point out the notes on someone's page if he is not keeping his eyes on the music. Quickly show the new students how to hold the trumpet, and follow new student instructions from the previous lessons.

The advanced students should play line 2. Review the new notes and rhythms with them so the new students also can observe and learn. Even though they will not be able to play that page for several days, they may gain some understanding of the notes and rhythms as they try to catch up with the other students. Pay close attention to the rhythms as the students play this line. Review half notes and half rests. If the students hold the notes a little longer than two beats, you can safely assume they are not understanding how to count two beats. Isolate the measure with the half note and half rest. Have everyone play the note for two beats and rest for two beats. Count out loud as they play. If they are not ending the note together, have them put their instruments on their laps. Everyone should count out loud: "1, 2, rest, rest." Have the students clap the beats during the half note, but not during the rest. Do this at least twice. Substitute the syllables "ta-ah" for the count "one-two." Then have everyone play that measure alone. Make sure they are still tapping their toes. That is the only way you can be sure they are counting. (I tell my students I can read their minds through their feet. If their toes are tapping in rhythm, I know they are counting properly in their heads.) After they can play that measure correctly, add the second measure. Then play the entire line. There should be improvement, though some of the students might forget to count to two on every half note.

Have the new students play a G. Quickly review how to read the note G, and the rhythm that is used in the line in the method book you are using. Have everyone, advanced and beginners, play the line together. You may need to play the line again to reinforce the pitch. Then, play the next line with an F. Make a point of showing the difference between the two notes. Have everyone play that line together. If this is moving quickly and well, have the students play the line with A on the page.

Lesson 4 usually has some songs the students know, such as "Go Tell Aunt Rhodie" and "Hot Cross Buns." Play these songs now. The students will usually rush and change tempos as they play these songs. Emphasize the need for a steady rhythm.

Have everyone, beginners and advanced, play "Mary Had a Little Lamb" together. In almost all beginning books, that will be the last line of the first page of notes. This may be easy for the advanced, but they should feel proud to have played it. The correct pitches of the more advanced students will make it easier for the beginning students to hear and play the correct pitches.

Quickly review any new notes and rhythms in Lesson 5 for the advanced students. If there is time, play as many lines as possible. Discuss any new rhythms and fingerings for new notes on this page and the next.

As always, give a specific assignment for all students. Beginners should practice playing high and low notes, and try playing all of the first page. Advanced students should work on Lesson 5, and if they feel they can go further, encourage them. However, they should feel that they can play one page well before they proceed to the next.

Figure 2-28
Music for Trumpet Lesson 5

The Whole Time

Jingle Bells

Ode to Joy

A Little Bit Longer

London Bridge

Duet

Be positive at all times. Whenever you correct mistakes, do it in a way that does not make the students feel they are not smart enough to play an instrument. Encouragement is necessary at all levels of instruction.

Further Thoughts and Suggestions

Some of the lessons in this resource may seem a bit optimistic. In many cases, they are. However, with a good group of students who are catching on to what you are saying, and with experience, you will find that many of the classes will move quickly. And there will be other classes, no matter how much experience you may have, that will move much more slowly than you would ever expect a class to learn any instrument. Experience will teach you when to push the students as hard as possible on a given day, and when to allow the students to move at a much slower pace.

This resource assumes a worst-case scenario that you must continually accept new students up to the fifth lesson. If you can control your recruitment situation, it is much better not to add new students after the third lesson. These students should be assigned to a new group so you do not slow down the progress of the advanced students.

Using the lessons in the *Kit* will help the students move quickly and learn how to control the pitches on the trumpet. Also encourage the students to use the warm-up exercises in Fig. 2-46 (pp. 122–123) as a daily practice routine.

Encouraging the students to practice daily is essential for all students, and especially for brass students. The students must realize that their lips are muscles and must be exercised daily in order to perform well on the trumpet.

Troubleshooting the Trumpet/Cornet

PROBLEM	CAUSE	SOLUTIONS
Tone quality	Instrument	(a) Check brand—must have a good quality instrument. (b) Check repair of the instrument—must be in good condition. (c) Check valves—must move easily and be in the correct cylinders. (d) Mouthpiece—size in relation to student's lips and in relation to student's ability.
Will not blow/ no air passing through the instrument	Valve placement or condition	(a) Make sure valves are in the cylinders correctly/not turned sideways. (b) Make sure valves or cylinders are not bent or dented. (c) Valves must be in the correct cylinders: check the numbers. If no numbers, take all three valves out. Put the first valve in the first cylinder. See if it allows air to pass through the cylinder or make a sound. If not, place another valve in the cylinder and keep trying until you find one that does. That will be valve number 1. Leave that valve in and try another valve in the second cylinder. When you find the valve that produces a sound or allows air to flow through the horn, then the valve left is valve number 3. This generally isn't a problem any more, but many years ago, there was a brand that did not number the valves. Students were always getting the valves mixed up.
Cannot buzz lips	Embouchure	(a) Top lip over bottom (slightly). (b) Have the students say: mmmmmm. (Do not allow them to hum when they do this.) (c) Ask the students, "What do you do when you eat a lemon?" "Eeeww." This brings the lips into a tight position. As soon as they do this, tell them to buzz. (d) Blow hard, play loud.
Blatty sound	Buzzing with the bottom lip	Put top lip slightly over the bottom lip. If the note is too high, gradually put less top lip over the bottom.
Cannot control pitch	1. All of the above 2. Too little practice 3. Not enough strength in lips	(a) Do all of the above exercises. (b) Practice the harmonic series. Start with C (below staff). Next play G, then C, third space, then D, and so on. Playing high is not important. Just have the student play the range that is easy for him (see warm-up exercise on pages 122–123). (c) Siren exercise.

Fingers moving too slowly	1. Stiff fingers 2. Not practicing	(a) Put fingers in an arch. (b) Do not put little finger in the hook. (c) Practice.
Cannot play higher pitches	1. Strength in muscles 2. Cannot hear pitches 3. Not enough practice	(a) The obvious: practice. (b) Sing the pitches, play them on the piano or another instrument in the same range. Have the students identify high and low pitches. (c) Use the "eat a lemon" technique (see p. 116). (d) Tell the students to tighten the corners of their lips. (e) Frown while buzzing the lips. (f) Think or imagine hearing a high note.
Cannot play low notes	1. Cannot hear the pitches 2. Too tense	(a) Same as (b) above. (b) Tell the student to loosen the lips. (c) Lower the jaw. (d) Think "ou" or "ah" while playing and make that shape with the throat. (e) Think or imagine hearing a low note. (f) Pull teeth apart while playing. (g) Buzzing with too much top lip over bottom. Put top lip higher on lower lip.
Puffing out cheeks	Muscle development	(a) Tighten lips. (b) Bring in cheeks. (c) Smile. (d) While sustaining an easy note, tell the student to bring in the cheeks. Say this over and over again, until the cheeks come in. This will work.
Not using the tongue	Does not understand	(a) Tell the student to start the note with the syllable "tah." (b) Put the tongue against lips or back of teeth before starting to release the air. After the air is released, then move the tongue. (c) See exercise on page 55 (from clarinet section). (d) Listen to other students tongue correctly—that is often the quickest solution.

Unfocused sound 1. Air support
2. Correct pressure
   to mouthpiece
3. Trumpet angle

(a) Blow harder and louder. You should not go into long and detailed explanations about air support during the first lessons.

(b) Make sure the student has the mouthpiece firmly against her lips. (See Photo 2-61.)

Photo 2-61

(c) The trumpet should not be facing the floor. A slight angle down from the mouth is correct.
(See Photo 2-62.)

Photo 2-62

(d) **Practice!**

B♭ Trumpet/Cornet
Fingering Chart
(Numbers indicate valve[s] to be pressed)

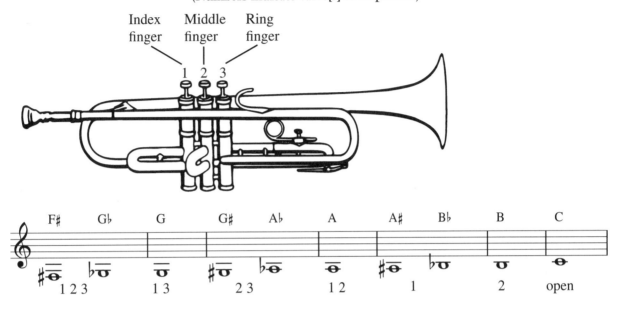

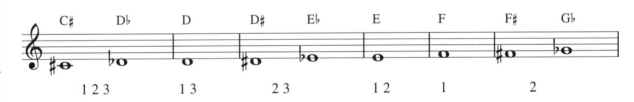

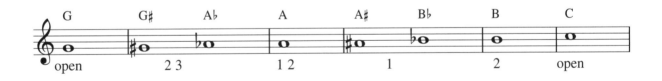

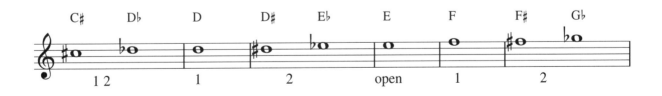

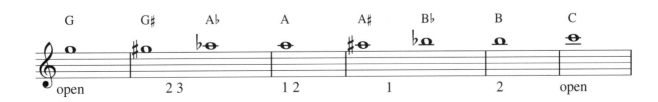

Trumpet Lessons Checklist

Lesson 1

- [ ] Chairs and stands in order
- [ ] Name tags on chairs
- [ ] Top of case
- [ ] How to open
- [ ] Assembly
- [ ] Instruct not to "pop" the mouthpiece
- [ ] Inspect instrument for quality/repair
- [ ] Hand position
- [ ] Buzz lips
- [ ] Buzz mouthpiece
- [ ] Siren sound
- [ ] No buzz—"eat a lemon" technique
- [ ] Top lip over bottom lip
- [ ] First note: G
- [ ] Adjust mouthpiece to mouth; mouthpiece firmly against lips
- [ ] Angle of trumpet
- [ ] Work on playing higher and lower—C & G
- [ ] Play C-G-C (third space)—the student has played his first song, "2001, A Space Odyssey"
- [ ] Tongue the note
- [ ] If time—play notes A and F
- [ ] Song: "Three Blind Mice"—only if time—challenge to learn by ear for next lesson
- [ ] Instructions on how to practice
- [ ] Disassemble the instrument
- [ ] Specific assignment
- [ ] ***Be Enthusiastic!***

Lesson 2

- [ ] Advanced students assemble instruments immediately
- [ ] While advanced are assembling instruments, show new students top of case
- [ ] Buzz check for advanced students
- [ ] Review and play notes with advanced students
- [ ] Continue to show new students how to assemble their instruments
- [ ] Posture
- [ ] Advanced: Play "Three Blind Mice"
- [ ] New students: G
- [ ] Advanced students start to play book, beginners follow along
- [ ] Show beginners C—work low and high notes
- [ ] Advanced: Continue with book
- [ ] Beginners: Work on C, G, C—"2001, A Space Odyssey"
- [ ] No book for beginners while playing
- [ ] Make sure advanced understand how to read the notes—no faking
- [ ] Only first page for advanced
- [ ] Beginners: Work on first three notes only
- [ ] Specific assignment
- [ ] ***Be Enthusiastic!***

Lesson 3

- [ ] Advanced: Start assembling instruments
- [ ] New students: Start showing top of case and assembly while advanced students are assembling instruments, reviewing, and playing their first notes
- [ ] Most advanced: Play lesson—reading notes
- [ ] Students who just played for the first time last week: Review notes
- [ ] Continue with beginners, as other students are playing their notes
- [ ] Keep reviewing all lessons
- [ ] Use baton/conduct

- [ ] Point to notes if students are not reading
- [ ] Have everyone follow along, even when not playing
- [ ] Posture
- [ ] Tonguing
- [ ] If the students are ready, start discussing intonation
- [ ] Specific assignment
- [ ] Notice their accomplishments and tell them how they have improved
- [ ] ***Be Enthusiastic!***

Lesson 4

- [ ] If possible, reschedule new students
- [ ] Advanced students start assembling instruments as they enter the room
- [ ] Start showing the new students top of case and assembly
- [ ] As soon as tones are stabilized, start tuning the instruments
- [ ] Continue to instruct beginners as you teach the advanced
- [ ] Counting/toe tapping
- [ ] Playing the notes (advanced—reading the notes)
- [ ] Embouchure—top lip slightly over bottom lip
- [ ] Posture—trumpet angle
- [ ] Show new notes and rhythms for next lesson
- [ ] Insist on practice
- [ ] Give specific assignment
- [ ] *Enthusiasm!*

Lesson 5

- [ ] New students should be rescheduled
- [ ] Assemble instruments immediately
- [ ] If you must have new students, teach instrument assembly while teaching the other students
- [ ] Advanced students: intonation
- [ ] As advanced play, watch eyes to make sure they are reading
- [ ] Posture
- [ ] Tonguing
- [ ] Breathing between notes
- [ ] *Discuss chair positions
- [ ] Embouchure
- [ ] Try to move as many students as possible to the same page
- [ ] Keep everyone playing—no more than a 5-minute break for anyone at any time
- [ ] Specific assignment
- [ ] *ENTHUSIASM!!*

*Though not discussed in text, it is important to inform students about chair positions and the responsibility of the first chair player: the best player in the section.

The first chair, or section leader, helps to keep his/her section together. Other students hear this person playing the music correctly and follow the section leader. Though chair auditions may still be a few weeks away, it is a good idea to introduce this concept by the fifth lesson.

Warm-ups for Brass Instruments

The following exercises should be practiced daily. It is not necessary to play the entire set of exercises on the first day of studying this warm-up exercise. Start with two lines on the first day and add one or two lines as the student feels comfortable. Do not continue to play if the lips are starting to hurt or getting too tired to play the correct pitches.

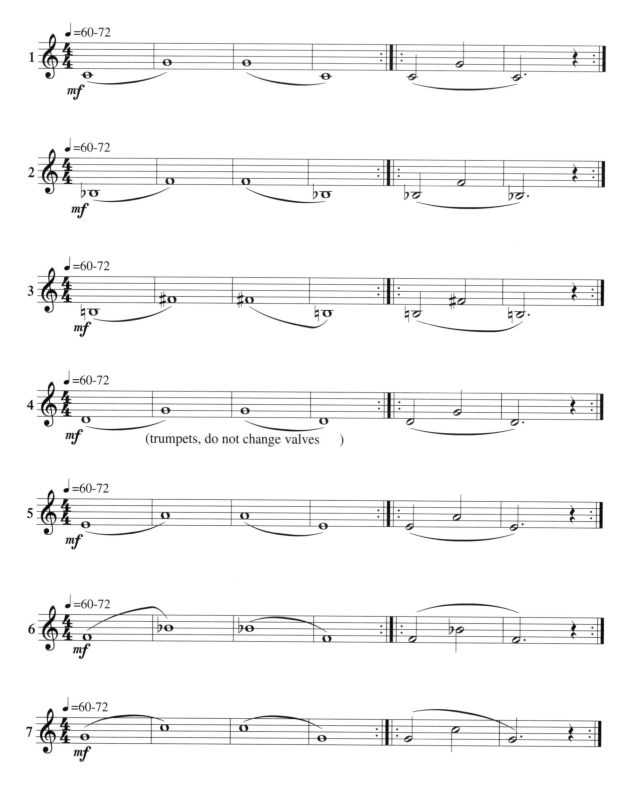

(trumpets, do not change valves   )

Brass Warm-up
(part 2)

BEGINNING F HORN LESSONS

Although the following guidelines for teaching F horn are not organized into five detailed lessons, this does not signify that the F horn is any less important than other band instruments. The basic pattern for teaching group lessons is quite similar for all instruments, especially when it comes to time management. Beginners usually start with the F horn as opposed to the double horn. Learning two sets of fingerings at the same time may become confusing for a beginner. Sometimes the B♭ horn is used for beginners; however, the F horn has become more common. Some beginning band methods no longer publish B♭ horn books, and most, if not all, band arrangements have only F horn parts. The F horn has a better tone quality, but the B♭ horn has better intonation tendencies. Students can be switched to the double horn later when they are in control of the instrument, usually not until after the second year. The size of the double horn may also be a problem for many young beginning students. It is more common for a high school student to play the double horn.

Selecting the F Horn Student

As with the oboe, care must be taken in selecting students. Because the fundamental harmonics are so low, valves are hardly necessary to play the correct pitches. (However, require your students to use the correct valves or there will be intonation problems.) In order for a student to be successful on the F horn, the student must listen carefully and have a very good ear for pitch. Choose a student who makes very good grades. A student who makes Cs probably does not listen carefully or pay enough attention to his teachers or his surroundings to be successful on this instrument.

Normally, I would not demonstrate the F horn to fourth graders. Though some students will be very successful, the horn is a little awkward to hold at this age. It is advisable to demonstrate the F horn at the sixth-grade level. The students are more mature and bigger and can handle the instrument more easily. If a student as young as nine does come to you and ask to play this instrument, there are some basic considerations and questions to ask him or her:

1. What kind of grades do you make? (You want to hear As, maybe a few Bs.)

2. Is the student academically inclined? (You may need to talk to teachers, principals, and parents to answer this question.)

3. Sing or play a pitch on the piano and ask the student to match it. (The student must be able to match pitches to become a good F horn player.)

4. Is there a keyboard instrument in the student's home, and can someone play the notes for him when he practices? (The success will be much greater and quicker if someone at home can play the notes so the student can match pitches. The person at home does not have to be a piano player, just as long as he or she can find the notes. The teacher will send home transposed notes. This should not be a requirement, but is worth considering.)

5. Does the student possess a positive personality? (You cannot ask the student this question, but is the student sure of him- or herself? A good F horn player is one who is self-confident and feels good about him- or herself. The classroom teacher may be the best person to answer this question.)

If you get a positive response to all of these questions, you should probably give the student a try on the F horn. The questions should be posed to any student who wants to play the F horn regardless of age or grade level. This is probably the most difficult instrument for a beginner to master. If a student does not respond positively to the preceding questions, he is more apt to be successful playing another instrument.

Getting Started

As in all instrumental music lessons, the teacher must be organized before the students enter the room. Have the chairs set up in the order in which you wish to teach. If you know the names of the students, have name tags on the chairs. The more organized you are, the more respect the students will give you. Once the students enter the room, have the students with instruments sit together and the other students sit where they can see what is taking place in the classroom. If you have name tags, the students should sit in their assigned seats. You may change the seating as necessary.

When the students are seated, tell them not to open their cases until you have instructed them to do so. At this moment, when you have their attention, state the rules of the class. Let them know the penalties for disturbing the class, making noise in the hall on the way to lessons, and anything else that may

Photo 2-63

pertain to your lessons. This is also the time to state the deadline for obtaining an instrument. You cannot have students continually coming to lessons with their instruments for the first time. After three lessons it is advisable to start a new group of beginners for lessons. If you allow students to join a group that is beginning their fourth or fifth lesson, you stand a chance that the students who started earlier will become bored, frustrated, and quit, or the new student will not be able to catch up with the other students, and quit.

You must demonstrate to the students how to open the case properly. The F horn dents very easily. Students should take special care in opening the case right side up and carefully removing the instrument. As with most cases, the top of the case has the brand name, and the bottom of the case has the handle. The latches move up when opening the case (Photo 2-63). Before the instrument is assembled, have the students take out the mouthpiece only.

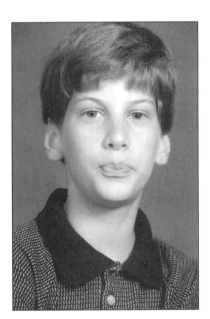

Photo 2-64

Embouchure

Before the entire instrument is played, make sure the students can buzz their lips. Ask the students to first wet their lips by licking them. Then have them put their lips tightly together and buzz. The teacher should demonstrate this first. Make sure the top lip is doing the majority of the buzzing. Tell the students to put the top lip slightly over the bottom lip (Photo 2-64). This may result in a very high pitched buzz, but that is okay. It is easier to lower the pitch than to have a student start with a low pitched buzz and tighten his lips later. After the students have buzzed their lips, have them buzz into the mouthpiece (Photo 2-65). The next step is to see how many students can make the siren sound. The siren sound is made by starting with as low a pitch as possible and tightening the lips to produce as high a pitch as possible and back down again, all in one breath. It is advisable for the teacher to demonstrate this first. Students will then see how easy it is to produce the sound.

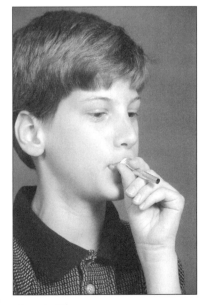

Photo 2-65

Once the students have tried making the siren sound, see if they can imitate pitches. The best example is for the teacher to play a pitch using the mouthpiece only, and see which students can produce the same note. These notes should not be random notes. Instead, play the notes that will appear in their first lesson. There is no point in having them imitate pitches with just the mouthpiece, when they may not play those notes for months or years to come. This is a good test to see who may be the more successful F horn students.

Assembling the Instrument

After everyone has had fun making sounds with the mouthpiece only, have the students put the mouthpiece into the F horn. Warn them not to twist or shove the mouthpiece too tightly. Also, they should not "pop" the mouthpiece. This will jam the mouthpiece into the F horn. If this does happen, the student must take the instrument to an instrument repair shop and have the mouthpiece removed with a mouthpiece puller. Instruct the students to not let their parents try to pull the mouthpiece out with a vise and a pair of pliers. This will definitely damage the instrument and, unfortunately, the mouthpiece will prob-

Photo 2-66

ably still be in the instrument. Some teachers carry their own mouthpiece pullers. If you do, require some penalty for getting a mouthpiece stuck. Otherwise, removing mouthpieces from instruments will become your daily routine.

Some F horns come with a removable bell. Most beginner-level instruments are not manufactured that way. However, if a student does enter with an instrument with a removable bell, have the student assemble the bell. Make sure the bell is firmly attached. You do not want the bell to fall off the instrument while playing.

Photo 2-67

Holding the Instrument

The student should sit on the edge and the corner of the chair (Photo 2-66). If a student sits all the way back in the seat and not at an angle, he or she will be facing the side of the room and it will be impossible see the conductor.

When holding the instrument, the student should bring the instrument to his mouth. Many times, a beginning student will set the instrument in his lap and bring his mouth to the mouthpiece, resulting in bad posture and a bad hand position. Tell the student to sit up straight, hold the instrument, and bring the mouthpiece to his mouth. The student is to be in command of the instrument, not the other way around. The ideal position is to have an even placement of upper and lower lip on the mouthpiece with a slight tilt forward of the upper body. However, many beginners are too short and have to reach up to meet the mouthpiece. The student may angle the horn as much as possible to alleviate this problem depending on his size. Unfortunately, he or she will just have to grow a little more. However, the student should still be able to play the instrument well even with this problem.

The hand position is very important in playing the F horn. The left hand holds the instrument on the left side of the F horn and is used to operate the valves (Photo 2-67). A young student may not be able to put his or her right hand in the correct position and control the instrument. It will be the easiest for a young player to hold the bell around the 10 o'clock position (Photo 2-68). The hand should be cupped as if catching raindrops. As the student becomes bigger and can handle the instrument better, the hand should move to the 5 o'clock position, touching the bottom of the bell (Photo 2-69).

Photo 2-68

Playing the F Horn

After the students have completed all of the above, have them play their first note on the F horn. The ideal situation is to find their "natural" open pitch. That is, the note they play with no valves down, and without music. The notes will most likely be in the treble clef, C, E, or G. If they play much higher or lower, ask them to tighten or loosen their lips until they play that range. Once they hit the same note several times in a row, then you know their "natural" pitch. If you are using the lessons in this book, and their "natural" note is G, then have them play down to the E. This will give students a way to find the pitches when they get home, when you are not there to guide them to the correct note. If their "natural" note is C, then they know to move the pitch up to E, and so on. If you have a chalkboard or some type of board on which to illustrate examples, then use the example in Fig. 2-29 so the students can see a picture of what you are talking about. This gives them

Photo 2-69

Figure 2-29
Finding the Student's Natural Note

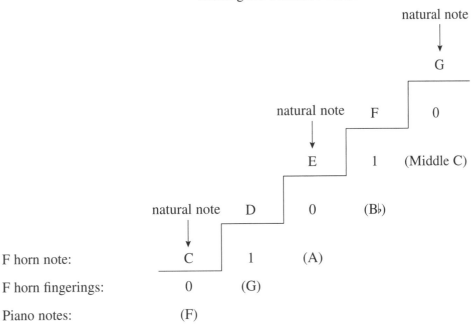

a visual example of moving up or down steps to the correct note. If you do not show students how to find correct pitches from their "natural" note, then when the student gets home it is just a "shot in the dark" as to whether the correct notes are being played. If this is the case, you may find in the next lesson that the students are playing the exercises several partials too high or too low, and they think they are playing the lesson perfectly. You will then have to keep retraining the ears to hear the right pitch, and that could be a very long process.

Once the students have found their "natural" pitch and know how to find E, then you may start with the lessons in this book (Figures 2-30 through 2-34) or the band method book of your choice. However, I strongly recommend using the lessons in this resource. In heterogeneous band method books, all instruments must play the same note at the same time and F horn players are usually put in the most difficult range of all the instruments. After following the first five lessons in the *Kit,* the students should easily be able to switch over to almost any of the heterogeneous band method books on the market.

It will be difficult to accomplish all of the above and all of the first lesson in one day. However, if you move quickly, you should at least be able to play the first three notes, which will allow the students to play "Three Blind Mice." Whether you finish Lesson 1 or not, emphasize the importance of finding the student's "natural" note and moving to the correct pitch for that note. If a student can learn to hear and move pitches up and down at will on the first lesson, he or she has a very good start to becoming a good F horn player.

As in all instrumental lessons, be positive to the students. Let them know how happy you are with their progress on the first day. Show your enthusiasm for their success. If you are not happy with what they have accomplished or happy with what you are doing, there is little hope of having a successful band. At the end of every lesson, tell the students to practice, how proud you are of them (though there will be times you will tell them they need more practice than they have recently given you), and to have a nice day.

Further Considerations

As lessons progress, it is a good idea from time to time to have the students buzz the song using only the mouthpiece. This is good for both their lips and ears. It helps them hear the pitch without the full sound of the F horn.

Strongly urge students to play at home with someone playing the pitches for them on a piano or another instrument. Offer to make a chart of piano or any other instrument's notes for the person at home (such as a parent or sibling) helping the student so he or she can find the correct pitches. Most parents will not know about transpositions, so if you give them a chart, the parent or sibling may play the notes on the piano while the student matches the pitches. F horn is the most difficult of all the instruments for young students to hear and play the correct pitches. The more they hear those pitches, the better they will be able to produce them on their own.

If you can get the F horn players to sing their parts, it will be a great aid in obtaining the correct pitches. It is not necessary to do this in front of the whole band, but ask students to hum or sing the pitch before playing. In a group lesson, they can all do it together, and in band see if they can sing or hum it very softly so only they can hear the pitch. The more confident a student is about humming or singing the pitch, the better the student will be able to produce the correct note.

Teachers may occasionally play along with the students during the class. It is not necessary that the teacher play the same instrument as long as the notes are in the same range. By hearing the correct pitches, the students will feel more secure and may remember the pitches or at least the range in which to play the notes.

F horn students can often be switched from other instruments such as the trumpet, trombone, or baritone. However, few trumpet players become good F horn players. The student must have a real desire to play F horn and meet the criteria given at the beginning of the F horn section.

Tuning

As with all instruments, the teacher should start tuning the instruments as soon as the tone starts to stabilize. Usually, that will take place around the fifth lesson. Do not wait too long to tune the players. They must start learning to listen for good intonation from early stages of development, or they will just ignore it and sound bad. Tune to an open pitch first. G or C in the treble clef staff is a good start. You may find that the better note may change from student to student. However, start tuning the players while they are still learning to listen to each other. After the horn is in tune to an open position, adjust the valve slides to get the entire horn in tune. With very young students, it is not necessary to tune all the valves individually. Find their open tuning pitch, then adjust the valve slides as necessary. However, let the students know what you are doing whenever adjusting an instrument for tuning. The more aware of tuning they are, the more correct pitches will be played. Eventually tune the valve slides as well as tuning the open pitch. Tuning for the double horn is discussed in the troubleshooting section.

Spit Removal

This may be a disgusting topic, but with the F horn it is necessary. More than any other instrument, the F horns can start gurgling and sound like they are drowning. There is no spit valve to alleviate the problem. There are several areas from which the student can drain the saliva out of the instrument.

1. Remove the tuning slide. This varies in location on models, but the removable slide is not attached to any of the valves. If the student is playing a double horn, then the other tuning slide must also be emptied. One of the slides is usually close to the student's body, and the other is on the opposite side of the player, usually on the other side of the horn as well.

2. Hold down the third valve, lean the horn down so the valve slides are at the bottom, and blow through the horn vigorously while "wiggling" the first and second valves. This will force the spit in the valves to slide into the third valve slide. Then remove the third valve slide. Be sure to have the third valve down before removing the slide. Otherwise, the slide could be damaged. This is a faster method than removing the saliva from each valve slide individually.

3. If still gurgling, remove the mouthpiece and revolve the horn until the spit falls from the lead pipe. There is a twisting pattern to match the tubing, but eventually the student will find the pattern and easily "dump" the spit from the horn. Also, remove the tuning slide when doing this procedure. It will help remove the spit more quickly.

Some students do not want to remove the spit because they think it is disgusting or embarrassing. However, if they do not, they will not be able to play the pitches and the rest of the band will start to make fun of them. Fortunately, this situation generally disappears in a short time.

Figure 2-30
Music for F Horn Lesson 1

This lesson is taught without showing the music to the student. Students should concentrate on producing a good sound. Attempting to read music will distract from all that is needed to produce a good sound.

(open, no fingers)

Find the natural note to locate E. The note is sustained for a comfortable length of time. Counting is not necessary for the first note.

Students should play the note four times in a steady count. All students not playing should count out loud with the band director.

valve 1

Follow the same procedure as above.

(open, no fingers)

Follow the same procedure as above.

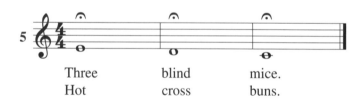

Three   blind   mice.
Hot   cross   buns.

First song. Counting rhythms is not necessary the first time. A quick accomplishment is paramount.

Mary Had a Little Lamb

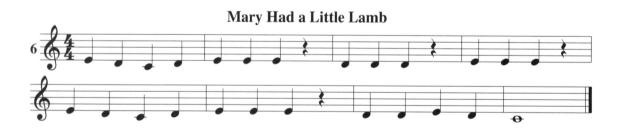

ASSIGNMENT: First, hold each note, then play each note four times.
Play "Three Blind Mice."
Challenge: Who can play "Mary Had a Little Lamb" using the three notes learned today? Be positive; wish everyone a nice day.
BE ENTHUSIASTIC!

Figure 2-31
Music for F Horn Lesson 2

Round One

(open, no fingers down)

Lookin' Up

(valve: 1)

Up and Down

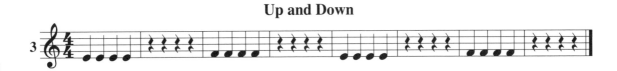

A New One

(open, no fingers down)

Take a Note

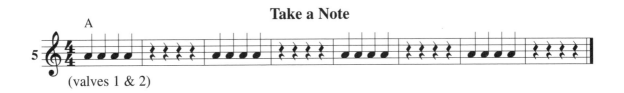

(valves 1 & 2)

Mary Had a Little Lamb

Tap toes: one foot tap per beat. Start with toes up; heels anchored on floor. Practice tapping toes while playing every line.

Figure 2-32
Music for F Horn Lesson 3

Steppin' Up

Down the Ladder

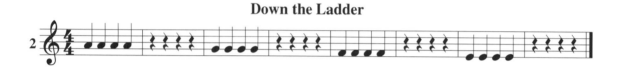

Over the Hill

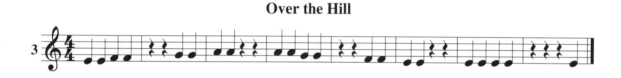

More to Play

Watch Out for That Rest!

Round and Round

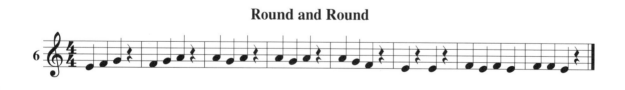

Waves

Figure 2-33
Music for F Horn Lesson 4

Remember This One

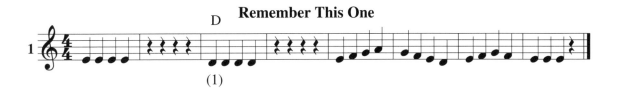

An Old Friend

Twice as Long

Say It Again

Hot Cross Buns

Go Tell Aunt Rhodie

Skippin' Around

Figure 2-34
Music for F Horn Lesson 5

The Whole Time

1   2   3   4   1–2   3–4   1–2–3–4   1–2–3–4   1   2   3   4   1–2   3–4   1–2–3–4   1–2–3–4

Jingle Bells

Ode to Joy

A Little Bit Longer

1–2–3 (4)   1–2–3 (4)

London Bridge

Duet

Troubleshooting the F Horn

Problem	Cause	Solutions
Defined and undefined difficulties		Make sure the instrument is in good playing order. This is true for all instruments. The instrument should play well. A good brand is also necessary.
Cannot make a sound	1. Dry lips	Wet lips
	2. Lip position	Make sure the student is buzzing with the top lip. The mouthpiece should be in about equal proportion to the top and bottom lips, but there may be some variation for some facial features.
	3. Angle of mouthpiece	If the student is large enough, there should be a slight angle down. However, because of size many young students may be looking up to reach the mouthpiece. Try to adjust the horn so the student can reach the mouthpiece without looking up, though that may not be possible.
Cannot play right pitch	1. Cannot hear the pitch	(a) Sing the pitch. (b) Hum the note. (c) Find the natural pitch (see p. 127). Work from that position to find the right note. (d) The right valves? (e) Sing the song or line. Maybe if he or she can hear the line as a whole entity, the student may be able to hear the pitches better. However, make sure the student starts singing on the right harmonic. (f) Play along with the students with an instrument in the same range.
	2. Too much saliva	Drain spit. (See p. 129)
Cannot play a higher note	1. Buzzing with bottom lip	Top lip over bottom
	2. Muscle control	Pretend to eat a lemon. That will result in the "eeewwww" shape of the mouth. Then buzz fast and hard. This could end up really high on the F horn. That is okay. Once the student has tightened the muscles, it is easier to have the student work his or her way down to the correct pitch.
Cannot play low note	Relax	(a) Lower jaw. (b) Pull teeth apart slightly. (c) Sing a low pitch. (d) Make an "oh" sound deep in the throat.

Intonation	1. Listening	(a) Listen to pitches.
		(b) Find the natural pitch.
	2. Hand position	In the beginning, the student will not be able to move right hand to adjust tuning. He must use his ear. As he advances, he will realize by moving the hand in and out slightly, he can effect subtle tuning.
	3. Too much spit in the horn	Drain the instrument (see p. 129).
	4. Tune the instrument (Single horn)	For B♭ or F, use open valve note. Adjust the tuning slide. Then after the student is a little more experienced, adjust the valve slides. Tune 2 & 3 together since there are no notes using only the third valve.
Tuning the double horn		Tune open third space written C to set open tuning. Then second valve B and first valve B♭. Third valve slide was tuned with 2 & 3 combination for A♭ and 1 & 3 is rare in the "normal" range. For B♭ side, tune open space F, second was E, first was E♭, and 2 & 3 was D♭ for the same reason as above. It is essential to have a good setting for all sides. Usually, after a good session setting the individual valves, it is only necessary to tune on one of the open pitches and set main tuning slides. Do not forget to tune both sides.
Gurgling	Too much spit in horn	See p. 129 for spit removal.

© 2001 by Parker Publishing Co.

F Horn/Double Horn Fingering Chart
(Numbers indicate valve[s] to be pressed)

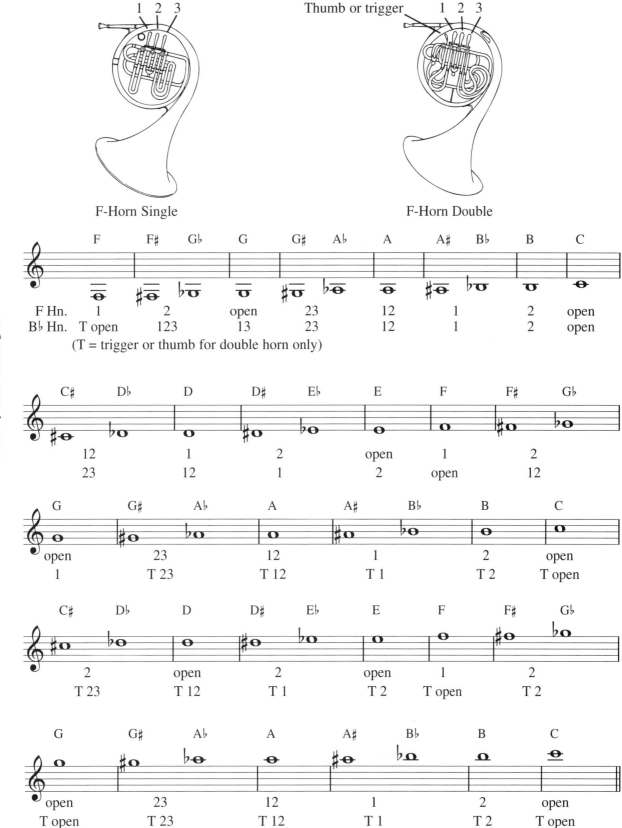

Finding the Student's Natural Note

Find the note in this range that the student plays naturally. In order to do that, have the student play several notes in a row. The one the student plays most often is his or her natural note. After the natural note is established, have the student play it several times, so he or she can hear and play the pitch on command. Then work the notes up and down so the student can find the correct note written on the music or the pitch he or she is attempting to match. Soon the student will be able to play the correct pitch on command. Once the natural note is established, the teacher may use the piano as an aid in finding the correct pitch. The parents or a sibling may also help the student at home if there is a piano or another instrument to help the student hear the correct notes.

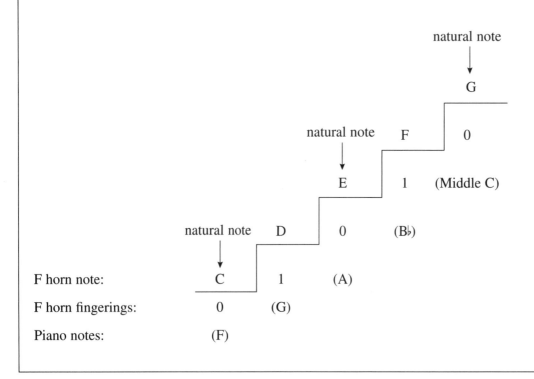

F Horn Lessons Checklist

Lesson 1

- [ ] Selecting the right student for F horn
- [ ] Chairs and stands in order
- [ ] Name tags on chairs
- [ ] Top of case
- [ ] How to open
- [ ] Assembly
- [ ] Instruct not to "pop" the mouthpiece
- [ ] Inspect instrument for quality/repair
- [ ] Hand position—hand to bell—consider child's size
- [ ] Wet lips
- [ ] Buzz lips
- [ ] Buzz mouthpiece
- [ ] Siren sound
- [ ] No buzz—"eat a lemon" technique
- [ ] Top lip over bottom lip
- [ ] Adjust mouthpiece to mouth—mouthpiece firmly against lips
- [ ] Angle of horn
- [ ] Work on playing higher and lower—C and G
- [ ] Play C-G-C (third space): the student has played his first song—"2001, A Space Odyssey"
- [ ] Find natural note
- [ ] Then locate E
- [ ] Tongue the note
- [ ] If time—play notes D and C
- [ ] Song: "Three Blind Mice"—only if time— challenge to learn by ear for next lesson
- [ ] Spit removal
- [ ] Instructions on how to practice
- [ ] Disassemble the instrument
- [ ] Specific assignment
- [ ] ***Be Enthusiastic!***

Lesson 2

- [ ] Advanced students assemble instruments immediately
- [ ] While advanced are assembling instruments, show new students top of case
- [ ] Buzz check for advanced students
- [ ] Review and play notes with advanced students
- [ ] Continue to show new students how to assemble their instruments
- [ ] Posture
- [ ] Advanced: Play "Three Blind Mice"
- [ ] Beginners: Play high and low
- [ ] Play C, G, C—"2001, A Space Odyssey"
- [ ] Find natural note
- [ ] Locate E
- [ ] Advanced students start to play book, beginners follow along
- [ ] Show beginners D, then C
- [ ] Advanced: Continue with book
- [ ] No book for beginners while playing
- [ ] Make sure advanced understand how to read the notes—no faking
- [ ] Only first page for advanced
- [ ] Beginners work on first three notes only
- [ ] Specific assignment
- [ ] ***Be Enthusiastic!***

Lesson 3

- [ ] Advanced: Start assembling instruments
- [ ] New students: Show top of case and assembly while advanced students are assembling instruments, reviewing and playing their first notes
- [ ] Most advanced: Play lesson—reading notes
- [ ] Students who just played for the first time last week: Review notes
- [ ] Continue with beginners, as other students are playing their notes—finding natural note first
- [ ] Keep reviewing all lessons
- [ ] Use baton/conduct
- [ ] Point to notes if students are not reading
- [ ] Have everyone follow along, even when not playing
- [ ] Posture
- [ ] Tonguing
- [ ] If the students are ready, start discussing intonation
- [ ] Specific assignment
- [ ] Notice their accomplishments and tell them how they have improved
- [ ] ***Be Enthusiastic!***

Lesson 4

- [ ] If possible, reschedule new students
- [ ] Advanced students start assembling instruments as they enter the room
- [ ] Start showing the new students top of case and assembly
- [ ] As soon as tones are stabilized, start tuning the instruments
- [ ] Continue to instruct beginners as you teach the advanced: natural note; then E, D, C
- [ ] Counting/toe tapping
- [ ] Playing the notes (advanced: reading the notes)
- [ ] Embouchure—top lip slightly over bottom lip
- [ ] Posture—F horn angle—hand position
- [ ] Show new notes and rhythms for next lesson
- [ ] Insist on practice
- [ ] Give specific assignment
- [ ] ***Enthusiasm!***

Lesson 5

- [ ] New students should be rescheduled
- [ ] Assemble instruments immediately
- [ ] If must have new students, teach instrument assembly while teaching the other students
- [ ] Advanced students: intonation
- [ ] As advanced play, watch eyes to make sure they are reading
- [ ] Posture
- [ ] Tonguing
- [ ] Breathing between notes
- [ ] *Discuss chair positions
- [ ] Embouchure
- [ ] Try to move as many students as possible to the same page
- [ ] Keep everyone playing—no more than a 5-minute break for anyone at any time
- [ ] Specific assignment
- [ ] ***ENTHUSIASM!!***

*Though not discussed in text, it is important to inform students about chair positions and the responsibility of the first chair player: the best player in the section.

The first chair, or section leader, helps to keep his/her section together. Other students hear this person playing the music correctly and follow the section leader. Though chair auditions may still be a few weeks away, it is a good idea to introduce this concept by the fifth lesson.

BEGINNING LOW BRASS LESSONS (TROMBONE, BARITONE, AND TUBA)

All the low brass instruments may be taught in the same group, though it is best not to have too large a group. An ideal small group is four or five students, though one should be able to handle eight students easily. If you are in a situation where you have 20 or more students per group, you will have to use your time very efficiently and have all students play at the same time.

There are many similarities between the trumpet and the low brass. However, I do recommend that you not put low brass in the same group as the trumpet players. The trumpets play an octave higher than trombones and the other low brass instruments. Some low brass students will try to play the same pitches the trumpets are playing, which will, of course, be too high. The low brass students will not play an octave too high, they will play up to the next partial or two higher, which will be wrong notes. You may put trombones or baritones with the saxophones. Even though the saxophones are playing an octave higher, the timbre is somewhat similar, and the low brass players are able to play their pitches an octave lower without too much difficulty. The tuba will be two octaves lower than the alto saxophones, so if they can be scheduled with low brass, or baritone saxophones, it will be easier for the tuba players to hear their pitches.

Students are often switched from trumpet to baritone horn. In these cases, the teacher frequently allows the student to play treble clef baritone. The fingerings are the same, but the transposition is up a major ninth. I strongly recommend having all baritone horn players read bass clef, even those converted from trumpet players. These players will quickly catch on to the bass clef fingerings and get used to reading bass clef. It is better to play in the same octave a student is reading. The ear seems to adjust to the correct pitches more quickly than when reading in treble clef. Also, there are some arrangements where there are no treble clef baritone or euphonium parts. In those cases, you will have a baritone horn player sitting, looking around, and missing a very important part of the arrangement.

Low Brass Lesson 1 (Figs. 2-36 and 2-37)

Before the students enter the room, have the chairs arranged as you wish them to be seated. If you know who is coming, put name tags on the chairs to avoid confusion and improve efficiency. You may wish to have chairs in straight lines or curved as in a band hall. I prefer the chairs curved if there is room. This allows the teacher to get to each student more quickly. The students usually can all see the instructor easily, and it gives them a feeling similar to playing in the band. The number of students attending the class will determine whether you have more than one row of chairs.

All students with instruments should sit in the front row or rows. Students who have not yet obtained instruments should sit together where they can easily see what the students with instruments are doing. As soon as the students have entered the room and are settled, explain the rules of behavior to them. They should understand that in order to stay in the lessons, with or without instruments, they must listen to the teacher and not make a disturbance. After two warnings, you should not hesitate to send a student back to his or her regular class for misbehaving. This is also the time to set deadlines for obtaining instruments. The students who are progressing quickly will lose interest if they are delayed and held back because there is a constant flow of new beginners in the class.

The students must know how to open the case and assemble the instrument properly. First, have each student set the instrument on the floor with the bottom of the case flat on the floor. The top of the case usually has the brand name on it, but the handle is always on the bottom portion of the case. Also, the latches always move in an upward direction to open the case. Instruct the students not to assemble the instruments until you have given them directions on how to put the instruments together properly (Photo 2-70).

Most of the low brass instruments require only insertion of the mouthpiece into the instrument, and the horn is assembled (Photo 2-71). The trombone has more to assemble than the other low brass instruments. First, the slide has to be attached to the bell. The bell goes to the left, and the slide to the right at

Figure 2-36
Music for Trombone and Baritone Horn Lesson 1

Teach this lesson without showing the music to the student. Students should concentrate on producing a good sound. Attempting to read music will distract from all that is needed to produce a good sound.

Slide position: 1
Baritone: (open)

The note is sustained for a comfortable length of time. Counting is not necessary for the first note.

Students should play the note four times in a steady count. All students not playing should count out loud with the band director.

3rd
(1)

Follow the same procedure as above.

4
(1,2)

Follow the same procedure as above.

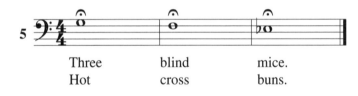

Three   blind   mice.
Hot   cross   buns.

First song. Counting rhythms is not necessary the first time. A quick accomplishment is paramount.

Mary Had a Little Lamb

ASSIGNMENT: First, hold each note, then play each note four times.
Play "Three Blind Mice."
Challenge: Who can play "Mary Had a Little Lamb" using the three notes learned today? Be positive; wish everyone a nice day.
BE ENTHUSIASTIC!

Figure 2-37
Music for Tuba Lesson 1

This lesson is taught without showing the music to the student. Students should concentrate on producing a good sound. Attempting to read music will distract from all that is needed to produce a good sound.

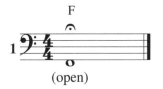

The note is sustained for a comfortable length of time. Counting is not necessary for the first note.

Students should play the note four times in a steady count. All students not playing should count out loud with the band director.

Follow the same procedure as above.

Follow the same procedure as above.

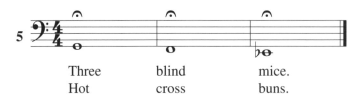

First song. Counting rhythms is not necessary the first time. A quick accomplishment is paramount.

Three   blind   mice.
Hot   cross   buns.

Mary Had a Little Lamb

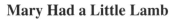

ASSIGNMENT: First, hold each note, then play each note four times.
Play "Three Blind Mice."
Challenge: Who can play "Mary Had a Little Lamb" using the three notes learned today? Be positive; wish everyone a nice day.
BE ENTHUSIASTIC!

a right angle to the bell (Photo 2-72). Often a student will put the slide too close to the bell. Demonstrate to the student that the slide may not go past the bell, because fingers may hit the bell first. There must be enough room for the fingers to easily slide by without hitting the bell. A right angle will take care of that problem. Once the angle is correct, the student may tighten the slide to the bell of the trombone. The next step is to gently set the mouthpiece into the instrument. The students must understand that the mouthpiece does not have to be forced or pushed as far as possible into the instrument. This applies to all brass instruments. If a student forces the mouthpiece as tightly as possible into the instrument, he or she

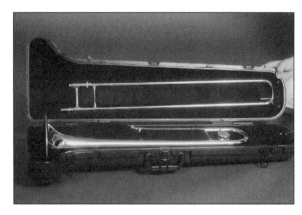

Photo 2-70

will not be able to remove the mouthpiece without a mouthpiece puller. Students also love to pop the mouthpiece into the instrument, thus making a "funny" noise. Warn the students severely that if they do

that, the mouthpiece will become jammed into the instrument and it cannot be removed without a special tool. Instruct the students not to let their parents put the instrument into a vise and try to remove the mouthpiece with a pair of pliers. Chances are the mouthpiece will not come out of the instrument, and the instrument may be seriously damaged. If the mouthpiece becomes jammed, it must be taken to a musical instrument repair shop to be removed. Some band directors keep a mouthpiece puller in their own repair boxes. If you decide to do that, make sure there is some penalty involved for you to remove the mouthpiece. Otherwise, the students will think it is great fun to "pop" the mouthpiece and you will be spending time daily removing mouthpieces from brass instruments.

How a student holds the instrument will vary with the size of the instrument and the size of the student. The baritone and tuba sit in the student's lap (some tubas may have stands or cradles). The right hand is for operating the valves, the left hand for holding the instrument. The right hand goes around or through the instrument over to the valve. If there is a thumb ring, the thumb should be placed into the ring with the first three fingers over the valves in an arch (Photo 2-73). Some euphoniums have a fourth valve. The little finger would be placed over the

Photo 2-71

fourth valve; however, few beginners start on the four-valve euphonium. Baritone horn is usually used for beginners. Some manufacturers now make a smaller, lighter version of the baritone which is excellent for very young students.

The left hand will hold the baritone or tuba. Usually the left hand will grip the instrument around the tubing toward the top of the instrument (Photo 2-74). A student with short arms may hold the instrument to the left side, gripping the side of the horn. How high up the baritone or tuba is held depends on size and arm length of the child as well as size of the instrument. Both the baritone and the tuba will rest in

Photo 2-72

Photo 2-73

the student's lap. If the baritone/tuba player sits at a slight angle in the chair, the student may be better able to adjust the stand so he or she can see the conductor and the notes at the same time. Because the bell of the baritone or tuba is coming straight up in front of the student, often the slight angle in the chair or slight tilt of the instrument will help the student find the best playing position (Photo 2-75).

The trombone is held with the left hand and the slide is moved with the right hand. The left thumb goes on the vertical bar behind the mouthpiece and the first two fingers should touch the top section of the slide just below the mouthpiece. Some students may try to grab the vertical bar; however, it is important that you stress and insist on the proper hand position. The slide is held with the thumb on the side of the bar attached to the movable part

Photo 2-74

of the slide closest to the student (Photo 2-76). Tell the student that the thumb should be in the position to put a thumbprint on the bar of the slide. The first two fingers are on the opposite side of the bar. Again, students will often want to grab the vertical bar. In the long run, this will slow down the student's ability to move the slide quickly and accurately. You must insist on a good hand position.

Photo 2-75

The trombone is placed on the left side of the student's head above the shoulder. The student's shoulder is *not* the proper resting place for the trombone. The trombone should have a slight angle down, but not directly toward the floor (Photo 2-77). You will have to constantly remind your trombone players to lift their bells up in order to be heard. Another problem for trombone players is the position of the music stand. Often the stands seem to be in the way (Photo 2-78). The student should position the stand so that the slide goes just below the stand. At the same time, the stand must be at a height that allows the student to see the conductor. This is not as difficult as it may seem, but you may need to assist your young players in finding the best position.

It is a good idea to have all brass players make a sound first with the mouthpiece only. Before attempting to make a sound, the students should first wet their lips. Have the students either all together or one at a time buzz into the mouthpiece. The buzz should be made with the top lip slightly over the bottom lip.

Photo 2-76

Then the mouthpiece is put firmly over the lip, but not with so much pressure it causes pain, or a pinching sound. Once the students have all made a sound, see if they can then make a siren sound with the mouthpiece. The siren sound is made by starting with as low a pitch as possible, or a loose buzz, and in one breath making the pitch go as high as possible and low again. This is usually fun for the students, and it is important for the teacher to emphasize that they do this daily before playing their instruments. In fact, they may perform this exercise without the mouthpiece. Suggest to the students that when they are alone, they should practice making the siren sound, with or without their mouthpieces. This will strengthen the lip

Photo 2-77

muscles and make it easier for them to control their pitches. It does not matter how high the pitch goes in the beginning—if they keep trying, the pitch will get higher as they continue to practice.

Photo 2-78

Once the students have a "good" buzz, have them put the mouthpiece into the instrument. If a student is having trouble producing a buzz, there are a few techniques that may help: Tell the student to put his lips together and make an "mmmm" sound with the lips shut tightly. Then blow the air out of the mouth as hard as possible. Make sure the student's lips are wet before he tries to buzz his lips. If that does not work, ask the student, "What do you do when you eat a lemon?" The sound "eeeewww" is made. With the lips tight in that position, blow the air out hard and make the lips buzz. This usually works when nothing else does.

There are students, however, who have a hard time buzzing their lips with or without the mouthpiece. Have them put the mouthpiece into the instrument and try to buzz. Many times those students will make some type of sound. Do not worry about a perfect sound. They are nervous about being able to make any sound at all, so be complimentary about any sound they make and go to the next student. Once you have a sound started, you can begin to improve the sound of the player. Also, you may need to push the mouthpiece firmly against the student's lips (Photo 2-79). If a student cannot get a buzz or a sound, then go on to the next student. Do not continue to try to have the student produce a sound. Sometimes, just hearing other students make a sound and seeing what they are doing is all they need to know to make a sound. However, even if that does not accomplish the task, do not embarrass or humiliate the student; go to the next student. When everyone has attempted to make a sound, you may ask the student to try again. If no sound is produced, have the student continue to try while everyone else is playing either the mouthpiece or the entire instrument. There is a reasonable chance the student will start to make a sound by the end of the class. If you single the person out too often, he may become so discouraged that he will quit.

Photo 2-79. Teacher helping student feel correct pressure against lips.

Have the students play high and low pitches before naming and requesting any particular note. When they can produce and control high and low notes, it is time for the students to play an F. F is a good first note. It is first position for the trombone or open for the valved instruments. Low B♭ is too low. Some students have trouble playing a low note first and then tightening up the lips to produce a higher note. Start from a position of tension, and then relax. Students will be more successful and advance more quickly on brass instruments by starting on higher pitches. Have the students hold the note for approximately four beats. The first time they play the note, do not tell them to play the note for any certain number of beats, but to hold the note until you cut them off. After they have played the first note successfully, have them play the note four times, one beat each. Insist that the students tap their toes while they play. If their feet are tapping a steady rhythm, they are most likely counting in their heads. Have them do this exercise a few times.

After they have all played the first note successfully (at a beginner's level), show the students how to play E♭. That is the first valve for the valved instruments, and third position for the trombone. Third position on the trombone is just before the bell, but try to have the students learn to feel where to stop the slide without using their fingers to find the correct position. Students should use their ears, not their fingers, to tune the instrument. For the trombone more than most other instruments, the students must listen to know when the notes are right in pitch. Some trombones' slide positions may be in a slightly different position for tuning than others. That could be related to the brand and condition of the instrument. The students should first hold the note on your cue, and then play the note four times, one beat apiece. Make sure they are tapping their toes.

Review F and E♭. The final note for the first day is G, fourth space (bottom line for the tuba). Then show the students how to play the notes by position or valves: fourth position for trombone and valves one and two for the valved instruments. Follow the same procedure as above: Hold the note on your cue, and then play the note four times, one beat each. Make sure the students are hearing the pitches sound higher as well as just playing the note. It is important that you emphasize to the students that they must listen to their pitches in order to become good brass players.

After they have played G, have the students play G, F, E♭, one beat apiece, slowly. Once they have accomplished that, they have played the first part of a song: "Three Blind Mice." If you have time, play this song a few times.

Challenge the students by telling them that with those same three notes, they can play "Mary Had a Little Lamb." You can make it a contest by saying anyone who can play "Mary Had a Little Lamb" by next week wins a prize (a couple of stickers, nothing expensive).

By this time you have come to the end of the class. In fact, it will be quite a matter of time organization to do all this in one class period, but it is extremely important that the students feel accomplishment no matter how small. If the class was able to play only two notes well, make sure they feel your pride in their achievement. Do not discourage students in the first lesson. If you did get to all three notes on the first day, and that should be your goal, make as big a fuss as possible about learning to play a song on the first day. Your enthusiasm will get the students through some of those tough beginning stages.

Give a specific assignment. Tell the students to practice each note one at a time. First, hold the note for as long as possible without straining. Tell them to tap their toes slowly and count the number of foot taps as they hold the note. Then, play the note four times in a row while tapping their toes. After each note is played in this manner, then play "Three Blind Mice." The remainder of their practice time can be used just playing notes, making "good" sounds, and trying to play "Mary Had a Little Lamb." Good sounds are sounds that are not so loud that the tone quality is poor, but it is important that beginning brass students play loudly. Playing softly will not give them proper air support for a good sound. However, you should not go into long dissertations about air support—a young student will have no idea what you are talking about. Just tell them to play loudly. If you try to explain proper breathing on the first lesson, you may be adding one thing too many for a student to accomplish. Remember this: On the first day the students have two great fears. The first fear is that they may sound bad. However, students are most scared that no sound will come out. If you add one more task to the list of things to do to get a sound, you may confuse them so they cannot play a note easily. When anyone is nervous, he does not breathe properly. If a student is breathing incorrectly, wait a few weeks. Once the student relaxes, he or she will most likely breathe from the proper position.

Be sure that the last thing students hear is your praise for their accomplishment of this day. Tell them to practice daily (at least 15 minutes for the first week) and to have fun because they sound great! Before they practice playing the notes on their instruments, instruct them to play just the mouthpiece and make the siren sound. Then they should start practicing the notes. If anyone gets home and cannot play a note, tell him to keep trying. By the end of the week, they all should be able to play the notes. Even if they do not, they should remember that they all got a sound today and with your help they will get it again, but it is extremely important that they keep trying every day!

Low Brass Lesson 2 (Figs. 2-38 and 2-39)

This lesson is more involved than the first lesson because it must cover students who played the previous week and students who are receiving their instruments for the first time. You must keep students interested and busy for the entire lesson. Review how to assemble the instrument, and have the students oil the slide from the very beginning so they do not have difficulty moving the slide. As a general rule, as you are going back and forth with the students who have played and those who are learning for the first time, try not to go more than five minutes without each group playing at least a note or a line. As you are teaching the beginners how to play their first note, have the advanced students (students who started the previous week) play along with them.

Before you start any lesson on any instrument, make sure you know all the fingers and slide positions that will be used during the first year. You do not want to give a bad impression by having a parent call your supervisor or principal and complain that you had to look up in the "manual" how to play the instrument. Be prepared ahead of time.

As the students enter the room, have the students who played the previous week sit together and students just receiving their instruments sit next to each other. If you have students who are attending the lesson but have not received instruments, instruct them to be quiet and pay attention to what the students who have their instruments are doing. If possible, this should be the last lesson students should attend without instruments. It is a good idea to allow the students to attend a couple of lessons without instruments so they will see what they are missing and hopefully obtain instruments and join the band. However, there is a point where they will be a distraction and possibly cost you more students than you will gain. Also, you want to discourage students who are just trying to get out of class. Be nice and courteous to them, occasionally remind them to pay attention, but if any of them become a distraction, immediately send him or her back to the regular class. You should have set a deadline for obtaining an instrument. Remind them of that date. It is important that you stick to your deadlines. It will make students next year be more aware of that date, and you do not want to lose students because the better students are being held back by a constant flow of new beginners into the classroom.

As the advanced students are putting their instruments together, instruct the beginners on how to find the top of the case, and put the case on the floor with the bottom on the floor. Follow the same procedure as in the previous lesson, but you will need to move quickly. There is a lot to be covered in this lesson, so you must keep all the students moving and paying attention to you for the entire lesson. This should not be too difficult since they are there to learn to play their instruments, but the teacher must know exactly what he or she is doing. Continue to show the beginners how to assemble their instruments while the advanced students are putting their instruments together. Since they have done this before, they should do it quickly and complete this task before the beginners have assembled their instruments. This whole process will take only a few minutes. You may have to give the trombones extra help in putting on the slide. Once the student understands how to attach the slide to the bell and adjust it to the correct angle, he or she will do this without your assistance.

Have the advanced students play F. Hold the note as you direct it, then have them play four quarter notes. If this goes well, and everybody is able to play the note, proceed to play E♭. If at any time a student

Figure 2-38
Music for Trombone and Baritone Horn Lesson 2

Round One

Slide position: 1
Baritone: (open)

Lookin' Down

Slide position: 3
Baritone: (1st valve)

Up and Down

A New One

4
(1, 2)

Three in One

Mary Had a Little Lamb

Tap toes: one foot tap per beat. Start with toes up; heels anchored on floor. Practice tapping toes while playing every line (see picture).

Figure 2-39
Music for Tuba Lesson 2

Tap toes: one foot tap per beat. Start with toes up; heels anchored on floor. Practice tapping toes while playing every line (see picture).

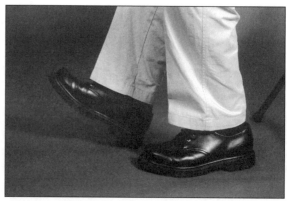

is having trouble producing a sound, work with him or her individually. Try the techniques discussed in the previous lesson or in the troubleshooting guide at the end of the Low Brass section (page 172) to help produce a sound. If it has not been five minutes, have the students play G.

Show the beginners how to play F. You may have an equal number of beginners as of advanced students on the first lesson, so you will have to move quickly to show them the valve or slide positions. If you chose to start using a heterogeneous band method book for the first lessons, rather than the lessons from this book, I would still advise that on the first lesson no music be used. Use these three easy notes to play first. It will be easy enough to show the students new notes next week. However, there is so much to learn for a young student that learning to read the notes on the same day may be too much to remember. After the new students have all played F, have the advanced join them in playing the note—first holding the note, and then four quarter notes.

Have all students look at Lesson 2 (Figs. 2-38 and 2-39) from this resource. If you must use a heterogeneous text, there is no rule that you must follow a book in the order in which the author thinks best. A book is a tool. It is up to you to use that tool to your best advantage. The first note to read should be an F. The music in this resource starts with the note F as the first line, and introduces the rhythm of quarter notes first. Make sure the students see what line indicates the note F. The note is on the fourth line (or space below the staff for tuba). It is that placement that is telling the student to play an F. Because the note is filled in and has a stem, the note is played for one beat only. Because there are four in a row, the students will play four Fs in a row. I believe this makes it easier, because holding a note for four beats is an abstract thought for young students, especially fourth graders. It is easier to count in your head to four if you are hearing four notes being played. This is especially true for young students. Have the advanced students play the first measure only. Explain to the students the rests in the next measure. Rests are moments of timed silence. They do not mean to stop thinking. Have the students count the rests out loud the first time they play the line. Once they have played the first two measures (one with notes, the second with rests), have the students play the entire first line. The beginners should not be playing, but following in their books.

Show the beginning students how to play E♭. Do this first by showing them the slide or fingering position and telling them that the sound is made in the same manner as playing the F, but the note this time will sound a little lower. Have all the students hold the note on your cue. The advanced may join in when all the beginners play together. Then have the students play four quarter notes. Have the students then play F, and ask them if they can hear the difference between the two notes. They should hear that the E♭ is a little lower than the F.

The advanced students should continue to the next line. First, you must show students how to distinguish between the F and E♭. F is on the fourth line, E♭ on the third space for trombones and baritones, and F below the staff for tuba and one leger line for E♭. Though this may seem overly simple, many students do not understand how to read music. They do not understand that the notes are marked on different lines and spaces. The teacher must demonstrate this. Point to the two different notes so the students can see the difference. This cannot be understated. We do not teach many new notes per day because we want the students to remember the notes and how to play them, but often as teachers who have been playing music for so many years, we forget that music is a foreign language to young children. Once they understand the difference in reading the two notes, they should play this line in the same manner as the previous line with F. The beginners should follow along in the book, but not play.

The beginners should then learn to play G. Do this in the same manner as before. Have the advanced students play with them when they play as a group. This will help the beginners hear the pitch, so they may learn more quickly. Next, show the advanced students how to play the line with G in it. You should follow the same procedure as before. Then try to play as much of this page as time will allow. Realistically, however, this will be about as far as you will be able to go in this day's class.

If you choose to use a band method book whose first page does not use these notes, start with the highest notes on the page. As I stated before, it is always easier to start from a point of more tension than with a low, more relaxed note. The muscles have not developed enough yet for all students to start with lower notes and tighten the lips to higher pitches.

As always, give a specific assignment. Do not assume the students will know what to practice. If you do not give a specific assignment, many of them will not practice. You must tell them what to do. Instruct all the students to practice buzzing their lips and making the siren sound at least five times before playing the instrument. Beginners should concentrate on making the three notes sound good. Practice "Three Blind Mice," and try to figure out how to play "Mary Had a Little Lamb." They may look at the book and start to practice reading the notes only after at least three days of practice working on sounds and holding notes and playing four notes on each tone. They should, however, review the notes on the staff immediately so they do not forget how to tell them apart.

Be positive. Give them words of encouragement. Let them know you are pleased with their progress and cannot wait until next week to teach them more new notes and songs. Your enthusiasm will make them want to play their instruments.

Low Brass Lesson 3 (Figs. 2-40 and 2-41)

As the students enter the room, have the students who played previously assemble their instruments. Have the new students sit together so you can instruct them on how to properly put their instruments together. Follow the same procedure as in the previous lesson for assembling the instruments. Give assistance whenever necessary. While the new students (beginners) are assembling their instruments, have the students who played last week (advanced) play and hold an F together, and then play it four times in a row. While doing this continue to help the beginners assemble their instruments. After the F, have the advanced students play an E♭ in a similar manner. If the beginners are still assembling their instruments, have the advanced students play a G, first holding the note and then playing it four times, one beat each.

The beginners should start by buzzing their lips without the mouthpiece and then with the mouthpiece up to their lips. Have a contest to see who can make the best siren sound. Once they can all make the siren sound (this does not have to be perfectly done), then have them put the mouthpiece into the instrument. Instruct them on the proper fingering or slide position for F, and have them each try playing an F. If you have a large class, have them play it all together. Use some of the techniques mentioned in previous lessons. When all the beginners have played F, have the beginners and advanced then play the note together.

After that is accomplished, have everyone open his or her book to the assignment, which should be the first page of notes in the method book, or the second lesson in this resource. Review the note F in the staff (just below for the tuba). Quickly discuss the rhythms indicated and have the advanced students play the first line. The beginners should follow along in the book, but not play. Continue with the next note, E♭, and follow the same procedure. If this process is moving quickly, continue on to the next line with G. Since the advanced students played these notes the previous week, the review should move quickly.

Now have the beginners play E♭. Show them the valve or slide position and have the students play the note in the same manner you just taught them to play F. If a student is puffing out her cheeks, first tell her not to—sometimes that will work. However, many students are not aware of the muscles around the mouth and how to use them. Ask the student to hold the note and while she is sustaining the note, tell her to bring in her cheeks. Say it over and over again, quickly. Just as she is about to run out of air, she will bring in her cheeks. By doing this, she will see she can control the muscles in her mouth and lips. You may have to do this a few times in a row, but soon she should be able to keep her cheeks from puffing out. Continue to remind students not to puff out the cheeks. This is important for tone development and pitch control.

If learning to play E♭ took less than five minutes, continue to show the beginners how to play G. Demonstrate the valve or slide position and have them play the note. Whenever the beginners play a note together, have the advanced join in. Because the advanced students will usually play the correct pitch, it will help the beginners hear and play the right sound. This also keeps both groups playing as much as possible.

Have the advanced students play as much of Lesson 3 as possible during the class. Most of the time will be taken up reviewing Lesson 2; however, be sure to play at least the first two lines of the page, discuss any new notes and/or rhythms, and discuss the importance of rests.

Figure 2-40
Music for Trombone and Baritone Horn Lesson 3

Figure 2-41
Music for Tuba Lesson 3

Steppin' Up

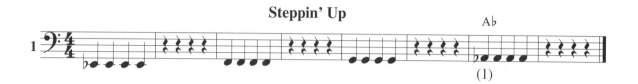

Down the Ladder

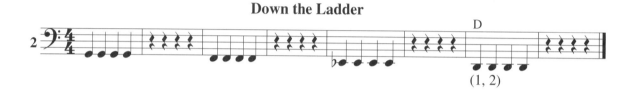

Over the Hill

More to Play

Watch Out for That Rest!

Round and Round

Waves

At the end of the lesson, give a specific assignment. All students should practice with just the mouthpiece before putting the instrument together. (The better and higher the students can make a siren sound, the better players they will become.) Then they should play the notes they have studied in class. Beginners should practice developing a good sound. First, play the notes as long as the student can with a good sound. Then play four notes, one foot tap each. Do this for each of the three new notes they just learned today. The advanced students should review the three notes, and then review Lesson 2. They should practice slowly. Speed is not important at this stage. Students need to take the time to listen to what they are doing. Since many notes can be played using the same valve or slide position, they must listen carefully to know if they are playing the correct pitch. After they have practiced Lesson 2, the advanced students should continue to the next lesson and play all of the page by the next week. If they have accomplished this, they may continue to the next lesson. Emphasize and encourage the students to look ahead. The more they can do on their own, the more the teacher can teach them.

Be positive. The students need to know you share their enthusiasm for learning to play an instrument. Let them feel that you are proud of their accomplishment. This will sustain them through any difficulties they may experience at home, or in future lessons. Make your band or instrument class a joy to attend.

Low Brass Lesson 4 (Figs. 2-42 and 2-43)

As the students enter the room, they should assemble their instruments immediately and put the instrument cases away from the chairs in which they will be sitting. If you have beginners coming to the lesson, have them sit together and await your instructions. I would advise that this be the last lesson to include beginners. It would be better to reschedule them into a different group by this lesson if at all possible. However, advice will be given should you not be able to reschedule a new class of students.

Immediately start to instruct the new students on how to take the instrument out of the case and assemble it while the advanced students are getting ready to play. Once all the advanced students are ready, review the notes learned previously. First, hold the note and have them play quarter notes on each tone. Continue to instruct the beginners on assembling their instruments in between having the advanced students review their notes.

The beginners should buzz the mouthpiece before playing the entire instrument. Making the siren sound is an excellent way to develop muscle control, and it is fun for the students to make as high a siren sound as possible. It is a good idea to have the advanced players do this from time to time, and encourage them to practice this at home. After they have buzzed their lips and made a siren sound, they should put the mouthpiece into the instrument and play their first note, F. As in previous classes, they should hold the note on your cue. The mouthpiece should be in the center of the mouth, not to the side or too high or too low. The buzz should be mostly with the top lip, not the bottom.

Review the previous lessons with the advanced students. It is not necessary to play every line since they have played this page before. Play one or two of the lines at the top of the page, and then play "Mary Had a Little Lamb" or the most familiar or fun song in each lesson. This should get everyone warmed up. It will also allow you to have all the students who played previously advance to the same page. As all students play, continue to watch for:

1. Holding the instrument at an angle where the player can see the music and the conductor.

2. Baritone/Tuba: The left hand is holding the instrument where it is easy to balance.

3. Trombone hand position: Left hand, the thumb should be around the back and bottom of the bar attached to the bell, and the fingers reaching up to touch the top of the trombone at this point. Right hand, the slide is held with the thumb and first two fingers. Neither hand should be "grabbing" the instrument.

4. Students should be buzzing mainly with the top lip, not the bottom.

5. The mouthpiece is firmly against the mouth, but not to the point of pinching the sound and hurting the lips (Photos 2-80 and 2-81).

Figure 2-42
Music for Trombone and Baritone Horn Lesson 4

Can You C This New Note?

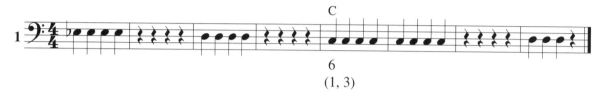

At the Bottom

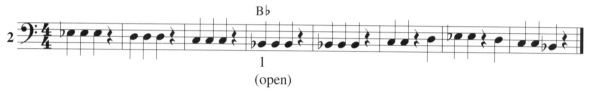

Twice as Long

Say It Again

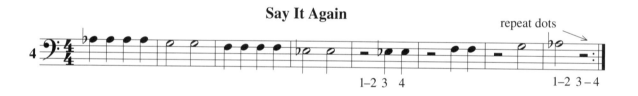

Hot Cross Buns

Go Tell Aunt Rhodie

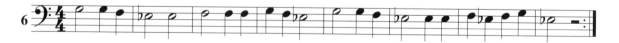

Skippin' Around

**Figure 2-43
Music for Tuba Lesson 4**

Can You C This New Note?

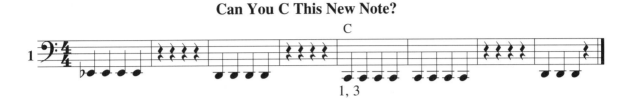

At the Bottom

Twice as Long

Say It Again

Hot Cross Buns

Go Tell Aunt Rhodie

Skippin' Around

6. As the students are reading music, watch their eyes to make sure they are really reading the notes and not just faking it and following along.

If you see eyes wandering and students looking at other students to find the note, you may assume they do not understand how to read the notes and, therefore, how to follow the notes on the page while playing a line. There is an easy procedure to correct this problem: First, make sure that everyone understands how the notes are positioned on the staff. This may seem simple to an experienced musician, but to an elementary student it is a new language. Point out the difference between the F and E♭. Let students see that one note is on a line and the other on a space. You

Photo 2-80

may need to point this out several times before it registers as a difference to some students. Then they have to understand that the rhythms are indicated by the shape of the note, not by the name or placement

on the staff. It is important to explain this thoroughly when you first introduce reading music to them, but you may have to do it more than once before everyone realizes how to distinguish notes and rhythms. The next problem a student may have is how to follow the notes as the line is being played. Sometimes a student may not understand reading music in the same manner as reading words. The music, just like printed text, is read from left to right. An easy way to help students realize this is to have everyone play a very easy line (such as the first line on the first page). While everyone is playing, walk over to the student having difficulties and point to the notes as everyone is playing. He should soon see that he has to keep looking at the next note in order to keep up with everyone. This is an easy way to demonstrate and does not embarrass anyone. Many times, other students are not aware that you started to point out the notes for a student. You may have to do this a few times before a student is able to read music, but it is a simple procedure that works (Photo 2-82).

Photo 2-81

Next, show the beginners how to play E♭ and G. Follow the

same procedure as in the previous lessons. Hopefully, you will only have one or two beginners in this class, if any. Move quickly, and do not spend a lot of time on the new students. They should catch on quickly because they have been watching for the previous three lessons—however, you cannot count on young students paying attention all the time! Do not hold up everyone else because a few students started late. They are expected to practice extra to catch up. It is better to lose one new beginner who started late and is not practicing than to lose five students who are doing well.

Have the advanced students turn to Lesson 3 (Figs. 2-40 and 2-41). Start at the top of the page and start playing each line. It is important not to skip lines in the first half of the book, even if the students may know the names of the notes and the rhythms. Students need the drill to remember how to play these notes and rhythms quickly. As the

Photo 2-82

class plays down the page, take the time to explain any new notes or rhythms. Conduct every line. This is important—students need to get used to a conductor. By conducting, you will help them keep a steady tempo, and they will become comfortable seeing a conductor beat time while they are playing. You do not have to go into details about conducting patterns, but it is a good idea to let them know that whenever your baton goes straight down, that is the first beat of the measure. That way, if they get lost or become insecure about where they are, there is a marker for them to get back on track.

If there are beginners in this class, continue playing Lesson 3 with the advanced students for about five or six minutes. Then have everyone, advanced and beginners, play the first three notes they learned. Review with the beginners how to read the notes on the page. Hopefully, they have paid attention and this will be a quick process. Then have everyone play line 1. This will help the beginners hear their pitch, and it will keep the advanced students playing their instruments. Then play the next lines that have the notes which they just learned. All students should play. Continue this review for about five minutes.

If there is time left, have the advanced students continue to Lesson 4. Show the students any new notes or rhythms on the next page. There may not be enough time to play anything on this page, but at least make a quick attempt to explain to the students how to perform these new items.

As always with all instruments, give a specific assignment. Tell the advanced students to finish Lesson 3 if it was not completed today. Then, try to play as much of the next lesson as possible. Anyone who completes Lesson 4 may look ahead and try songs from other lessons. Always encourage students to move ahead. The beginners and advanced should practice the siren sound every day. Beginners should review the first three notes they learned to play. After they feel confident that they can play those three notes, they may start practicing the lessons in this resource. Encourage them to try to catch up with the advanced students as quickly as possible.

Again, the last things the students should hear from you are words of encouragement, your feeling of pride for their accomplishments, and reminders to practice! Students should always feel good about coming to lessons, even on the teacher's worst day.

Low Brass Lesson 5 (Figs. 2-44 and 2-45)

This is the lesson where you should start to get all the students playing the same page. However, if you accept beginners now, that will delay getting everyone to play together. If you choose to allow new students to start playing at this point, you must move very quickly and spend most of your time with the students who have already started playing their instruments. If you take too much time with the one student who just obtained an instrument, you could lose several others because of boredom and frustration. Tips will be given on how to handle this type of situation; however, it is strongly advised to have your deadline set by the fourth lesson at the latest. It is best to schedule a new group if you have students continually signing up this late for instrumental lessons.

As the students enter the room, they should start assembling their instruments. If a new student enters, immediately start helping him assemble his instrument. Follow the same procedures as in the previous lessons.

It will be a good warm-up and review to start playing the first page of the book or the lessons from this book (Lesson 2). Play one or two lines and then have everyone play "Mary Had a Little Lamb." This should take about five minutes to complete.

Have the new student play an F. Then quickly have the student play an E♭ and then a G. After the beginner has played the three notes separately, have him or her then play the three notes in a row so the student will have played "Three Blind Mice."

Tell the beginning student to pay close attention to the advanced students as they continue to play more music today. The student should follow along in the book and try to recognize the notes on the staff. They may need more time, but it is crucial that you not lose the momentum of the advanced students. That does not mean that you will ignore the beginners from this point on; you will have them play from time to time, but your main concentration will be on advancing the students who have played before.

Figure 2-44
Music for Trombone and Baritone Horn Lesson 5

The Whole Time

Jingle Bells

Ode to Joy

A Little Bit Longer

London Bridge

Duet

Figure 2-45
Music for Tuba Lesson 5

The Whole Time

Jingle Bells

Ode to Joy

A Little Bit Longer

London Bridge

Duet

(2)

By this lesson, the advanced student's tone should be improving and becoming stable. If the students can hold a steady pitch, it is time to start tuning their instruments. You may tune the low brass to F or B♭ depending on which note they can play better. Since both notes are in first position or open valves, either will do. However, if low B♭ is stable, I prefer that note since that is the tuning note for the entire band.

Have the first student play the tuning note and then the next student play the same note. Ask the students in the lesson which pitch is higher. If they give you the wrong answer, instead of correcting them, ask the students to listen again. Make sure they are not confusing volume with pitch. In this age of television and computer games, many people judge volume as higher or lower. If the two students' pitches are fairly close, have one student pull her tuning slide out. Then let the students hear the difference in the sounds. As the student who pulled the tuning slide out pushes the slide further in, the class will hear the pitches come closer together. Thus, you are training the students to use their ears. When the two pitches finally match, the students will hear what is meant by good intonation. Tune all of the advanced students in the class. As soon as the beginners can stabilize their pitches, start tuning them. For one thing it will make your day more pleasant, but it will also make the entire band as well as the students in the group lessons sound better, and the students are more likely to stay in the band. Tuning the students for the first time may take a while, maybe the entire period. This is time well spent. However, while tuning the advanced students, do not forget about any beginners in the class. Make sure you continually teach them how to play their instruments while you tune the advanced band. No student should go more than five minutes without playing his or her instrument.

If, in the previous lesson, you did play most of Lesson 4, give it a quick review. Otherwise, play the entire page. It can be tempting to skip lines if the students seem to be progressing quickly; however, they need the drill of doing things over and over again in order to maintain consistency in their playing. Review the time values for half notes and half rests. It is okay to have the new students participate in this event—they do need to start recognizing the notes and rhythms in order to catch up with the other students. As the students play this page, make sure they are tapping their toes. It is a good practice to have the students clap the rhythms before they play the lines. You may not need to do this with every line, but if you have a class with particularly bad rhythm, it is advisable to spend as much time as necessary on rhythm.

When the students play lines with repeat dots at the end, make them repeat. If you do not do this now, when they play an arrangement with repeat dots, they will ignore them just as they did in your beginning classes. Teach them to pay attention to the details. The details are not too complicated at this point, so heeding them should not be asking too much of the students.

After about five minutes, review the first three notes with the beginners by playing them as four quarter notes each. Then show them the first page with notes. Have them play the line with F. If that goes well, proceed to the next lines. Spend no more than five minutes with this group. This will give them the information they need to play the notes and start to catch up with the other students. Emphasize to them that the only way they will catch up with the other students is to practice every day, at least 30 minutes a day or more.

Return to the advanced students. Complete any lines from Lesson 4 and play as much of Lesson 5 as you can. Carefully explain to them the different rhythmic values. Make sure they see the difference between the kind of note (rhythmic values) and the different notes on the page. Even though you may have gone over this before, you may need to review it for some students. Make sure they can see that notes are on a particular line or space, and that the position is what is telling them what note, slide position, or valve to push down. As simple as this seems, it may not be an easy concept for some beginners. They must learn to read the notes in these early lessons.

As the students play, watch for:

1. Holding the instrument at an angle where they can see the music and the conductor.

2. Posture: Sitting up straight at the edge of the chair, with both feet flat on the floor. No crossing legs, sitting on legs, or slumped posture.

3. The left hand is holding the instrument where it is easy to balance (baritone and tuba).

4. Trombone hand position: Left hand, the thumb should be around the back and bottom of the bar attached to the bell, and the fingers reaching up to touch the top of the trombone at this point. Right hand, the slide is held with the thumb and first two fingers. Neither hand should be "grabbing" the instrument.

5. Students should be buzzing with the top lip, not the bottom.

6. The mouthpiece is firmly against the mouth (but not to the point of pinching the sound and hurting the lips).

7. Tapping toes.

8. Students counting the rhythms correctly.

9. As the students are reading music, watch their eyes to make sure they are reading the notes.

At the end of the lesson, give an assignment. Tell the beginners to play the first three notes without the book for the first few days. After two days, and if the sound is good, tell them to start reading and playing the lines in the book. The advanced students should complete Lesson 4 and play Lesson 5 by the next session. All students should concentrate on a good sound and playing the correct rhythms. Again, students may look ahead, but it is important to try to play as much of the assignment as possible by the next lesson.

Be cheerful. Tell them to have a nice day. And, most important, let them know you are pleased with their progress and expect to hear some great sounds from the low brass section of the band.

Further Considerations

It is important to make band fun and play music that is fun right away. However, for brass players, it is important to play long tones as soon as possible. One way to make this fun is to have a contest to see who can hold the note the longest with a good tone. If they keep practicing, they will be able to hold the notes a little longer each week.

Practicing arpeggios is also important for all brass students. It will develop lip control and also help the students to hear the different pitches. Arpeggios should start very simply with just a fifth. In the beginning it is not important to know each note the students are playing; just have them play two notes without playing change valves or changing slide position. As time goes on, that can be extended (see exercises in Figs. 2-46 and 2-47).

Teaching the Tuba
(Considerations specifically for teaching the tuba)

Who Should Be Switched to Tuba?

Most students start on instruments other than the tuba. The two most obvious reasons are student size and the cost of the instrument. However, there are students who will want to play the tuba as their first instrument. If the student's size does not pose a problem, then the student should be allowed to play the instrument of his or her choice (Photo 2-83).

Trumpet, trombone, and baritone horn players are usually the easiest students to switch over to the tuba, though it is not advisable to refuse a woodwind student the right to switch to tuba. If a student really wants to play an instrument, in most cases he or she will practice and succeed. Candidates for the tuba should be of a physical size that will allow them to handle the instrument. A thick lip construction is helpful but not necessary for success when playing the tuba. Many times a trumpet player who is struggling to play with a good sound on his trumpet will switch to the baritone horn or tuba and do extremely well. It is important to note that the trumpet player is not having trouble because he is a poor musician. He is simply better suited physically to play a larger mouthpiece.

Figure 2-46
Warm-ups for Brass Instruments

The following exercises should be practiced daily. It is not necessary to play the entire set of exercises on the first day. Start with two lines on the first day and add one or two lines as the student feels comfortable. Do not continue to play if the lips are starting to hurt or getting too tired to play the correct pitches.

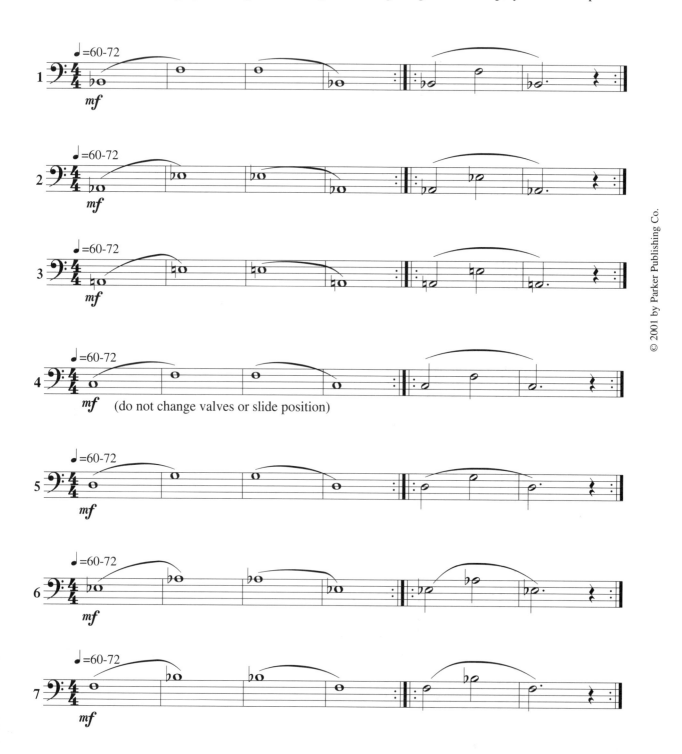

Brass Warm-up
(Part 2)

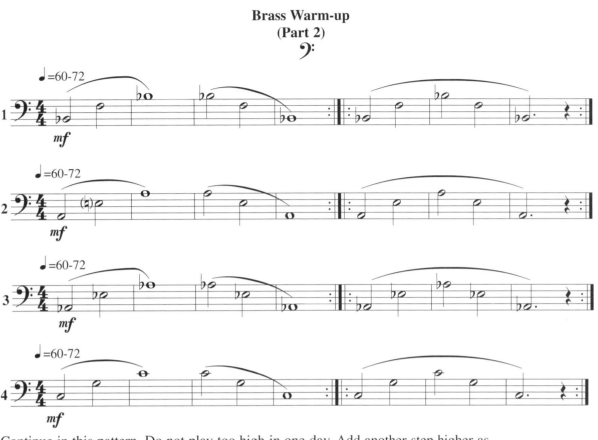

Continue in this pattern. Do not play too high in one day. Add another step higher as one feels comfortable.

Continue in this pattern. Do not play too high in one day. Add another step higher as one feels comfortable.

Figure 2-47
Warm-ups for Brass Instruments

𝄢

Tuba

The following exercises should be practiced daily. It is not necessary to play the entire set of exercises on the first day. Start with two lines on the first day and add one or two lines as the student feels comfortable. Do not continue to play if the lips are starting to hurt or getting too tired to play the correct pitches.

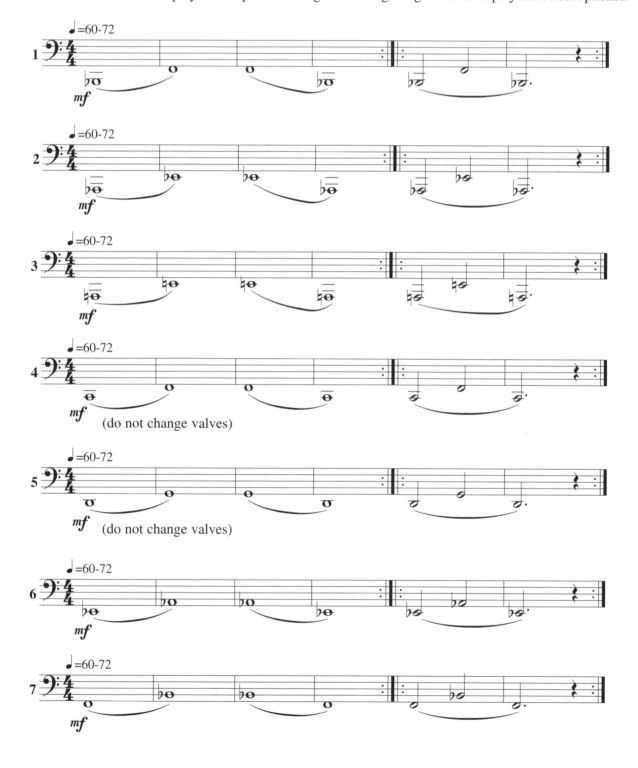

Brass Warm-up
(Part 2)

Tuba

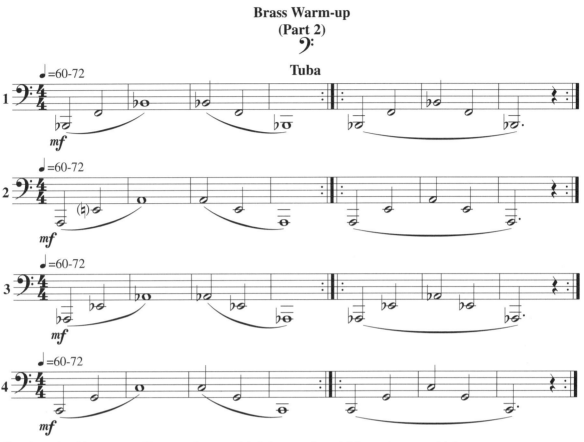

Continue in this pattern. Do not play too high in one day. Add another step higher as one feels comfortable.

Continue in this pattern. Do not play too high in one day. Add another step higher as one feels comfortable.

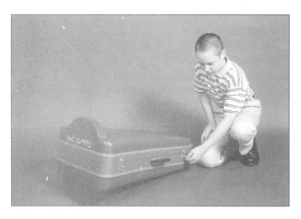

Photo 2-83. Opening case.

Making the Switch from Trumpet, Trombone, and Baritone

A logical progression for switching a trumpet player to the tuba is to switch first to baritone horn, and then after he or she is comfortable with that instrument, switch to the tuba. I strongly recommend that when you switch a trumpet player to baritone, have him start reading bass clef immediately. If you do not, it will be much harder later to make him read a different clef of music. While the student is switching to a new instrument, make it part of the procedure to change to a new clef.

Trombone and baritone horn players should very easily make the switch to the lower sounding instrument. The baritone horn player will only have to get used to reading the lower notes of the bass clef and producing a lower buzz (Photo 2-84). Fingerings instead of slide positions will have to be learned by the trombone player, but it should still be a very easy switch (Photo 2-85).

Posture

Good posture should be enforced at all times (Photo 2-86). This, of course, should be enforced for all instrumental players, not just the tuba player. Performance problems can be the result of poor posture. The student should sit up straight, on the edge of the chair, feet flat on the floor, and hold the chin up so the throat is unrestricted.

Lap Type Horn

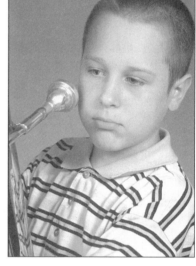

Photo 2-84. A lower buzz.

Photo 2-85. Hand position.

A stand should be used whenever available for your young tuba player. If one is not available you can make a platform on which to rest the instrument (see Fig. 2-49 on page 171). If a stand is not available and one cannot be constructed for the student, then the student will have to learn to hold the instrument in his or her lap. That is why the size of the student is an important consideration when allowing someone to play the tuba.

Air Support

A lack of air support can cause a student to have a buzzing "whirr" sound. Playing the tuba does not take a lot of air pressure, but it does require a large volume of air moving constantly, especially in the low register. Suggest the student sing the phrase using the syllable "la" and then play the phrase. Do not go into long explanations of air support with a young student. He will not understand what you are talking about. Tell him to blow loud, push the air out hard, and make the throat in the "la" shape as he is playing the instrument.

Increasing Range and Improving Tone and Pitch

Due to the large volume of air that is required to play the instrument, and the low amount of resistance, a good amount of buzzing on the mouthpiece alone can produce improved results. When the student is working in the high range, it is very easy to find the proper amount of air pressure to support the buzz. In the low to extremely low register, placing the tip of the finger over the end of the mouthpiece will adjust the back pressure to duplicate the instrument's natural resistance.

Photo 2-86

No Tuba at Home

Photo 2-87

A great disadvantage of playing tuba is the size of the instrument and the hassle of transporting the instrument back and forth to school. Some schools are well equipped enough to provide two tubas, so the child can have one at home and one at school. Unfortunately, that is often not the case. Here is a suggestion for how to practice the tuba without having one at home:

Purchase a piece of clear rubber tube, $5/_8$ inch outside diameter, $1/_2$ inch inside diameter, from your hardware store (Photo 2-87). Cut the tube 24 inches in length. Place the tube in the freezer. When it becomes rigid, take it out and drill a $1/_8$-inch hole through one side only, about $1 1/_2$ inches from the end (Photo 2-88). Insert the tuba mouthpiece into the tube (Photo 2-89). This tube can be used to practice all music and/or exercises, covering the hole in the medium to low range. Cover the hole from the second space C down. The tube gives the same resistance as playing the instrument.

Buzzing Exercises/Tuning

Fig. 2-48 presents some exercises that will increase range and tone. Once the student has developed a controlled sound, it is time to work on tuning. I strongly recommend first playing the note on a piano or an

Photo 2-88

instrument that is in tune and in the same range as the tuba. Practicing the B♭ scale with a tuner may be helpful, but only after hearing the pitches from a tuned instrument. As the players become more advanced, you may want to show them how to pull certain slides for key pitches. At any rate, do not wait long to discuss tuning with any instrument. The sooner a student is taught to listen and work on tuning, the sooner your band will play in tune and sound good.

Figure 2-48
Buzzing Exercises
(Play with tuba mouthpiece or mouthpiece and tube or with the instrument)

Cover hole of tube

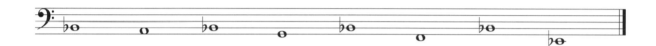

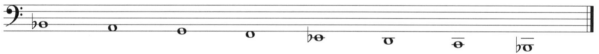

Once playable in this range, play 8va bassa

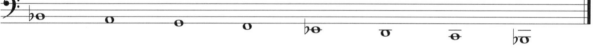

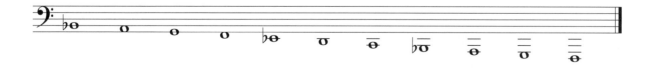

Photo 2-89

Mouthpiece Selection

There are many mouthpieces on the market. The rim can be either flat, rounded, or a combination of both. The main consideration of the shape is the comfort and ease of holding the proper placement of the embouchure. A flat rim is better for large lips. The contour of the cup is another consideration. A younger student needs a shallower cupped mouthpiece while the older student will find the V shape more suited to his or her needs. The player with thin lips may need a shallow cupped mouthpiece for a better response. The bore of the mouthpiece will affect the tone, response, and pitch. Beginners will probably be more successful with a small bore.

Figure 2-49
Tuba Stand (for Chair)

Materials:
1 piece 1″ x 4″ x 8″ pine
1 piece 1″ x 4″ x 4″ pine
1 piece 4″ x 4″ rubber foam

Note: The width and length of stand may be cut to the individual size of the student to fit between the legs of the player.

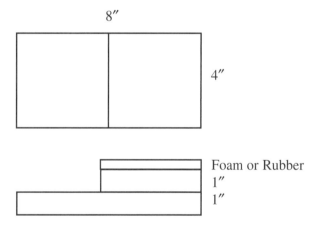

Troubleshooting the Low Brass

PROBLEM	CAUSE	SOLUTIONS
No sound	No buzz	(a) Must have a good brand of instrument in excellent playing order. (b) Wet lips. (c) Top lip slightly over bottom lip. (d) Pretend to eat a lemon, making an "eeewww" sound. (e) Push mouthpiece against lips. (f) Play louder.
Cannot change pitch	Muscle control	(a) See all of the above. (b) Make "mmmmm" sound. (c) Practice siren sound on mouthpiece. (d) Blow louder and harder.
Poor sound	Embouchure	(a) Play with mouthpiece center to lips, not to one side. (b) Buzz with top lip. (c) Bring in puffed cheeks.
Gurgling sound	Spit in instrument	Open spit valve.
Difficulty in high register	Mouthpiece too low	Center mouthpiece on lips.
Difficulty in low register	Mouthpiece too high	Center mouthpiece on lips.
Wobbly sound	Air speed	Tell student to blow louder.
Muffled stuffy tone	Lips wrapped around teeth	(a) Good embouchure. (b) Work on buzz.
Thin tone	Embouchure too tight	Relax—especially for tuba.
Cannot play high notes	Tighten embouchure	(a) Tell student to tighten corners of lips. (b) Tell the student to pretend to eat a lemon. This makes the "eeewww" effect, which allows the student to tighten lips and play higher.

Cannot play low Embouchure

(a) Loosen lips.
(b) Lower jaw.
(c) Upper lip too much over lower lip. Bring lower lip down. Both lips buzz, but the upper lip does most of the buzzing.

Puffing out cheeks

(a) Tell student to bring in cheeks.
(b) The "eat a lemon" technique often works.
(c) Have the student sustain an easy note. While holding the note, continue to tell the student to bring in cheeks. Usually, just about the time the student runs out of air, the cheeks come in. Now the student can feel how the muscles work. Have student do this a few more times in a row. Soon the student will be able to control the cheek muscles.
(d) Pretend to suck the air out of the instrument. This brings in the cheeks, and the student can feel the muscles tighten up around his or her mouth.

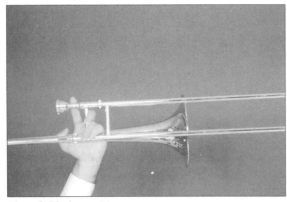

Photo 2-90: 1st position

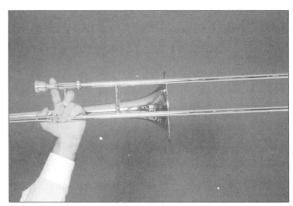

Photo 2-91: 2nd position

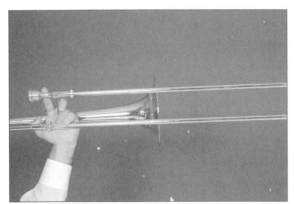

Photo 2-92: 3rd position

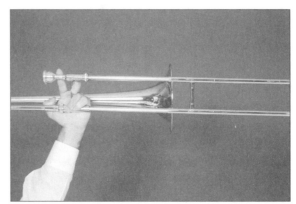

Photo 2-93: 4th position

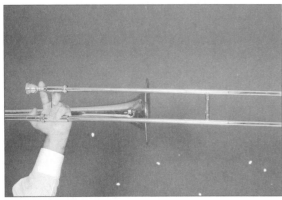

Photo 2-94: 5th position

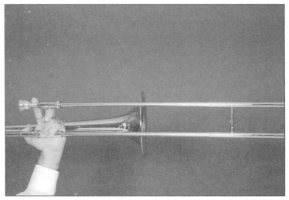

Photo 2-95: 6th position

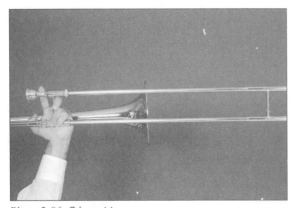

Photo 2-96: 7th position

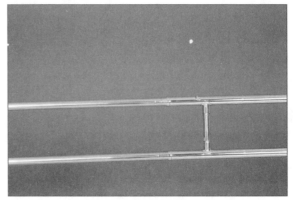

Photo 2-97: 7th position close-up

Trombone Slide Position Chart
(Numbers indicate slide positions)

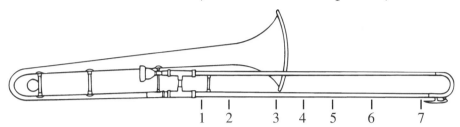

HINT: 2nd position: just a little of the inside slide is in view.

HINT: 3rd position: just before the bell.

HINT: 4th position: just beyond the bell.

HINT: 5th position: halfway in between 4th & 6th—feel it

HINT: 6th position: arm extended, but the raised portion of inner slide is not in view.

HINT: 7th position: arm extended, the raised portion of inner slide just in view.

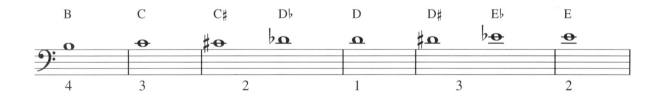

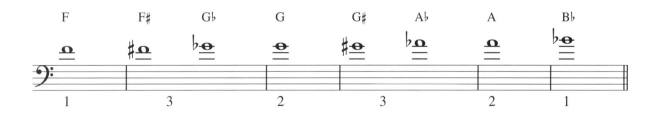

Baritone Horn-Bass Clef Fingering Chart
(Numbers indicate valve[s] to be pressed)

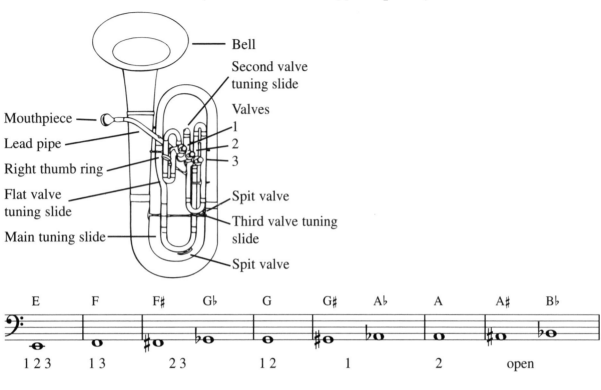

Bell

Second valve
tuning slide

Valves

Mouthpiece

Lead pipe

Right thumb ring

Flat valve
tuning slide

Main tuning slide

Spit valve

Third valve tuning
slide

Spit valve

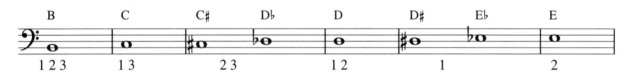

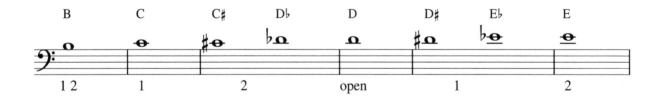

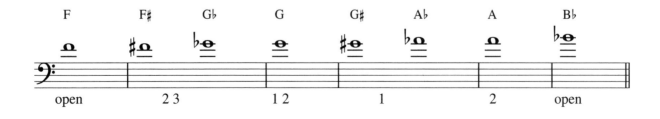

Baritone Horn-Treble Clef Fingering Chart
(Numbers indicate valve[s] to be pressed)

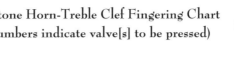

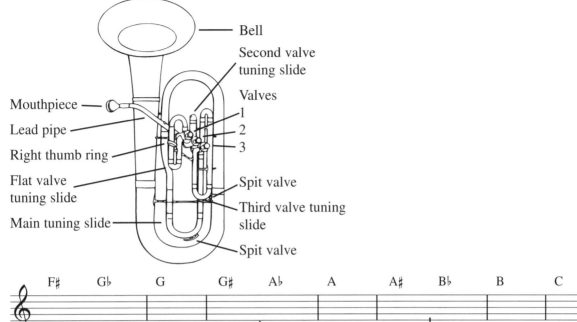

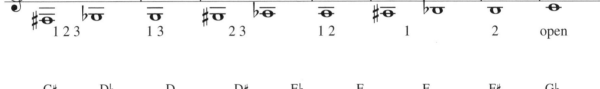

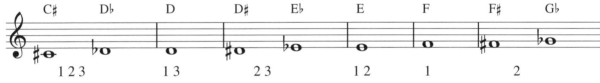

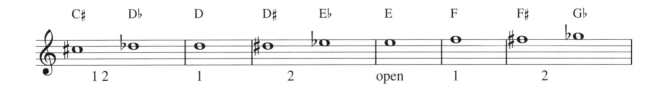

Tuba Fingering Chart
(Numbers indicate valve[s] to be pressed)

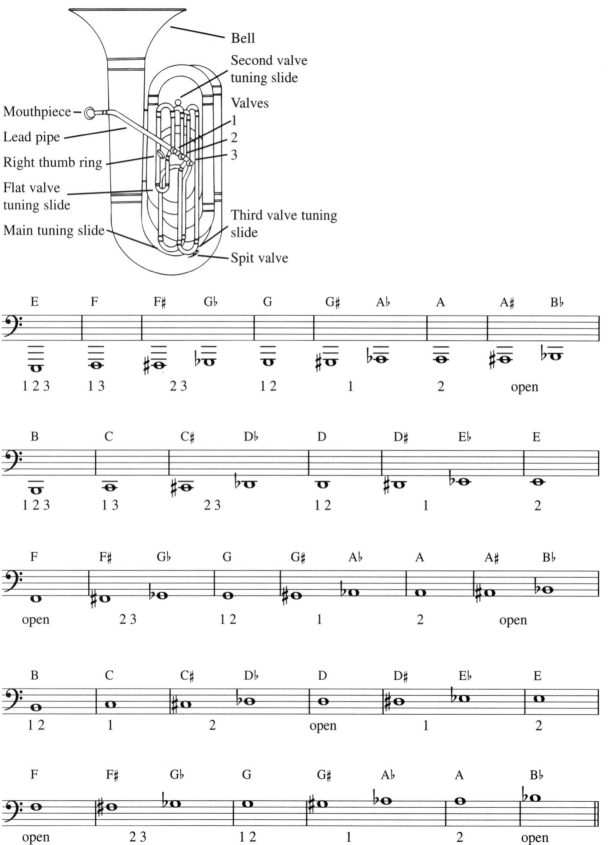

Low Brass (Trombone/Baritone/Tuba) Lessons Checklist

Lesson 1

- [ ] Chairs and stands in order
- [ ] Name tags on chairs
- [ ] Top of case
- [ ] How to open
- [ ] Assembly
- [ ] Instruct not to "pop" the mouthpiece
- [ ] Inspect instrument for quality/repair
- [ ] Hand position
- [ ] Buzz lips
- [ ] Buzz mouthpiece
- [ ] Siren sound
- [ ] No buzz—"eat a lemon" technique
- [ ] Top lip over bottom lip
- [ ] Work on playing higher and lower—B♭ & F
- [ ] Angle of instrument
- [ ] First note: F
- [ ] Adjust mouthpiece to mouth—mouthpiece firmly against lips
- [ ] Play C-G-C (third space)—"2001, A Space Odyssey"
- [ ] Tongue the note
- [ ] If time—play notes E♭ and G
- [ ] Song: "Three Blind Mice"—only if time—challenge to learn by ear for next lesson
- [ ] Instructions on how to practice
- [ ] Disassemble the instrument
- [ ] Specific assignment
- [ ] ***Be Enthusiastic!***

Lesson 2

- [ ] Advanced students assemble instruments immediately
- [ ] While advanced are assembling instruments, show new students top of case
- [ ] Buzz check for advanced students
- [ ] Review and play notes with advanced students
- [ ] Continue to show new students how to assemble their instruments
- [ ] Posture
- [ ] Advanced: Play "Three Blind Mice"
- [ ] Show beginners B♭—work low and high notes
- [ ] Beginners: Work on B♭, F, B♭—"2001, A Space Odyssey"
- [ ] Beginning students: high/low, then F
- [ ] Advanced students start to play book, beginners follow along
- [ ] Advanced: continue with book
- [ ] No book for beginners while playing
- [ ] Make sure advanced understand how to read the notes—no faking
- [ ] Only first page for advanced
- [ ] Beginners work on first three notes only
- [ ] Specific assignment
- [ ] ***Be Enthusiastic!***

Lesson 3

- [ ] Advanced: Start assembling instruments
- [ ] New students: Start showing top of case and assembly while advanced students are assembling instruments, reviewing and playing their first notes
- [ ] Most advanced: Play lesson—reading notes
- [ ] Students who just played for the first time last week: Review notes
- [ ] Continue with beginners, as other students are playing their notes
- [ ] Keep reviewing all lessons
- [ ] Use baton/conduct
- [ ] Point to notes if students are not reading
- [ ] Have everyone follow along, even when not playing
- [ ] Posture
- [ ] Tonguing
- [ ] If the students are ready, start discussing intonation
- [ ] Specific assignment
- [ ] Notice their accomplishments and tell them how they have improved
- [ ] ***Be Enthusiastic!***

Lesson 4

☐ If possible, reschedule new students
☐ Advanced students start assembling instruments as they enter the room
☐ Start showing the new students top of case and assembly
☐ As soon as tones are stabilized, start tuning the instruments
☐ Continue to instruct beginners as you teach the advanced
☐ Counting/toe tapping
☐ Playing the notes (advanced: reading the notes)
☐ Embouchure—top lip slightly over bottom lip
☐ Posture—trombone/baritone/tuba angle
☐ Intonation—if not introduced yet and there is time
☐ Show new notes and rhythms for next lesson
☐ Insist on practice
☐ Give specific assignment
☐ ***Enthusiasm!***

Lesson 5

☐ New students should be rescheduled
☐ Assemble instruments immediately
☐ If must have new students, teach instrument assembly while teaching the other students
☐ Advanced students: intonation
☐ As advanced play, watch eyes to make sure they are reading
☐ Posture
☐ Tonguing
☐ Breathing in between notes
☐ Discuss chair positions
☐ Embouchure
☐ Try to move as many students as possible to the same page
☐ Keep everyone playing—no more than a 5-minute break for anyone at any time
☐ Specific assignment
☐ ***ENTHUSIASM!!***

BEGINNING DRUM LESSONS

Snare Drum Lesson 1 (Fig. 2-50)

Several decisions must be made before the students enter the room. The first is whether they are required to purchase or rent the drum kit versus buying just the pad, sticks, and book. An advantage of requiring only pads is they are inexpensive and easy to carry. One advantage to the drum kit is that it will be more fun playing on the instrument than on the pad, thus sustaining interest in the instrument. The drum class has the highest mortality rate of all the instrument classes. A drum kit is the least expensive instrument in the band, but requiring the student to obtain an instrument will more likely induce the better or more serious students to sign up for drums.

The second decision is whether to require the students to use pads or drums in class. If you have a permanent band room, definitely use the drums. If there is a space problem that requires the use of pads, then you may be forced to use pads in class. My recommendation is that students use the drums in school whenever possible. The students signed up to play the drum, not a rubber pad. They may rapidly lose enthusiasm without hearing the instrument. Another problem with drum pads is that students often strike the pad too hard in order to hear themselves. When they finally do switch over to a real snare drum, they play too loudly. Also, playing the drum helps make them feel important, and that they have the same responsibilities as the other band members.

I recommend that all students start playing the snare drum. In later lessons, students may take turns playing the bass drum, but in the beginning, they should all work on hand positions and control.

In some schools, you may have students who want to sign up for bells but not drums. Welcome them. They will be a nice addition to the band and will do wonders in helping to carry the melody in weak sections of the band. Bell players often do not consider themselves drummers since the drum is not the instrument they want to play. Put each group in a separate class and both will advance quickly. As your drummers become proficient on the snare drum and you have time, you may teach them to play mallet percussion also. However, in the first year, students should concentrate on playing one instrument very well before adding more instruments. Your drummers will concentrate on the snare and bass drums, and the bell players will play only bells. Later in the first year, your drummers will start to play triangle and other percussion instruments, but most likely your bell players will only want to play bells.

Before the students enter the room, have the chairs and stands in an order most convenient to you. If you know who is coming, put their names on the chairs. Group the students with instruments together. Students who have not obtained instruments should sit where they can observe others receiving the first lesson with their instruments. If this is a situation where anyone in the school who is interested in drums may attend, beware—you may have a large group, mostly without instruments. If you have only a small room for instruction, limit the class to a grade level at a time. Have a tablet or sheet of paper ready to have all students sign the paper with their name, grade, and homeroom. Next week you should call only those who have expressed an interest in playing the drums. Each week, you should expect fewer students to attend until you have only interested students in the class. This process will take only two to three weeks, but you must be organized in order to facilitate it. Because the drum class can be large and the instrument itself tends to lend itself to discipline problems, you must be organized and in control from the very first lesson. Get their attention and state the rules immediately. You may need to be stricter in the drum class than with the other sections.

Assembly is a very important part of the beginning lesson for all instruments. The first step in assembly is opening the case. This can be more difficult for drums than for other instruments because it is sometimes difficult to tell the top of the case from the bottom of the case. Some snare drum kits come in backpack-style cases. It is easy to determine the top from the bottom of these cases because of the location of the zipper (Photo 2-98). However, it is much more difficult to distinguish the top and bottom of the instrument case with some of the hard-shell cases because the case is divided evenly in half and the brand name is on both sides. The only way to tell the top of the case from the bottom on these instruments

Figure 2-50
Music for Snare Drum Lesson 1

This lesson is taught without showing the music to the student. Students should concentrate on producing a good sound and hand position. Attempting to read music will distract from all that is needed for becoming a good percussionist.

Tap the drumhead once. Make sure the student has a good hand position and the stick is not left on the drum after the note is played. The student should be standing with the feet slightly apart.

Students should play the note four times in a steady count. All students not playing should count out loud with the band director. After the drum is tapped, immediately lift the stick off the drumhead as though the sound is drawn out of the instrument.

Follow the same procedure as above.

Everyone should count the beats out loud while playing. Reverse the sticking. Motion should be in the wrist. The arms should not be moving up and down.

Continue with this pattern. Do not allow the students to rush. Everyone should count out loud.

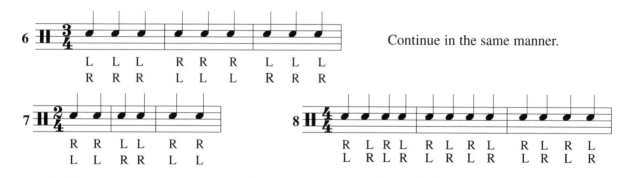

Continue in the same manner.

Assignment: Make sure the hand position is correct. Once the hand position is correct, play one tap on the drumhead. Then play four taps, making sure of the proper hand position and no arm movement. Challenge: Who can play the longest without speeding up? Practice the sticking as on this page. Teacher: ***Be enthusiastic!***

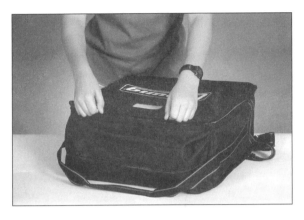

Photo 2-98

is to note whether the latches turn or twist up to release the case halves. I strongly recommend that students purchase or rent the backpack-style cases. They are easy to carry, lighter than the hard-shell cases, easy to distinguish top from bottom, and most manufacturers are now making the backpack-style case.

Once the case is opened, the students should remove the stand. The teacher should demonstrate to the first student how to put the stand together, then put the snare drum on the stand and adjust the batter head about two to four inches below the belt (Photos 2-99 and 2-100). Have all the students assemble the stand and place the instrument on its cradle. Tell the students to remove the snare drum from the stand before adjusting the height of the stand. Be aware that the drum is heavy, and it could come down very quickly and pinch or cut the student's hand. When the students tighten the wing nuts, make sure they do not tighten them too much (hand tight should be enough to hold the drum in position). Students should stand in front of their instruments when they have completed assembly. Adjust the stand height to the appropriate level for each student (two to four inches below the belt). Require drummers to stand when they play. Sitting is not an acceptable position for playing the snare drum. If you are going to teach the matched grip, the batter head should be parallel or horizontal to the floor.

Photo 2-99

The teacher must make the decision to teach the matched or traditional grip. I strongly recommend the matched grip. It is easy to use, easy to learn, and uses the correct hand position for mallet instruments. The traditional grip is used less frequently today. It is good for marching bands where the drum is hanging from a strap, but in most cases today, special carrying straps or brackets hold the drum straight in front of the drummer.

It is very important to make sure that the students start with the correct hand position. Have the student hold the stick with the first finger and the thumb. The first finger does not point, but goes around the drumstick with the thumb and first finger on opposite sides of the stick. The thumb lies flat on the stick as if to make a thumbprint (Photo 2-101). Next, the student should wrap the rest of her fingers under the stick (Photo 2-102). The majority of the stick should be sticking out the front of the hand (Photo 2-103). The student should feel a balance with the bead (front) of the stick wanting to lean down (Photo 2-104). The butt (back) of the stick should come out just to the right of the wrist between the wrist and the knuckle of the little finger touching the back of the hand. The stick should not be directly under the arm. If you are teaching the matched grip, the hand position is the same for both sticks. The angle of the sticks should be as if the sticks have sliced out about one-third of the drumhead (Photo 2-105). The wrist

Photo 2-100

Photo 2-101

should be parallel to the ground, or the back of the hand facing the ceiling. A good exercise is to have the student put a quarter on her hand and tap the drum. If the student is playing properly, the quarter will not drop. This will help keep the students from lifting their hands too high in between notes. The motion is in the wrist, not in the arms. Emphasize this to the students. You may need to do this over and over again.

If you are teaching the traditional grip, the right hand is the same as with the match grip. However, the grip is different for the left hand. First, have the student hold the stick between the thumb and first finger only. It is best if you place the stick in each student's hand the first time. Place the stick about two-thirds of the way from the bead to the butt of the stick. Have the student close her thumb over the stick, but not around it (Photo 2-106). The student should then tap the drum using that position only. Tell the student to tap the drumhead once. If she can maintain control of the stick, then ask her to tap the drumhead four times. She should be able to control the stick without the use of the other fingers. Once she has learned where to balance and control the stick, go to the next student. Have all the students learn this much of the hand position before proceeding. After all the students have played the left hand with the thumb and first finger position, instruct them to then take the bottom two fingers and put them under the stick. The top two fingers go over the stick (Photo 2-107). The students do not need to hold the sticks as tightly as possible, nor should they. They should hold them only tightly enough to keep the sticks from falling

Photo 2-102

out of their hands, and that is done mostly with the thumb and first finger. The other fingers are used for control of rolls and other rudiments. The motion to strike the drumhead is all in the wrist. The arm should not move up and down. A good example of how to strike the drumhead is to ask the student to pretend she has a glass of water in her hand. She is now going to throw the water on the person next to her without moving her arms, only the wrists. That will give her the motion she needs to control the stick and hit the drumhead correctly. The angle of the sticks to the drumhead is similar to that of the matched grip. As the students strike the head, watch for arm movement.

Photo 2-103

The sticks included in most drum kits are usually an appropriate size for beginning students. However, if they need to buy sticks, 2B is an excellent pair for beginners. 2A has a rounded bead and is very easy for teaching rolls. Do not allow the students to use the very thin drumsticks used by many drum set players. Size 5B is also an acceptable drumstick for young drummers; it is thinner than the 2A and may be easier for students with small hands. Vic Firth's SD1 Generals are also very good for beginners.

The book should not be used for the first lesson. Concentrate on developing a good hand position and a steady rhythm.

Have the first student tap the drumhead with the right stick once. Notice if the arm moved. Was the motion in the wrist only? Some students will have a tendency to hold the sticks away from their hands (Photo 2-108); make sure the stick is close to the palm of the hand. The first finger should not be pointing in the direction of the stick, but wrapped around the stick. If the hand position is correct, have her tap the drumhead again, one time. Both hands should be over the drumhead, even though you are having the student use only

Photo 104

one hand at a time. The proper angle of the sticks should be maintained at all times.

Instruct the students to draw the sound out of the drum, not to beat the sound into the drumhead. Many times a student will strike the drumhead and then leave the drumstick on the head of the drum. As soon as she taps the drumhead, she should pull the drumstick up immediately, being careful not to lift her arm, but only the wrist. If this is done correctly, have her then tap the drumhead four times. Count off the tempo. (It is critical that the director counts with a steady tempo.) The director should continue to count out loud as the student plays. Ask the student to count out loud with you. Use your baton as you direct. Even with individual students, this will be beneficial. Every student should do this exercise one at a time. If you have several students with their drums on the first day, you must move very quickly. In some cases, you may have groups of twenty or more. If that is the case, have the students play together in groups to save time. Keep an eye on all of the basics listed above. It will be hard to do, but you must be alert. It is always better if you can arrange your group lessons in groups of six or fewer, but in many cases that is impossible. Once everyone has played separately or in small groups, have the

Photo 2-105

entire class play together. Do not forget to praise the students at every step of the way. Positive reinforcement is critical if you want students to stay in your program.

If there are students without instruments and/or drumsticks and pads, keep them involved. Ask them questions from time to time, and have them count the beats out loud with you when the other students are playing. If they become disciplinary problems, remove them from the class.

The same procedure should follow for the left hand. While students are playing, check for the following:

1. Grip

2. Wrist motion

3. Arm motion (There should be none.)

4. Are the sticks hitting the head firmly?

Photo 106

5. Did the student draw the sound out of the instrument or leave the bead lying on the drumhead?

6. The sticks should not bounce.

7. When the student played four notes in a row, was the tempo steady?

Do not forget to count off for the students every time they play. Students need to hear a steady beat. The teacher should count off "one, two, ready, play," or "one, two, three, four." They will play on the next beat and have a feeling of the tempo you are giving. It is best to give a medium tempo, not too fast or too slow, about 80 to 90 beats per minute. Praise each student for every accomplishment.

Photo 107

Once the students have played the two hands separately, instruct them to play four counts in each hand: four taps in the right hand, four taps in the left hand. Count off the students with a steady tempo, and use your baton. Your baton is a visual that will help them to keep a steady beat. If they get used to seeing and following it now, it will be easier for them to follow you in the band rehearsal. The first instruction will be to count four taps in the right stick and four taps in the left stick, then stop. Some students will have trouble with the concept of counting to four while playing. It may be easier if you require all of them to count out loud. Make sure they are all counting. If a student's lips are not moving, tell her you cannot hear her. Ask her to count out loud. Those students counting silently may not be counting at all. It is not necessary that they tap their toes at this point—as they become more comfortable counting out loud, they may start tapping their toes. However, if some students start tapping their toes naturally, do not stop them. Also, students should tap only their toes—it is too much effort to move the entire foot up and down while standing. Continue to watch for arm movement. The longer you have the students play, the more the tendency to rush or drag. Count louder, and keep them in the same tempo. Watch for stick control. Notice if their sticks are bouncing or just lying on the head after the student taps the drum. Hand position is extremely important. Some students will start to point their first fingers, and some will start to allow the sticks to move away from the palms of their hands. Constantly remind them of the proper hand position.

Photo 2-108

Once the students have control of tapping the drumhead with four counts in each stick, have them continue the exercise with three taps in each stick. The students should count to three for each measure. Continue to watch for all the possible errors mentioned above. Be especially aware of tempo problems. Make the students follow a steady beat, and emphasize to them that it is very important that they try to keep a steady tempo as they practice at home. The easiest way for students to tell if they are changing tempos is to count out loud. They should be able to hear if they start to rush or drag the tempo.

After the students have played three taps in the right, three taps in the left, have them play two in the right and two in the left hand. Count to two for each hand. Follow the same procedures as for the above exercises.

Finally, have the students alternate every other hand: right, left, right, left, while counting one, two, one, two.

As the students practice during this lesson, and in all lessons, continue to watch for:

1. Posture: Stand up straight, feet slightly apart (no sitting while playing!).
2. Stick position
   - Angle
   - Holding sticks close to palm
   - Choking (hand too close to bead or head—Keep an eye out for this constantly.)
   - Thumb and finger position (a big problem with young students—Develop the correct hand position now.)
   - Pointing finger
3. Wrist movement
4. Arm movement
5. Tempo changes
6. Tapping toes
7. Counting out loud

Students should concentrate on hand position and keeping a steady tempo. It will probably take you the full period to accomplish all that has been discussed so far; however, if you have extra time, drill these exercises. Do not add more. In some cases you may have a group that is catching on quickly and it will be tempting to add more or to start reading notes. Do not do this. Practice all of the items mentioned above—this is more than enough for the first lesson.

Give a specific assignment. Tell the students to practice just the right stick once, then several times in a row, and then the left stick once and then several times in a row. Once they have done that, then play four sticks right, four sticks left. They should practice that exercise for at least one minute without stopping. Tell them to stand in front of a clock with a second hand and to continue until an entire minute has passed. One minute may seem longer than they expect. While doing this, they should concentrate on whether they are speeding up or slowing down. Also, since they are not using a book, it is okay for them to look at their hands to make sure they keep a good angle with the sticks and a good hand position. After they have practiced four taps in the right hand, four taps in the left hand, they should practice three times with each stick, then two, then every other stick. Each time the student practices this, she should practice the exercise for at least one minute without stopping, continuing to be aware of tempo changes and stick positions. Advise students to try to practice 30 minutes a day, but if it is a busy day with homework, please try to practice at least 15 minutes. Inform them that they need to practice every day so they will develop the muscles in their hands and wrists in order to become good drummers and to play well and fast (this is important to students). The concept of playing relaxed and letting the sticks do most of the work is paramount. Strongly encourage students without instruments to obtain them by next week. If you have set a deadline for receiving instruments, remind them of that date or lesson. The students without instruments should practice clapping their hands and counting out loud. As the students leave, tell them to practice, and praise them for their accomplishments that day. Let them see your enthusiasm for music and your joy in their progress as new musicians.

Snare Drum Lesson 2 (Fig. 2-51)

In this lesson you will now have three different groups of students: students who have played before (advanced), students who are learning to play for the first time (beginners), and students who have not yet obtained instruments. You must manage all three groups at the same time.

As the students enter the room, have the advanced students begin assembling their instruments immediately. They should be grouped together. The beginners should also be placed in a group, and students without instruments should also be grouped together. Now is a good time to strongly advise students

Figure 2-51
Music for Snare Drum Lesson 2

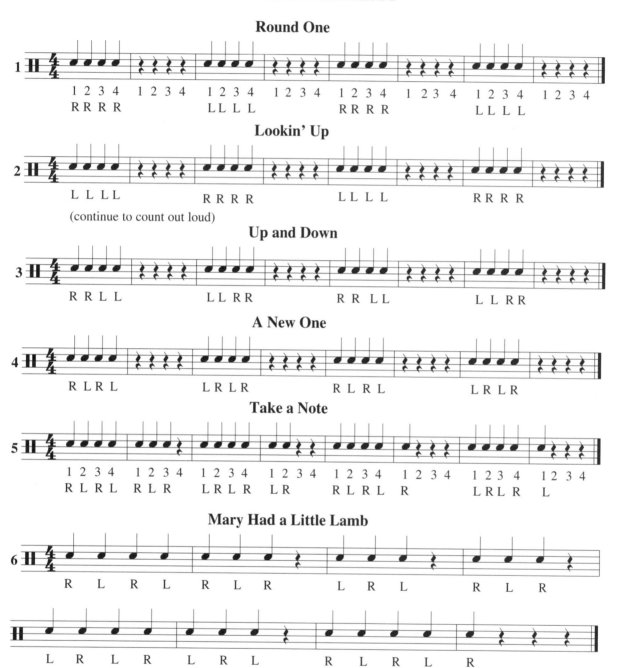

Round One

1 2 3 4 1 2 3 4 1 2 3 4 1 2 3 4 1 2 3 4 1 2 3 4 1 2 3 4 1 2 3 4
R R R R   L L L L   R R R R   L L L L

Lookin' Up

L L L L   R R R R   L L L L   R R R R

(continue to count out loud)

Up and Down

R R L L   L L R R   R R L L   L L R R

A New One

R L R L   L R L R   R L R L   L R L R

Take a Note

1 2 3 4 1 2 3 4 1 2 3 4 1 2 3 4 1 2 3 4 1 2 3 4 1 2 3 4 1 2 3 4
R L R L R L R   L R L R L R   R L R L R   L R L R L

Mary Had a Little Lamb

R L R L R L R   L R L R L R   R L R L R   L R L R L

L R L R L R L   R L R L R

Tap toes: one foot tap per beat. Start with toes up; heels anchored on floor. Practice tapping toes while playing every line.

without instruments to try very hard to have their drums by next week. Otherwise they will soon get behind in their study of drums and have a difficult time catching up with the others. You may tell students that without instruments they will not be allowed to attend the lesson next week.

Instruct the beginners on how to assemble their instruments while the advanced students are assembling their instruments on their own. The advanced students should complete this process very quickly. As you are helping the beginners assemble the stand and place the drum at the appropriate height, you can review the previous week's lesson with the advanced students. First, have the advanced students play four taps with the right hand and four taps with the left hand. They may continue this pattern as you observe:

1. Hand position.

2. Posture (stand up straight—do not pull hand in front of stomach—and keep the elbow a few inches out from ribs).

3. Arm movement.

4. Drawing the sound out of the drum.

5. Keeping a steady tempo.

During this time, you should also continue to help the new students assemble the drum stand and adjust the drum so they will be ready to play. If the beginners are not ready to play, then have the advanced drummers play three taps with the right stick and three taps with the left stick.

By this time the beginners should have their drums assembled. Make sure the drum is about two to four inches below their belt line. Students should not have to reach down to tap the drum, nor should they have to raise their arms to elbow level to play. A relaxed position with the elbows slightly bent is a very good position for a drummer to comfortably play the instrument (Photo 2-109). Show the new students how to hold the drumstick between the thumb and first finger. Then wrap the other fingers around the stick and bring the stick close to the palm of the hand (see pictures in previous lesson). The student should not have too much stick out the back of her hand—usually about four inches is fine, depending on the size of the student. There should be a nice bal-

Photo 2-109

ance so the student can easily control the stick. Check posture. The students should be standing with their feet slightly apart, back straight.

Have the first beginning student tap once with the right hand. Make sure there is no arm movement. After the tap, the student should lift the stick away from the drum as though drawing the sound out of the drumhead. After she has tapped the drum once successfully, ask her to then tap the drumhead four times in a row using the right hand only. Once the student has performed this task successfully, have the other students perform it. If there are not too many students, follow this procedure one at a time. If you have a large class, you may have several students perform it together. Soon you should learn to develop a quick eye and ear and find any problems.

Do not leave the advanced students idle too long. You should complete the preceding task within five or six minutes. If you cannot accomplish it due to the number of new students or special problems, have the advanced students join in when the beginners play the four taps together. Concentrate your attention on the beginning students, but keep the advanced drummers active. Young students may easily become distracted and unfocused when they are allowed to be inactive for very long. It is sometimes difficult to then get them back on task.

Continue to review the pattern of playing with three taps per hand, two taps per hand, and alternating sticks every beat with the advanced students. Watch for hand position, arm movement, and tempo. You may have to show students when the sticks are slipping out of position. Do it often now, so they will develop a good hand position.

Ask the beginning students to play four taps with each stick. The advanced may play with them. New students may now play three taps per stick, two taps per stick, and finally alternating sticks every beat. Students should be counting out loud during each exercise. Students without instruments should also count out loud. Have them participate as much as possible. Do not allow them to gather in the back of the room and start talking. Never hesitate to send anyone back to class if he or she creates a disturbance.

Have everyone look at Lesson 2 (Fig. 2-51) or the first page of the method book with notes in it (I strongly recommend using the music in this resource if possible). Quickly discuss the staff and how the notes are placed on the staff. The snare-drum notes are always in the third space, so that makes it very easy for drummers. Do not get into long explanations about the staff and music. (The staff is a chart where the notes are placed so drummers know what rhythms and what kind of drums to play.) Do not confuse them with too many details. Explain to the students that the note filled in solid with a stem is a quarter note and gets one beat. You do not have to explain the proportions of all rhythmic values at this time. Right now, your main objective is to get them playing the drums quickly and as much as possible. After you have shown them how to count the first note, show them how a rest is executed. (A rest is a silent note. Silence is an important dramatic effect in music.) Discuss the rhythmic value of the notes on the page. Once the students understand the rhythms on the first line, have them play the first measure only.

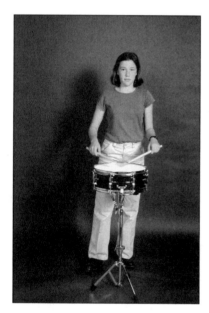

Photo 2-110

Advanced and beginning students should play and count out loud. I like to have students tap their toes if they can do it comfortably. Standing and tapping toes is a little more difficult than it is for wind instrument students who are sitting, but it is still an important concept for drummers to understand. Since they can count out loud, toe tapping is not essential, but it is very helpful for understanding the divisions of the beat and just feeling the pulse of the song. If the student puts one foot slightly forward (Photo 2-110), this will make toe tapping possible. Once they have played the first measure correctly, have the students play the first two measures together. The second measure has four beats of rest. Still, have them play the first two measures only. Try to help them understand the concept of playing a rest, or being silent for a certain number of beats. After the first two measures are played correctly, have the students play the entire line. Watch for wandering eyes. If a student is not looking at the music but at other students' drums, sticks, hands, etc., then that person does not understand how to read music. This is easy to correct: Have everyone play the line again. This time, walk over to the student who is having trouble focusing on the notes. Point to the notes with your baton as the line is being played. You do not have to say anything to the class. As you point to each note as it is being played, the student should start to see how to read the notes. Students are familiar with reading words from left to right on a page, but they do not always understand that it is the same process with music. You may need to do this with several students. Do not make an issue of it. Simply walk over to that student while everyone is playing and point to the notes.

Once the students have successfully played the first line, continue with the next line. Explain any differences of new rhythms. The second line is often the same as the first, but with a different sticking indicated. Make sure they follow the sticking suggested. Another way to see if the students are reading music is to conduct the exercise with your baton. When the students reach the end of the line, continue to conduct. You will know who is faking it if anyone continues to play. Tell them the heavy double bar at the end of the line means to stop. Make a game of it and see who plays a solo at the end of the line. The students will enjoy it, and you will make a strong point about reading the notes.

All the time you are teaching, you must continue to pay attention to the following:

1. Hand position.
2. Arm movement.
3. Posture.
4. Tempo.
5. In the beginning, counting out loud.
6. Watching for roaming eyes (do not let them fake it now—learn to read while it is easy).

Continue in this pattern until the end of the lesson.

Always give an assignment to the students. Never assume they will know what to practice. Tell all the students to practice first without the book. Then, once they have the correct hand position and they are sure they are not moving their arms, they may start to play out of the book. Everyone should practice the entire first page for the next lesson. You may wish to advise the students to play each line four times as they do their daily practice. No matter how well they have done on the first lesson, do not assign more. If they wish to look ahead, they may do so. However, you want to encourage them to make sure they feel secure about the assignment first before moving ahead. Beginning students should spend most of the practice time without the book and concentrate on a good hand position and steady tempo. They may read music from the book after they feel they have control of playing the drum.

Compliment them for their progress. Be enthusiastic for them. Let them know you are really pleased with how well they played today. Wish them a nice day and remind them to practice every day.

Snare Drum Lesson 3 (Fig. 2-52)

As students enter the room, have the advanced students assemble their instruments. New students should sit together, and students who are without instruments should sit in one area. You must be organized and be in control of the situation. Students without instruments should be instructed that they will no longer be allowed to come to lessons without instruments. If you decide they may remain during this lesson, make sure they understand that they must remain quiet and pay attention to what is happening during the lesson. My advice is to send them back to class. They have witnessed two lessons without instruments. They know the fun that is happening, and what they are missing. If you send them back to class now, they will either obtain instruments or drop out of the program. You do not need students coming to drum lessons who only want to get out of a class.

Immediately start to show the new students how to assemble their instruments. When the advanced students are ready to play, start reviewing the previous lessons. First, have them play the exercises of four taps with the right stick/four taps with the left stick. Then three each, two each, and finally alternate sticking. Continue to help the beginners assemble their instruments as you review with the advanced students.

When the beginners have their instruments assembled and set at the right height, about two to four inches below the belt, show them how to hold the sticks properly. Check each child's hand position. Once the hand positions are correct, have the first student tap the drum. Make sure the sound is drawn out of the drumhead by lifting the stick immediately off the instrument. Do not allow her to let the stick rest on the drumhead after the instrument is struck. After she has accomplished that task, ask her to tap the drum four times with the right stick. Continue to watch for:

1. Hand position.
2. Stick angle.
3. Thumb/first finger.
4. Wrist position.

Figure 2-52
Music for Snare Drum Lesson 3

Steppin' Up

Down the Ladder

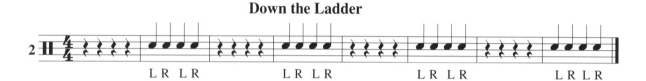

Over the Hill

More to Play

Watch Out for That Rest!

Round and Round

Waves

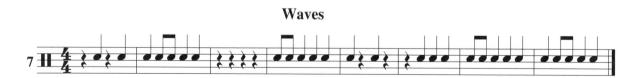

5. Arm movement.

6. Counting out loud.

Go to the next student and continue this process.

After five minutes, review Lesson 2, which was studied the previous week by the advanced students. If every beginner has not progressed to the point of playing four taps with the right hand and four taps with the left hand, then play only the first line of the book with the advanced students. Have all beginners play four taps in the right hand and four in the left, then have the advanced students play the next line. The beginners should play three taps in the right hand/three taps in the left hand. Advanced students should now play the next line in Lesson 2. Continue in this manner until every beginner has played the drum with the correct hand position. As you watch for hand position and all of the points mentioned above, also be aware if a student is starting to rush. If someone is rushing, count louder and ask all students to count out loud with you.

The advanced students should finish the first page (Lesson 2 in the *Kit*). As soon as the first page is completed, then start on the second page (Lesson 3 in the *Kit*). Continue to work on this page as far as possible for five minutes. It is not necessary to complete the page in five minutes. Play as many lines as possible, then switch to the beginning students. In addition to observing all the items mentioned before, watch carefully for students' eyes wandering, not looking directly at the page, or observing other students' hands, and notice if they play in rests, or continue to play after the line is over. These students are not reading music. Go to the student's stand, and, using your baton, point to the notes as the line progresses. When not pointing to the notes, insist that the students watch you conduct with your baton. This is essential.

The beginners should practice playing four taps with each hand, three sticks with each hand, two sticks with each hand, and finally every other stick. When all beginners play together, have the advanced join in. Keep as many students involved as possible. Practice each exercise for one or two minutes nonstop. Continue to watch for:

1. Posture.

2. Hand position.

3. Wrist movement.

4. Stick position.

5. Arm movement.

6. Keeping a steady tempo.

If you have not started Lesson 3 by now, the advanced students should be ready for this page. Play as many lines as possible. Discuss any new music concepts introduced on this page.

By this time the class should be coming to an end. Give a specific assignment. Beginners should practice without music. They should practice the different exercises learned in class. After a few days if they feel comfortable, they may start Lesson 2, but that is not essential. What is essential is that they obtain a good hand position, not move their arms, and try not to speed up or slow down while playing. Advanced students should first review without the music, then practice the assignment. The assignment should be very specific. Tell them to review the previous lessons, and then practice the new page. They may look ahead if they can first play the assigned pages.

Tell the students they are doing well and that you look forward to teaching them next week. Tell them to have a nice day and be enthusiastic.

Snare Drum Lesson 4 (Fig. 2-53)

As in previous lessons, advanced and beginning students should stand next to each other. Advanced students should start assembling their drums immediately. If a student shows up without an instrument, you should tell him that he must have an instrument by the deadline you have set. If he does not have an instrument by that date, he must wait until next school year (or sign-up time) to learn to play the drum.

Figure 2-53
Music for Snare Drum Lesson 4

Remember This One

An Old Friend (In a New Place)

1 2 3 & 4   1 2 3 & 4   etc.

Twice as Long

1 2 3-4   1 2 3-4   1 2 3 4   1-2 3-4   1 2 3 4   1-2 3-4   1 2 3 4   1-2 3-4

Say It Again

1-2 3 4   1-2 3 & 4   1-2 3-4

Hot Cross Buns

Go Tell Aunt Rhodie

1 2 3 4 &

Skippin' Around

Send him back to the regular class. You do not need students without instruments disturbing the music class at this point of study. Also, sending them back to the nonmusic class will reinforce your statement that they should get instruments immediately or it will be too late to learn to play an instrument this school year. It would be better from this point forward to take any new students and reschedule them into a different group if that is possible. However, the next two lessons will assume that the teacher must take on new beginners. Time management becomes the real problem in this instance.

As the advanced students are assembling their instruments, start showing the new students how to put their instruments together. If they have attended the previous classes, they should be able to do most of this quickly on their own. You will need to check their instruments and make sure the batter head is about two to four inches below belt level.

Review Lesson 3 with the advanced students as you are getting the beginners ready to play. It is not necessary to play every line, but play enough to make sure they understand what was introduced on that page. However, if Lesson 3 was not played at the last session, the students should play every line. Once that is done, start on Lesson 4 in the *Kit*. Start with the first line. If anything new is introduced on this line, discuss it first.

As with Lessons 3 and 4 in this resource, most books will introduce eighth notes on one of these pages. Explain to the class that for an eighth note, the beat is divided into two parts. All students, advanced and beginners, should pay attention to this discussion. If you have required your students to tap their toes, you will have an easier time demonstrating to them how to play a note for one half of a beat. Tell the students that notes are not counted in seconds, but in beats. The beat is the pulse of the music, and it can be felt just like a strong heartbeat. Often you may see someone tapping their toes while listening to music. They may not even be thinking about it. It is a natural thing to do. Musicians tap their toes in order to count the rhythms so their music will have a steady beat. We tap our toes because it is the easiest way to count a beat. One beat equals one foot tap. The foot starts in the up position, goes all the way to the floor (see photo in Fig. 2-51) and back up again. A quarter note gets one foot tap. The first half of the foot tap is with the toes up and lasts until the toes hit the floor. The second half of the beat is when the foot comes back up. There are two eighth notes per beat. The first note is when the foot goes down, and the second, when the foot comes back up. Thus, there are two notes in one beat if there are two eighth notes written. Discuss the notation and how it is written. The eighth note is indicated by the beam attached to the stem. It does not affect the name of the note. It may seem confusing to some students as you explain the rhythm to them, but when they play the rhythm, it will become easier for them to comprehend. Before playing the line, have all the students play only the first note. They start with the foot in the up position. Play the first note. When they have played the note, the foot is flat on the floor. Next they will play two notes: one when the foot goes down, and the second when the foot returns to the up position. The second time they play, have them say out loud, "down/up." Once they can do that, then have them count the rhythm, "one-and." Make sure they continue to tap their toes. The advanced students may then play one beat of eighth notes, while counting "one-and," and tapping their toes. Possibly you will have time to allow the students to play eight eighth notes while counting: "one/and, two/and, three/and, four/and." It is never too early to start the students counting rhythms.

By this point it is time to show the new students how to play their instruments. As in previous lessons, make sure they are standing directly in front of the drums. Show them the correct hand position, making sure the angle of the sticks is correct. Have the first new student tap once with the right hand. Then have the student tap four times with the right hand. Go down the line, having all new students tapping with the right stick only. Next follow the same procedure with the left stick. Have all students, advanced and beginners, play four times with the right hand and four times with the left hand for about one minute, keeping an eye out for moving arms, good stick angles, and a steady tempo.

Turn your attention again to the advanced students. Quickly review the eighth note rhythm. Now play the first measure of the line that has eighth notes. While the students play, the director should count out loud. The students should also count out loud with you. Make sure they are looking at the notes. There may be students who need you to point to the notes while the line is being played. Quietly walk over to the stand and point to the notes. Play the first measure until everyone understands how to play that measure, then play the entire line. When you are not pointing to notes, conduct. Always count out loud (at least for the first several lessons). Continue to play with this group for five minutes. You may wish to play the bass drum or the piano to help provide a steady beat for the students. However, while doing this, you must keep your focus on the students. If you can play more than one line, continue; however, the number of lines performed today is not important. Accuracy is the major objective. It is best if you do not play every line at the same tempo. Do not start the lines too fast. A moderately slow tempo will make it easier for the students to think the rhythms and count out loud while they play. Continually watch for wandering eyes. Once the students have played the line fairly well, sing the melody the band will play while they play and count. This will help them keep in tempo and rhythm when they meet with the entire band.

The beginners should now play four taps with the right stick, four taps with the left stick. After about a minute of that exercise, have the beginners play three taps with each stick, then two, and finally tap the drumhead with alternating sticks. Continue to watch for:

1. Stick angle.
2. Hand position.
3. Wrist movement.
4. Arm movement.
5. Thumb/first finger position—do not let them point their index fingers—**this is critical.**
6. Posture.
7. Toe tapping.
8. Steady tempo.
9. Counting out loud.

Use your baton. This gives a visual representation of the beat and helps the students feel that they are part of a band. It is also easier to point to notes with a baton when students are having trouble following the notes on the page. Do not give the same tempo for every exercise. Vary it slightly; however, a fast speed at this time is not advisable.

The advanced students should continue on the same page. Try to finish the page if you can. Many books start to put more variations and complications in the exercises. Insist on accuracy. Be careful of rushing and student counting. At this point, do not skip lines. Even though the lines may be basically the same, it is the drill and routine that helps the students to become more secure drummers. Make sure you go over everything on this page: rests, repeat dots, new rhythms, and so on. Do not expect the students to figure it out on their own; they need your help. When the student hears your voice telling him what to do, there is a fairly good chance he may be able to remember what to do. Continue with the advanced students for about five minutes.

Review with the beginners about sticking and counting. Introduce the first page of musical notes to the students. Remind them about the rhythmic notation. The students should be concerned with playing only the snare drum part at this time. Bass drum can be added later.

Give a specific assignment to all students. Tell the beginners to play without the book at first. They should pay attention to their hand position and try to get as clear a sound as possible on the snare drum. They should practice in front of a clock with a second hand. Play each exercise learned today for at least one full minute each, without stopping. After they feel they are in control of the sticks, they may start practicing from the book.

Advanced students should review and/or complete the page worked on today, then practice the following page. If there is a new rhythm, explain it to them quickly. You are probably out of time by this point, so you should talk quickly and clearly.

Tell all the students to practice daily even if for only a few minutes. It is best to practice at least 30 minutes a day if they wish to become good drummers.

Congratulate them on their progress. Be pleasant and wish them a good day.

Snare Drum Lesson 5 (Fig. 2-54)

The advanced students should start to assemble their instruments as soon as they enter the room. Beginning students should sit together. Immediately start to help them assemble their instruments. Give the same instructions as in the first lesson, but proceed more quickly. Anyone reporting without an instrument should be sent back to class. If you cannot start another section of drum lessons, it should be made clear that it is too late for drum lessons this school year. Stick to your deadlines. It will make students in the future see that you mean what you say and will follow through. Starting anyone this late or later could be a problem. These students will be so far behind the others that it will be very hard for them to catch up. They may become discouraged and quit.

As you are instructing the new students on how to assemble the stand and drum, have the advanced students review the previous lesson. Do not play every line that was previously played in class, but just two or three to see if they remember what was covered and how to play the rhythms. By the time you have the advanced students play a few lines, the beginners should be ready to play.

Instruct the beginners how to hold the drumstick. Make sure they are using the thumb and first finger as indicated in the first lesson. Then have the beginners play with the right stick only. They should tap four times with the right stick. Have every new student perform this procedure. Then have them play four taps with the left stick. Then have the beginners and advanced play four taps with the right hand and four taps with the left hand. Have the advanced play with the beginners to keep them practicing and help the beginners keep a steady tempo.

The advanced students should continue on Lesson 4. They should play every line that was not played in class before. It is important that students play these exercises so they can drill in the rhythms and note values learned. Continue on this page for about five minutes. While the students are playing continue to watch for:

1. Posture.
2. Hand position.
3. Wrist movement.
4. Stick angle.
5. Choking (the hand too close to the bead of the stick).
6. Arm movement.
7. Steady tempo.
8. Dynamics (if introduced by this time).
9. Counting out loud.
10. Tapping toes.

Review with the beginners by playing four taps in each hand. Continue this for about one minute. Next have the beginners play three taps with each hand.

The advanced students may join in. Keep them busy. Then play two taps with each stick. And finally, they should tap the drumhead with alternate sticks. It is extremely important that you insist that all the students maintain a steady tempo. Continue to watch for students' arms moving up and down—there should be little arm movement. Work with the beginners for about five minutes.

Continue with Lesson 4 for the advanced group. When finished with Lesson 4, discuss any new rhythms or other information presented in Lesson 5. Play as many lines as possible on this page, but do not have the beginners idle for more than five minutes.

Have everyone look at Lesson 2. Your attention will be focused on the beginners; however, the advanced students should play along. Let some of the advanced students explain the rhythms to the beginners. If you have time, have all the students play the first line. At the end of the line, continue to conduct. If some of the students play when the line is finished, you know they are not reading the music. Have everyone play the line again and point to the notes on the page as they should be played. It is important

Figure 2-54
Music for Snare Drum Lesson 5

The Whole Time

Jingle Bells

Ode to Joy

A Little Bit Longer

London Bridge

Duet

to watch for wandering eyes. Students must learn to read music while it is easy. If they do not catch on to this now, they will be lost within the next few pages. Continue five minutes with each group until the end of the lesson.

As always, give a specific assignment. Be enthusiastic, and let them know your pleasure with their progress. Let them know how you look forward to teaching them.

Future Considerations

Start rudiments (Fig. 2-55) as soon as possible. Many beginning method books pay little attention to rudiments. If your students start rudiments very early on, they will become better percussionists.

With experience you will know when to push the students to learn more, or when to be precise with the notation. There will also be days you will know that you can take this class only so far. Be aware of the body language: It will often tell you the student is no longer absorbing information. When that happens, review previous materials or skip ahead to music that does not involve the current problem. Do not forget to be enthusiastic. Even as they progress and become good percussionists, they still need your enthusiastic support.

Tuning the drums has not been mentioned because there is little time to tune them during the first five lessons. However, a child will often come in with a new instrument from the store that has not been unpacked or tuned. Do not spend time teaching such a student how to tune his drum during these first lessons. It is important that all students start playing immediately. The teacher should quickly tune the drum for them. At a later lesson, explain to them what you are doing and have everyone practice tuning their drums. Look in the troubleshooting part of this section to see how to tune a drum.

As the students progress in the book, you may not need to play every line on every page. Sometimes playing just the lines introducing new materials, plus a few extra lines, may be all that is needed for that day or that particular rhythm. Move ahead whenever possible, but only after the first several lessons, not in the first five.

Many band method books do not give enough attention to rudiments or teaching the students enough rhythms in the first book. If you are teaching in a band situation, you must start with the band method; however, as quickly as possible, finish book one and start using a drum method book. You may want to introduce those books before they finish Book 1. If you do not do this, the drummers may become bored. They only have rhythms to play, so they must play more than quarter notes and eighth notes to enjoy playing drums. Make playing the drum a fun challenge.

Figure 2-55
The Standard 26 American Drum Rudiments

L L R R L L R R LL RR LL etc.

The Long Roll. Start slowly, gradually get faster until the roll is sounded, then gradually slow down until the sound comes to a stop. TIP: When slowing the roll, let the sticks bounce a little higher.

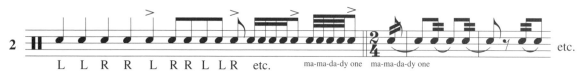

L L R R L R R L L R etc.   ma-ma-da-dy one   ma-ma-da-dy one

The Five-Stroke Roll. TIP: Count each bounce using the words: "mama-daddy."

L L R R L L R R R L L R R L etc.   ma-ma-da-dy-ma-ma-dad

The Seven-Stroke Roll. TIP: Count each bounce using the words: "ma-ma-dad-dy-ma-ma-dad." Don't forget the accent.

ᴸR ᴿL ᴸR ᴿL ᴸR ᴿL etc.   fl-am   fl-am

The Flam. TIP: Start with lower stick about one inch above drumhead; the higher stick about chest level. Try to have both sticks hit the drumhead at the same time. Do not raise the lower stick. The sound will mimic the name of the rudiment: "fl-am."

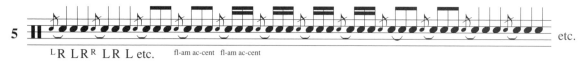

ᴸR LRᴿ LR L etc.   fl-am ac-cent fl-am ac-cent

The Flam Accent. TIP: Sing: "fl-am ac-cent" to count rhythm. Be sure to alternate sticks.

ᴸR L R R ᴿL R L L L Fl-am-a-did-dle Fl-am-a-did-dle

The Flam Paradiddle. TIP: When going at the faster speed, let the repeated sticking bounce: at first bounce slowly and high, then smaller bounces as you speed up.

The Standard 26 American Drum Rudiments (cont.)

7   L R L R L L R   R L R L R R L   It's a flam–a–cue   etc.

The Flamacue. TIP: There is no official syllable for this, but the student may use: "It's a flamacue." Be careful to play the flams and accents.

8   L L R   R R L   It's a ruff   etc.

The Ruff. TIP: Play in the same manner as a flam. Lower stick near the drumhead and the higher stick about chest level. Use the phrase "It's a ruff" to play the rhythm.

9   L L R   L R R L   R L L R   L R R L   R etc.   It's a ruff drag   etc.

The Single Drag. TIP: Similar to ruff or flam. Use the syllable: "It's a ruff drag."

10   L L R L L R   L R R L R R L   R L L R L L R   L etc.   It's a ruff, it's a ruff, drag.   etc.

The Double Drag. TIP: Similar to ruff. Count syllables: "It's a ruff, it's a ruff, drag."

11   L R L R L L R L R L R R R etc. It's a par–a did–le   etc.

The Double Paradiddle. TIP: As the percussionist speeds up, allow the repeated stick to bounce. (High bounce at slower speeds.) Use the sentence "It's a par-a-did-dle" to keep up with the notes.

12   L L R L R L R R L R L R L L R L R etc.   It's a rat– a– ma– cue   etc.

The Single Ratamacue. TIP: Starts with ruff. Use the sentence "It's a ratamacue" to help play the rhythm.

The Standard 26 American Drum Rudiments (cont.)

L L R   L L R   L L R   L R L   R R L   R R L   R R L R L R etc.
It's a rat–It's a rat– It's a rat–a– ma– cue.

The Triple Ratamacue. TIP: Three ruffs. Use sentence in second measure for rhythm.

L   R   L   R   L   R   L   R   L R L R etc.

The Single-Stroke Roll. TIP: Do not try to go too fast too quickly. Take your time and control your hands before you try for very fast tempos. The object is even strokes and steady timing.

R L R R L L R R L   R R L L R R L L R   ma- ma- dad-dy ma- ma dad-dy one

The Nine-Stroke Roll. TIP: Count the mama daddies as in the previous rolls.

L R R L L R R L L R or L L R R L L R R L R

The Ten-Stroke Roll.

L L R R L L R R L L R   R R L L R R L L R R L

The Eleven-Stroke Roll.

L L R R L L R R L L R R L   R R L L R R L L R R L L R etc.
TIP: ma- ma dad- dy mama dad- dy ma- ma dad- dy tap

The Thirteen-Stroke Roll.

L L R R L L R R L L R R L L R   R R L L R R L L R R L L R R L etc.

The Fifteen-Stroke Roll.

The Standard 26 American Drum Rudiments (cont.)

20   L R R R L L   L R R etc.   fl- am tap   etc.

The Flam Tap. TIP: The rudiment says its name: "flam-tap."

21   L R L L R L R R L R L L R L R R etc.   etc.

The Single Paradiddle. TIP: This rudiment says its name: "par-a-did-dle."

22   R L L R L R R L R R L R L L R LLR L R R Oh! It's a drag a–did–dle etc.   etc.

The Drag Paradiddle No. 1. TIP: Keep count by singing: "Oh! It's a drag-a-did-dle."

23   R L L R L L R L R R R LLR LLR L R R L RR L RR L R L L Oh! It's a ruff It's a par–a–did–dle   etc.

The Flam Paradiddle No. 2. TIP: Use the following sentence to keep count of the notes: "Oh! It's a ruff, it's a par-a-did-dle."

24   L R L R R L L R L R L L R R etc.   fl–am a did–dle–did–dle   etc.

The Flam Paradiddle-diddle. TIP: Think: "Flam-a-did-dle-did-dle."

25   L L R L R R R L R L etc.   (inverted)   etc.

Lesson 25. (Yes, that is the name, Lesson 25. Guess they couldn't think of anything else.)

26   L L R L L R L R L RR L RRL R L R etc.   etc.

The Double Ratamacue. TIP: Think: "It's a rat, it's a rat-a-ma-cue."

Troubleshooting the Drums

PROBLEM	CAUSE	SOLUTIONS
Uneven rhythm	Hand position	Stick at the correct angle (see Photo 2-105, p. 185). Butt of stick must go between wrist and finger knuckle. Sticks never go directly under arms. Practice a slow steady count in quarter notes, first, four taps in each hand. Band director and student must count out loud for one minute, nonstop. Do not allow the tempo to change. Then go to three in each stick, two, and then every other stick. Do not have the student look at music. It is better that the students watch their hands in the correct position.
	Tension	(a) Hand positions. (b) Ease tension with this relaxing exercise: The student should hold both sticks in the same direction. Hold the sticks at each end, palms up. See page 211 for photos. The right hand goes under the left hand, and the left hand twists around until both hands have twisted around back to palms up, but thumbs pointing in the opposite direction. Reverse the procedure. This will relax the muscles and get the blood flowing.
Can play the music during the lessons, but when the band plays, the student is lost, and the rhythm is incorrect	Panic/insecurity	(a) In class: Learn the part perfectly in one tempo. Then conduct directly in front of the drum section. However, change the tempo. At first, wait eight measures or more before changing tempo, and then more often. Make sure students are learning to watch you and your every gesture. They should reach a point where they can follow you no matter what changes you make in tempo or how often. (b) Practice. They just do not know the music well enough. (c) If the problem persists, write a simple part that is the same every measure, even as simple as quarter note/quarter rest. Work this pattern as in suggestion (a), changing tempos often in the lesson. During band rehearsal, students should not play the written music from the arrangement, but the part you have written. The student(s) should look at you the entire time the song is playing. The part should be so easy they should not play incorrectly and if they play in the rests you can quickly get them back on the beat. Tell the student(s) to follow your baton for the beat at all times (you do not have to explain meter patterns at this time; however, letting the student[s] know where the down beat is may be very helpful). Even if they're having rhythmic problems at this time, it might be one thing too many on which to concentrate. Once they can

follow you and stay in tempo, you may start to reintroduce the original drum part. If the students get lost, they can always go back to the simple part they memorized.

Connecting rolls	Hand/finger position	(a) Must hold sticks with the thumb and first finger.
		(b) Balance: Hold the stick away from fingers.
		(c-d-e) Balance the sticks (though the balance should not be in the center of the stick). Tap the drumhead with the stick slightly away from the palm of the hand. Single taps. Once in control, hold the stick in proper position. Do this with both hands in proper position. Start with just one stick at a time, then switch and alternate hands: 4/4, 3/3, 2/2, R/L.
Control rolls	Stick control/hearing the beats	(a) Slow—right and left until the end of the roll with stick bouncing properly.
		(b) If still a problem, subdivide it more. *Example:* Five-stroke roll: Start with the right stick, and have the student do one bounce. Then the left stick one bounce. A slight pause before each so the student can hear and count the beats. Then the final tap to end the roll: ma-ma, dad-dy, one. Gradually speed it up until it sounds like a roll. This procedure can be followed for all rolls.
Out-of-tune drum	Weather/packing and shipping	A new student will often come in with a new drum that the store has not unwrapped or has not tuned for the child. Start the tuning process by tightening one corner of the drum with the drum key. Tap the batter head halfway between the rim and the center of the drum. For beginners and for the sake of quickly getting everyone playing, tune the drum until it has a nice sound. The actual tuning pitch for the snare drum is A440. If the snares are also too loose

or out of adjustment, release the snares while tuning. When the drum has a full sound, not too tight but not too flat, then tune the area of the drum opposite the section you just tuned (Photo 2-116). After that part is tuned move over one lug, tune it and then go across. Continue in this manner until the drum is tuned. Adjust the snares so that when the batter head is tapped, it has a nice sound with the snares vibrating under the drum. Tighten the snare head in the same manner as the batter head. The snare head should be slightly tighter than the batter head. Do not strike the snare head hard. It is not as tough as the batter head and can tear.

Photo 2-116

Slowing down	Lifting arm	(a) Teacher places hand just above student's hand. Whenever the student lifts the arm too high, it will hit the teacher's hand. (b) Play with motion from the wrist.
Too long to assemble instruments	Talking to each other, etc.	(a) Obvious: Tell them not to talk. It is important to assemble instruments as quickly as possible so they will have time to learn more about playing the drums. (b) Have a contest. See who can assemble his or her instrument first. Winner can play a solo today or something musical. (I do not recommend cookie and candy rewards.)
Having trouble playing rolls	Needs a progression of learning to control the bouncing of the sticks	(a) Play single strokes: quarter notes, eighth notes, sixteenth notes, etc. (b) Next work on bounces: one stick at a time —bounces as long as they can —try four bounces, then left stick —three bounces —two bounces —two bounces back and forth: sixteenth notes—right/right/left/left (c) Work on flams and ruffs. (d) After the preliminary strokes are mastered, put together to make rudimentary rolls.
Students are bored	Poor method book	Almost all heterogeneous band method books are too simple to develop good drummers. You must require supplementary method books designed especially for beginning drummers. Some suggestions are: —*Alfred's Beginning Drum Method* (Alfred Publishing, 1987) —*Roy Burns' Beginning Drum Method* (Warner Bros., 1962) —*Stick Control* by George Stone (George B. Stone & Son, 1935) —*Progressive Steps to Modern Syncopation* by Ted Reed (Copyright assigned to Alfred Publishing, 1996)

Drums Lessons Checklist

Lesson 1

- ☐ Drum pad vs. drum kit
- ☐ Bring drum kit to class?
- ☐ Room setup
- ☐ Assemble the drum
- ☐ If necessary, tune drum—teach it to students later
- ☐ Height of drum: 2" to 4" below belt
- ☐ Traditional/match grip
- ☐ Hand position
- ☐ Check—pointing fingers
- ☐ Stick size
- ☐ Tap drumhead once
- ☐ Check hand position
- ☐ Draw sound out of drum
- ☐ Tap four times
- ☐ Conduct with baton
- ☐ Count out loud
- ☐ Wrist motion?
- ☐ No bouncing sticks (yet)
- ☐ Four counts in each hand
- ☐ Three counts in each hand
- ☐ Two counts in each hand
- ☐ Tap alternating sticks
- ☐ Maintain steady beat
- ☐ Hand position
- ☐ Thumbprint on stick
- ☐ Wrist movement
- ☐ Arm movement
- ☐ Tapping toes
- ☐ Specific assignment
- ☐ *Enthusiasm!*

Lesson 2

- ☐ New beginners together/advanced together
- ☐ Advanced start assembling instruments as soon as they enter the room
- ☐ Start to teach beginners to assemble instruments
- ☐ Advanced students should have the drums assembled before you complete instructions for assemblage of the drum to new students
- ☐ Have advanced play four taps in each hand
- ☐ Watch for hand position
- ☐ Arm movement
- ☐ Toe tapping
- ☐ Wrist motion
- ☐ Bouncing sticks
- ☐ Steady tempo
- ☐ Posture
- ☐ Beginners: hand position
- ☐ Beginners: tap—watch for above
- ☐ Beginners follow same pattern as advanced: 4/4, 3/3, 2/2, alternate sticks
- ☐ Look at first page with notes
- ☐ Alternate between advanced and beginning students
- ☐ Specific assignment
- ☐ *Enthusiasm!*

Lesson 3

- ☐ Advanced students start assembling instruments immediately
- ☐ Work with new students—assembly
- ☐ Advanced: Play lesson from previous week
- ☐ No student idle for more than five minutes (alternate groups)
- ☐ Beginners: hand position
- ☐ Advanced continue in book
- ☐ Beginners: tapping drums—alternating hands
- ☐ Advanced play with beginners
- ☐ Alternate advanced just reading with advanced on second page of book
- ☐ Continue to watch for hand position, posture, steady beat, etc.
- ☐ Specific assignment
- ☐ *Enthusiasm!*

Lesson 4

- ☐ Send students without instruments back to class
- ☐ Advanced: Assemble instruments
- ☐ Start to instruct beginners on assembly
- ☐ Advanced: Start reading and playing
- ☐ Hand position for beginners
- ☐ Beginners start to play
- ☐ Advanced play with beginners
- ☐ Advanced should learn eighth notes
- ☐ Work with beginners
- ☐ For all, watch: hand position, posture, etc.
- ☐ All students look at reading exercises
- ☐ Count out loud
- ☐ Specific assignment
- ☐ ***Enthusiasm!***

Lesson 5

- ☐ Advanced start to assemble instruments
- ☐ If possible, reschedule beginners
- ☐ If not, start instructing them on assembly
- ☐ Advanced: Start to play; review earlier pages
- ☐ Beginners: hand position and play one note
- ☐ Advanced: Play more music
- ☐ Continue to switch groups—5 minutes each
- ☐ Advanced start to watch for dynamics
- ☐ Continue to watch for:
  - ☐ posture
  - ☐ hand position (thumbprint)
  - ☐ wrist movement
  - ☐ stick angle
  - ☐ arm movement
  - ☐ tempo
  - ☐ dynamics
- ☐ Count out loud
- ☐ Tapping toes
- ☐ Continue to switch groups
- ☐ Specific assignment
- ☐ ***Enthusiasm!***

BEGINNING BELLS/PERCUSSION LESSONS

The bells can be a very important addition to a beginning band and if they are offered as a band instrument, many students who are studying piano are likely to sign up for band. These students do not consider themselves drummers, nor do they want to learn to play the snare drum. It is advisable to demonstrate the bells and offer these students the chance to sign up as bell players. Students who do not play piano will also sign up for bells and learn quickly. Do not confuse or frustrate the students by requiring them to play the snare drum at the same time. They will either not sign up or drop out quickly, because it is not what they want to play.

It is best not to schedule bell students with the snare drum class. As I mentioned before, bell players do not consider themselves drummers; they want to be in their own class. Also, other than grip, the snare drum is a different class to teach. The drummers do not need to know the names of the notes on the staff. Both groups will progress much more quickly if you schedule them separately. This is not to say that at some point you will not want to teach your drummers to become percussionists and play all percussion instruments, but at this time, the bells and drums should be considered two different instruments.

If you have only one bell player and cannot have a private lesson, schedule the student with oboes or saxophones, or almost any other group. However, do not schedule the bell player with the flutes. Though they are both C instruments, the flutes have to play with the mouthpiece only for the first week. The instructions for the two instruments are too different to combine into one group until they have passed the beginning stages of playing.

The beginning bell lessons are not spelled out in a step-by-step fashion as they are for most other instruments covered in the *Kit*. By this point, the reader should be able to understand time management within a lesson group. This is very similar for all instrumental classes other than the flute class. Although a troubleshooting chart is provided for the bells, it is also advisable to refer to the drum troubleshooting chart. The emphasis is different in teaching the two groups, but there are common problems with the two instruments. If the reader uses both troubleshooting sections, he or she will have a more complete guide to teaching bells.

Instrument Assembly

There are many different styles of cases for bell kits. The most practical for young students is the style designed as a backpack. The hard-shell, heavy cases of most older models will be more discouraging for the children to play because of their weight and awkwardness and the difficulty in carrying them. If your dealer or rental supplier does not carry the backpack style, request that they start doing so immediately. Your retention rate will improve with the lighter backpack style (Photo 2-117).

Another advantage of the backpack is the ease with which it opens. A zipper is used to open the cloth case. The top will have the brand name, but it will also be obvious because the bottom section will have the shoulder straps. If you are using the hard-shell case, the top of the case should have the brand name on it. If it does not, or the brand name is on top and bottom (which is not that unusual), notice that the latches will move up to release to two sections of the case. Some of the cases will have a handle on the top and the bottom of the case, so your students will have to know how to tell which way the latches are moving before they completely open the case.

The first thing to do in assembling the instrument is to put the stand together. That is usually very easy. Spread the legs apart on the bottom half and tighten the wing nut so the stand will not slip. Then insert the top half and push up the braces so the support brackets will

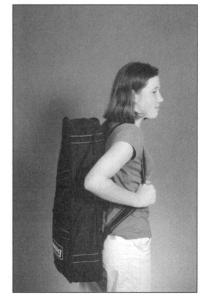

Photo 2-117

be parallel to the floor. Most bells will sit easily in this cradle. Some manufacturers have designed the stand so the bells are screwed onto the top of the stand. This is also not difficult to do and can quickly be accomplished. The height of the stand should be set about two to four inches below the belt when the student is standing (bell students should stand while playing). The student should be able to stand in front of the bell with the arms slightly bent and in a relaxed position. While playing, the arms should not be stiff and straight, nor should they be bent so much that the student is rasing his or her arms. If the child is stressing the arm muscles, it will be more difficult to control rhythm and play rapidly (Photo 2-118).

Photo 2-118

Hand Position

Students playing the bells use the match grip, the same as used with most other percussion instruments. Make sure the butt of the stick goes beyond the hand in between the wrist and knuckle of the little finger. The stick should not go directly under the wrist and arm (Photo 2-119). Hold the stick about one-third from the back end or butt of the mallet.

The hand should not be too close to the ball of the mallet. A good place with which to start is about three-quarters of the way to the back of the stick. However, it will rely somewhat on the size of the mallet and weight of the ball. The student should be able to comfortably hold the mallet and strike the instrument when he or she intends to play a note.

Photo 2-119

Do not allow the student to let the stick rest on the bar after it is struck. As soon as the bar is struck, the student should immediately lift the ball of the mallet off the bar as if to draw the music up and off the bar with the rise of the mallet. The result of leaving the mallet on the bar will be a "thud" sound instead of a nice clear tone that results from striking the instrument properly. Usually one or two reminders are all that are necessary for the students to remember how to play the instrument properly.

There should not be lots of arm motion. The motion is in the wrist. If the student is moving the arms up and down, the arms will soon tire and rhythm will become a problem. The appearance of arms moving up and down to an exaggerated extent may look comical to the audience. The less motion, the more quickly the student will be able to move from one note to another. Also, the student should keep the hands about the same level as, or just above, the keyboard. Do not play down at an angle.

Method Book

Generally, most method books are acceptable for the bell player. Since producing a sound is not usually a problem, it does not matter which notes are in the first lessons. However, the bell notes should not be too high. Notes above the staff and in the upper portion of the staff sound fairly high. Again, high notes are not difficult to play, but they may not blend so well with the band. You may choose to use your heterogeneous band method book or the lessons in this resource. The lessons included in the *Kit* concentrate on developing a good rhythmic sense while having fun. Since they start with quarter notes instead of whole notes, it is easy for young students to understand how to count and play the notes at the same time. It is very confusing for young students on the first day to play a whole note and count to four, when the note on the bell does not last usually for more than one beat anyway. The easier it is for a student in the first lessons, the better the chances he or she will stay with the program.

Muscle Relaxing Exercise Demonstration

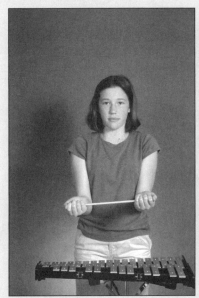
Photo 2-111

Photo 2-112

Photo 2-113

Photo 2-114

Photo 2-115

Figure 2-56—Music for Bells Lesson 1

This lesson is taught without showing the music to the student. Students should concentrate on producing a good, clear sound. Attempting to read music will distract from all that is needed to produce a good sound.

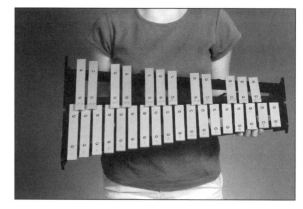

Photo 120

The note is played and allowed to decay. Counting is not necessary for the first note.

Students should play the note four times in a steady count. All students not playing should count out loud with the band director.

Follow the same procedure as above.

Follow the same procedure as above.

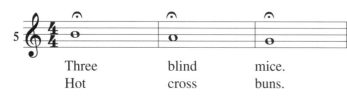

Three   blind   mice.
Hot   cross   buns.

First song. Counting rhythms is not necessary the first time. A quick accomplishment is paramount.

Mary Had a Little Lamb

ASSIGNMENT: First, hold each note, then play each note four times.
Play "Three Blind Mice."
Challenge: Who can play "Mary Had a Little Lamb" using the three notes learned today? Be positive; wish everyone a nice day.
BE ENTHUSIASTIC!

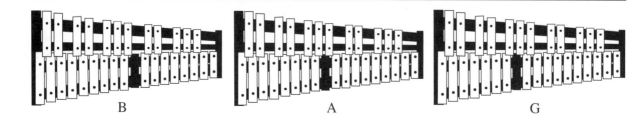

B   A   G

Figure 2-57—Music for Bells Lesson 2

Round One

Lookin' Up

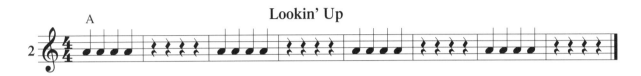

Up and Down

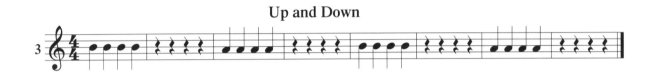

A New One

Take A Note

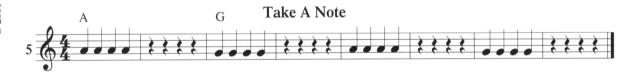

Mary Had a Little Lamb

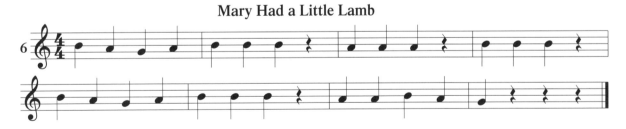

Tap toes: one foot tap per beat. Start with toes up; heels anchored on floor. Practice tapping toes while playing every line.

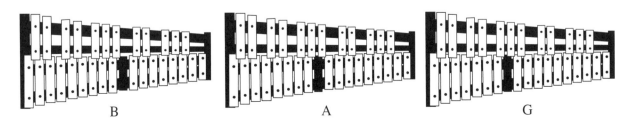

Figure 2-58
Music for Bells Lesson 3

Figure 2-59
Music for Bells Lesson 4

Figure 2-60
Music for Bells Lesson 5

The Whole Time

Jingle Bells

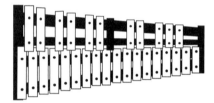

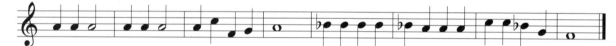

Ode to Joy

A Little Bit Longer

London Bridge

Duet

TROUBLESHOOTING THE BELLS*

PROBLEM	CAUSE	SOLUTIONS
Uneven rhythm	Hand position	(a) Stick at the correct angle. (See Photo 2-105 on p. 185.) Butt of stick must go between the wrist and finger knuckle. Sticks never go directly under arms.
		(b) Practice a slow steady beat in quarter notes. First, tap four times in each hand. The band director and students must count out loud for one minute, nonstop. Do not allow the tempo to change. Then go to three taps with each stick. Then two taps with each stick, and finally alternate sticks for every tap. Do not have the student look at the music. At this stage, it is better to concentrate on a steady rhythm, correct hand position, and using the correct sticking. (Play any note.)
	Tension	(a) Correct hand position.
		(b) Gripping the stick too tightly—loosen up.
		(c) Ease tension and fatigue with this relaxing exercise: The student should hold both sticks in the same direction. (See Photos 2-111 to 2-115.) Hold the sticks at each end, palms up. The right hand goes under the left hand, and the left hand twists around until both hands have twisted around back to palms up, but the thumbs point in the opposite direction. Reverse the procedure.
Slowing down	Lifting arm	(a) Teacher places hand just above student's hand. Whenever the student lifts the arm too high, it will hit the teacher's hand.
		(b) Play with motion from the wrist.
		(c) Make sure the students are alternating their sticks. Bell players sometimes will use only one hand to play all the notes. Do not let this become a habit. It is very difficult to break.

*Check "Troubleshooting the Drums." Many problems and solutions are the same.

Too long to assemble instruments	Talking to each other, etc.	(a) Obvious: Tell them not to talk so much. It is important to assemble the instruments as quickly as possible so they will have time for more instruction and help during the lesson.
		(b) Have a contest: See who can assemble his or her instrument first. The winner can play a solo today. (I do not recommend cookie and candy rewards.)
Student having trouble seeing notes and the director at the same time	The student has not learned to use his peripheral vision.	(a) Practice enough to become familiar with the notes and where they are.
		(b) Have the student look straight ahead. The band director should stand to his or her side and ask if he or she can see the conductor. It is the same principle that the student can see the notes and conductor at the same time.
		(c) Practice alternating the sticks so one does not have to look down at every single note played.

All of the above is applicable to other percussion instruments and vice versa. Drums and mallet instruments usually encounter similar difficulties.

Bells Lessons Checklist

Lesson 1

- [ ] Bells—Schedule lessons with saxophones, oboes or other groups, but not flutes or snare drums
- [ ] Room setup
- [ ] Assemble the bells
- [ ] Height of bells—two to four inches below belt
- [ ] Match grip
- [ ] Hand position
- [ ] Check—pointing fingers
- [ ] Stick size (mallet)
- [ ] Play note once
- [ ] Check hand position
- [ ] Draw sound out of bells
- [ ] Tap four times
- [ ] Conduct with baton
- [ ] Count out loud
- [ ] Wrist motion?
- [ ] Four counts in each hand
- [ ] Three counts in each hand
- [ ] Two counts in each hand
- [ ] Alternate sticks
- [ ] Maintain steady beat
- [ ] Hand position
- [ ] Thumbprint on stick
- [ ] Wrist movement
- [ ] Arm movement
- [ ] Tapping toes
- [ ] First notes: B, A, G
- [ ] First song: "Three Blind Mice"—B, A, G
- [ ] Challenge to play "Mary Had a Little Lamb" using only those notes
- [ ] Specific assignment
- [ ] *Enthusiasm!*

Lesson 2

- [ ] New beginners together/advanced together
- [ ] Advanced start assembling instruments as soon as they enter the room
- [ ] Start to teach beginners to assemble instruments
- [ ] Advanced students should have the bells assembled before new students' instructions for assembling the bells are complete
- [ ] Have advanced play four taps in each hand
- [ ] Watch for hand position
- [ ] Arm movement
- [ ] Toe tapping
- [ ] Wrist motion
- [ ] Steady tempo
- [ ] Posture
- [ ] Beginners: hand position
- [ ] Beginners: tap—watch for above
- [ ] Beginners follow same pattern as advanced: 4/4, 3/3, 2/2, alternate sticks
- [ ] Look at first page with notes
- [ ] Alternate between advanced and beginning students
- [ ] Specific assignment
- [ ] *Enthusiasm!*

Lesson 3

- [ ] Advanced students start assembling instruments immediately
- [ ] Work with new students—assembly
- [ ] Advanced: Play lesson from last week
- [ ] No student idle for more than five minutes (alternate groups)
- [ ] Beginners: Hand position
- [ ] Advanced: Continue in book
- [ ] Beginners: Tapping bells—alternating hands
- [ ] Advanced: Play with beginners
- [ ] Alternate advanced just reading with advanced on second page in book
- [ ] Continue to watch for hand position, posture, steady beat, etc.
- [ ] Specific assignment
- [ ] *Enthusiasm!*

Lesson 4

- [ ] Send students back to class without instruments
- [ ] Advanced: Assemble instruments
- [ ] Start to instruct beginners on assembly
- [ ] Advanced: Start reading and playing
- [ ] Hand position for beginners
- [ ] Beginners: Start to play
- [ ] Advanced: Play with beginners
- [ ] Work with beginners
- [ ] For all: Watch hand position, posture, etc.
- [ ] All students look at reading exercises
- [ ] Count out loud
- [ ] Specific assignment
- [ ] ***Enthusiasm!***

Lesson 5

- [ ] Advanced start to assemble instruments
- [ ] If possible, reschedule beginners
- [ ] If not, start instructing them on assembly
- [ ] Advanced: Start to play; review earlier pages
- [ ] Beginners: Hand position and play one note
- [ ] Advanced: Play more music
- [ ] Continue to switch groups—five minutes each
- [ ] Advanced: Start to watch for dynamics
- [ ] Continue to watch for:
  - [ ] Posture
  - [ ] Hand position (thumbprint)
  - [ ] Wrist movement
  - [ ] Stick angle (mallet)
  - [ ] Arm movement
  - [ ] Tempo
  - [ ] Dynamics
  - [ ] Counting out loud
- [ ] Tapping toes
- [ ] Continue to switch groups
- [ ] Specific assignment
- [ ] ***Enthusiasm!***

BEGINNING OBOE LESSONS

Not many students sign up for oboe. That is most likely a good thing. Can you imagine a band with 15 oboes! A band director must be careful about allowing students to start or switch to oboe. It is an instrument that requires a person to listen carefully. The student who succeeds on this instrument is usually one who makes very good grades and has learned to listen carefully and follow instructions. That is a key to the successful oboe player. I often ask a player what her grades are when she asks to play an oboe. If the student says she makes all As or almost all As, I feel confident that she will be able to

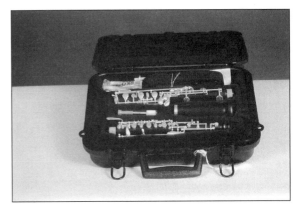

successfully play the instrument. This does not mean that I would not let someone who makes As and Bs play the instrument, but if she tells me she also makes Cs, I will try to convince the student to play another instrument. Since tuning and controlling the tone on the oboe requires much more discipline than needed for most other instruments, I want a student who listens to what is happening around her and the instructions given her in order to play the instrument well.

Because you may have only one oboe student as a beginner, you may require that she attend lessons with a different instrument. The first instrument to consider combining with the oboe is the bells. They often play in the same range, and they can often share the same music if one of the players forgets his or her book. The oboe can also be combined with the saxophone group. The notes are not the same, but many of the fingerings are very similar, and they should progress at the same rate. Oboes also do very well playing along with the clarinets. I do not recommend

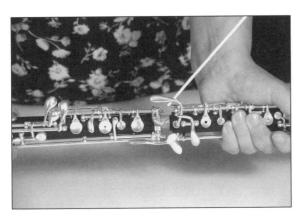

Photo 2-122

having the oboes play with the flutes. Because the flute players should play the head joint only for the first week, it will be very difficult to manage enough time to teach the flute players and the oboes all they need to know in each lesson. Trying to correct individual problems may be next to impossible. Flutes need to be in a group unto themselves.

If the new oboe student is switching from another instrument, I would strongly recommend that he or she play the lessons provided in this resource before continuing in a band method book. Students can easily switch from just about any instrument to the oboe. Saxophone players often have the easiest time switching. Only students who truly want to play oboe should play this instrument. I do not recommend persuading anyone who shows the slightest signs of resistance to playing the oboe.

Instrument Assembly

As with all instruments, the first order of business is to know how to open the case. The brand name is usually on the top of the case, and the handle is

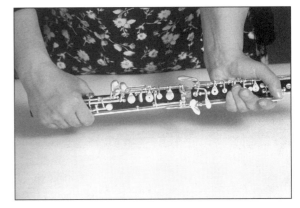

Photo 2-123

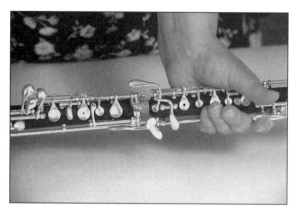

Photo 2-124

usually on the bottom portion of the case. If the handle is located on the bottom or there is no brand name, the latches are always pulled or pushed up in order to release the two halves of the case. Students should put the bottom of the case on the floor in front of them. It is not recommended to assemble any instrument with the case in the student's lap. If the student loses the balance of the case on her lap, it could fall and damage the instrument (Photo 2-121).

The oboe can be a rather delicate instrument to assemble. One must be careful not to bend the keys when putting the instrument together. The two major body parts are assembled in a manner similar to those of the clarinet. The upper body joint should be placed in the left hand with the long row of keys down and the heel of the hand pressing the bridge keys up (Photo 2-122). The lower body joint is held with the right hand toward the bottom of the oboe, near the bell (Photo 2-123). There are two sets of bridge keys for which the student must watch. If the body joints are held so the keys are down, the student can keep an eye on both bridge keys since they are easily bent. The two body parts should be pushed together with a slight twisting of the two body joints back and forth until the two parts have completely come together (Photo 2-124). The bridge keys on the side of the instrument should be connected (Photo 2-125).

The cork on the reed should be greased before inserting it into the instrument. Also, the reed needs to be soaked in water before playing the instrument. The student may put the cane portion of the reed in a small cup or glass while she is assembling the instrument. An

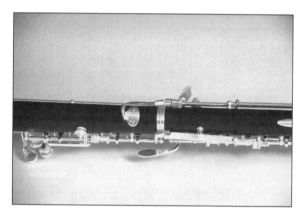

Photo 2-125

ideal container for soaking the reed is a 35mm film canister filled about halfway up with water. When the canister is sealed, it will not leak, so it can be carried in the instrument case or a backpack. If that is not possible, the oboe student may place the cane portion of the reed in her mouth and dampen the reed with the saliva in her mouth while assembling the oboe. However, the band director should discourage soaking a reed with saliva since it will break down the reed much faster than water. For the first time, have the student insert the reed into the oboe completely. Tuning and reed placement are to be discussed at a different lesson. The first goal of instrumental instruction is to have the student make a sound as soon as possible. Playing in tune on the first day is not the main consideration, but must be kept in mind as instructions progress. Good intonation is crucial for this instrument. As soon as the tone starts to stabilize, start teaching the student to listen to the notes and tune the instrument. See the position and angle of the reed to the oboe—the flat part of the reed should be parallel to the row of keys on the oboe (Photo 2-126).

Photo 2-126

Hand Position

The hand position is similar to that on the clarinet. The left hand goes on the top, right hand on the bottom, as with all woodwind instruments (Photos 2-127, 2-128 and 2-129). Fingers should have a slight arch to them. The thumb should be perpendicular to the oboe, and the nail of the thumb, not the knuckle, should line up with the thumb rest. If the thumb rest is uncomfortable and brings discomfort to the student, you can suggest a commercial thumb pad or you can make a very comfortable and inexpensive thumb pad by cutting a very short piece of surgical tubing and placing it over the thumb rest. This can be obtained at a medical supply store.

Photo 2-127

Reeds

The oboe student will not be able to play the instrument without a reed in good playable condition. You cannot expect beginning students, especially at an elementary school age, to make their own reeds. Unless you play oboe or you can make good reeds quickly for your students, your students will need to buy their reeds. Even if you can make playable oboe reeds, it is unlikely you will have time to make reeds for your students. The reeds found in music stores will work for beginners. They are not the best sounding reeds, but they play easily. And a quick and easy sound is the first step to having a student continue to play the instrument. After the student can play the oboe and complete the first book, if he shows a strong interest in continuing with the instrument, strongly encourage him to take private lessons and find a good oboe teacher who plays oboe. A good oboe teacher may possibly supply the student with good reeds. The main problem with commercial oboe reeds is that they are made to play easily, so much of the heart, or much of the wood in the center of the cane, is cut out, thus making a thin sound. (See the Appendix at the end for a list of suppliers of good oboe and bassoon reeds.)

Photo 2-128

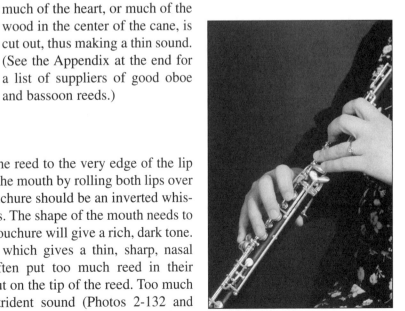

Photo 2-129

Embouchure

The student should put the tip of the reed to the very edge of the lip (Photo 2-130). Insert the reed into the mouth by rolling both lips over the reed (Photo 2-131). The embouchure should be an inverted whistle with equal tension from all sides. The shape of the mouth needs to be in the "awh" position. This embouchure will give a rich, dark tone. Avoid the "smiling" embouchure which gives a thin, sharp, nasal sound. Beginning oboists will often put too much reed in their mouths. Encourage them to stay out on the tip of the reed. Too much reed causes a sharp pitch and strident sound (Photos 2-132 and 2-133). Most of the time the reed should stay in the middle of the lower lip. Do not bite down or squeeze the reed. That will cut off the air supply to the instrument in the same way as pinching the reed will do to the clarinet. The bell of the oboe should be at about a 45-degree angle from the mouth which would be around the knees or just above them (Photo 2-134). That will give the proper angle in which the reed and mouth should be positioned. The mouth should be kept shut tight, and the cheeks should not puff out when blowing air into the instrument. For some children, that will be difficult in the beginning. The oboe provides more air resistance than most other instruments, and for some beginners, it is more difficult not to allow the cheeks to puff out. The mouth and lips must remain shut as tightly as possible, but still allow the reed to vibrate. This is not so difficult as it may sound, but you must be continually reminding the students not to puff out their cheeks. Practice is essential for success in playing the oboe. Inform the student that if she does not practice daily, she will not play the oboe well. Only through practice will the muscles develop strongly and the ear develop so the student can learn to play all the notes in tune. It is also extremely important that the teacher insist the instrument be kept in good playing order and the reed in playable condition. Any instrument must be in good playing condition for a student to be successful playing it, but with the oboe, it is essential that the reed and instrument be in good playing order. The student will not know if something is wrong with the instrument. She may blame herself for not being able to play the instrument well and quit. It is the teacher's responsibility to let the student and his or her parents know that the instrument is in need of repair and/or that a new reed is necessary to play the instrument.

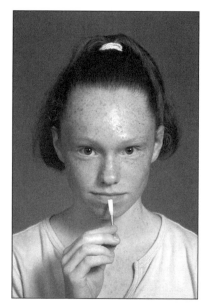

Photo 2-130

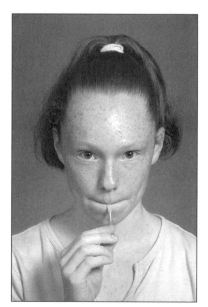

Photo 2-131

The First Note (Figs. 2-61–2-65)

Before the first note is played, show the student the fingering for B, third line. This is an easy note for most students to play. As the student is holding the oboe with the correct fingering for B, follow the procedure stated above for instructing the student how to put the reed into his mouth. Once the embouchure and fingers are in position, have the student blow into the instrument starting the note with the tongue using the syllable "tu." Do not discuss breathing at this time other than to tell the student to take a deep breath. The student should not puff out his cheeks. For many students, the embouchure of both lips curled over the teeth helps to keep the cheeks from being puffed out. If the student's cheeks do come out, tell him to tighten the corners of his mouth, and while sustaining the note, tell the student to bring in his cheeks. When the cheeks finally come in, he will feel the muscles working. Once the student can play B, teach him how to play A. This should be an easy task. The final note for the first day is G. Now the student can play the first part of "Three Blind Mice." Challenge the

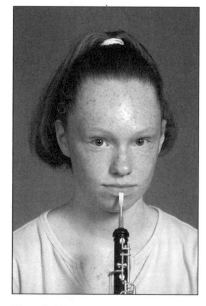

Photo 2-132

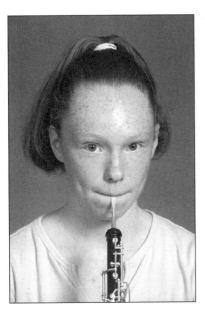

Photo 2-133

student to play "Mary Had a Little Lamb" using only those three notes by the next lesson.

If you are giving group lessons, you will have to take turns having the students play if you are using these lessons for the first instructions. There is nothing wrong with having students wait while the other students are learning, but make sure that you keep everyone playing. A good basic rule to follow is that once all the students can play their first note, no one should go more than five minutes without playing his or her instrument. This will prevent complaints from parents, and keep a higher retention rate in your classes.

Remember to give a very specific assignment every lesson. The oboe student should not feel as if he or she is playing an instrument that no one wants to play, or that it is an unimportant instrument. Give the oboe player all the attention necessary to help her become a productive member of your band. And always be enthusiastic. Every accomplishment must be rewarded with your enthusiasm.

Photo 2-134

Figure 2-61
Music for Oboe Lesson 1

Teach this lesson without showing the music to the student. Students should concentrate on producing a good sound. Attempting to read music will distract from all that is needed to produce a good sound.

1.   B

The note is sustained for a comfortable length of time. Counting is not necessary for the first note.

2.   1 2 3 4

Students should play the note four times in a steady count. All students not playing should count out loud with the band director.

3.   A

Follow the same procedure as above.

4.   G

Follow the same procedure as above.

5.

Three   blind   mice.
Hot   cross   buns.

First song. Counting rhythms is not necessary the first time. A quick accomplishment is paramount.

Mary Had a Little Lamb

6.

ASSIGNMENT: First, hold each note, then play each note four times.
Play "Three Blind Mice."
Challenge: Who can play "Mary Had a Little Lamb" using the three notes learned today? Be positive; wish everyone a nice day.
BE ENTHUSIASTIC!

Figure 2-62
Music for Oboe Lesson 2

Round One

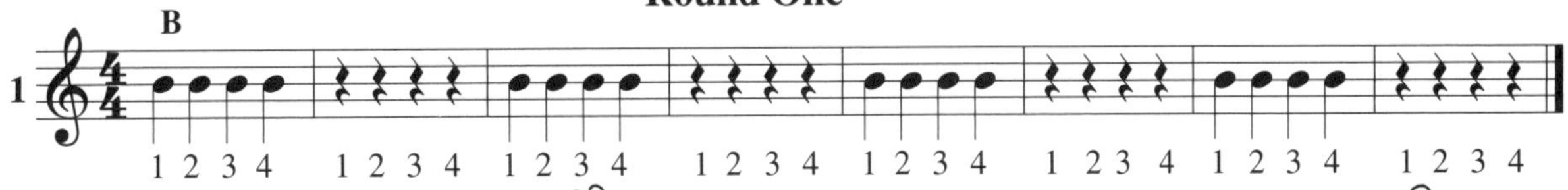

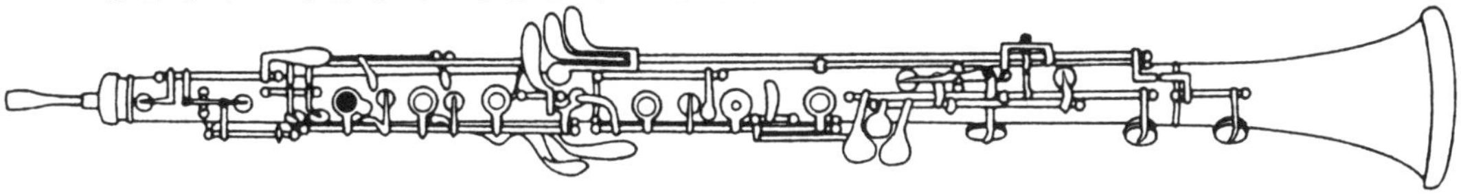

Lookin' Up

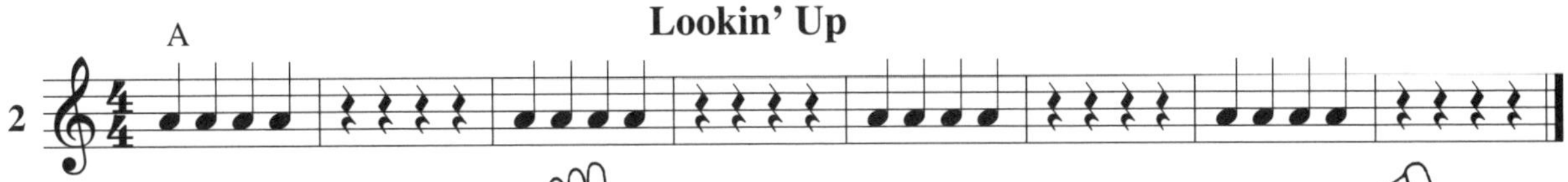

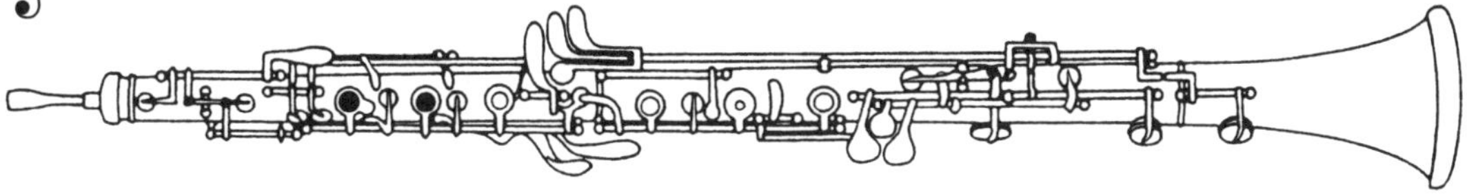

Up and Down

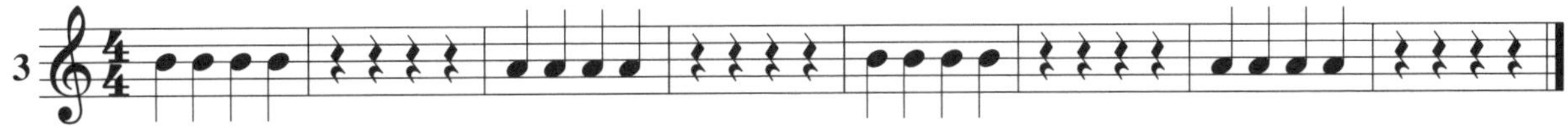

A New One

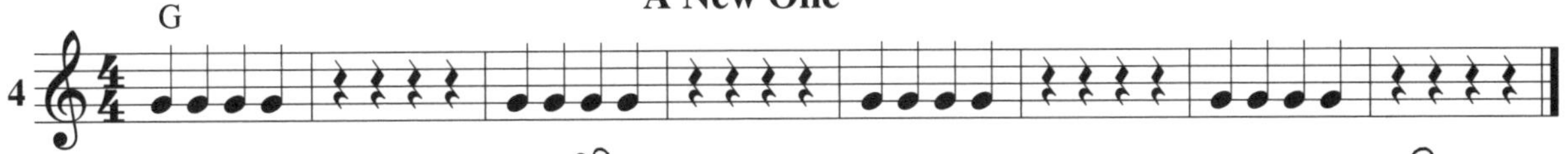

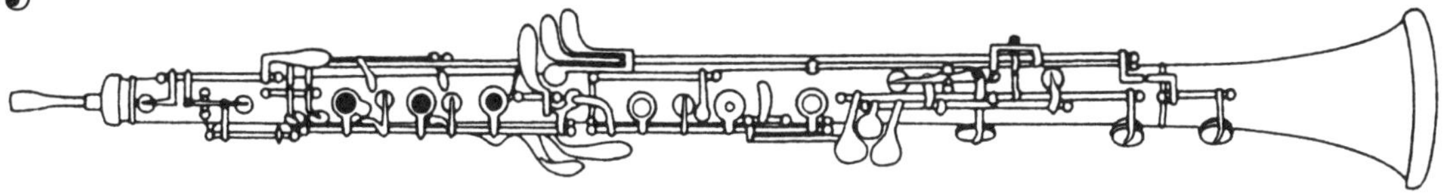

Take a Note

A G

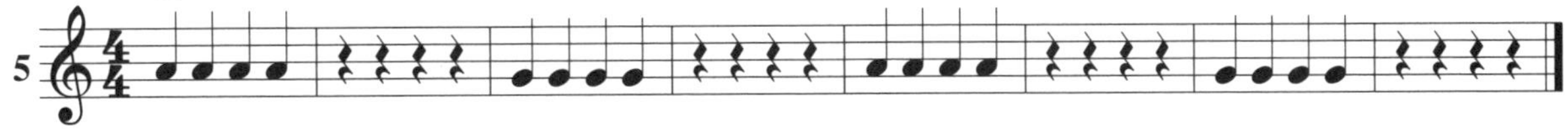

Mary Had a Little Lamb

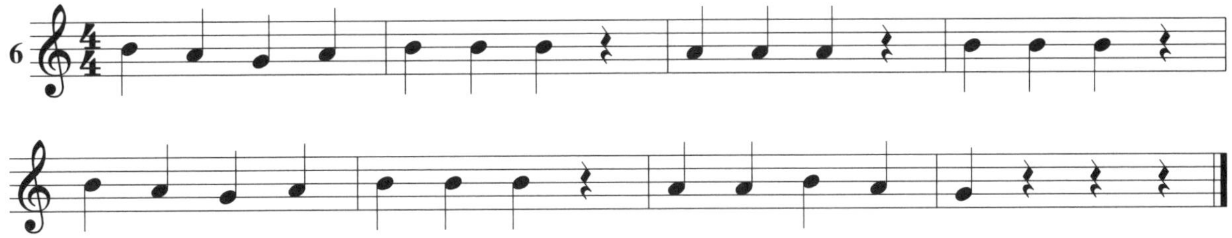

Tap toes: one foot tap per beat. Start with toes up; heels anchored on floor. Practice tapping toes while playing every line.

Figure 2-63
Music for Oboe Lesson 3

Steppin' Up

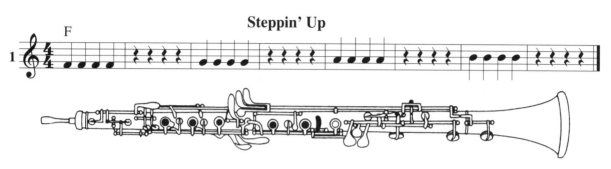

Down the Ladder

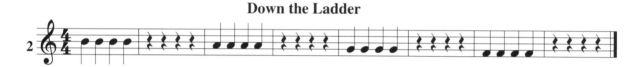

Over the Hill

More to Play

Watch Out for That Rest!

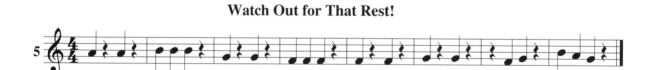

Round and Round

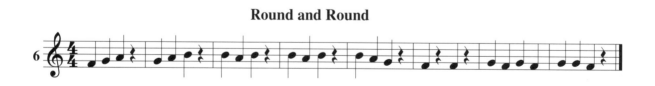

Waves

Figure 2-64
Music for Oboe Lesson 4

Try This One

One Higher

Twice as Long

Say It Again

Hot Cross Buns

Go Tell Aunt Rhodie

Skippin' Around

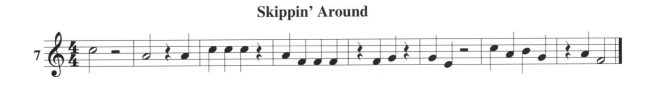

Figure 2-65
Music for Oboe Lesson 5

The Whole Time

Jingle Bells

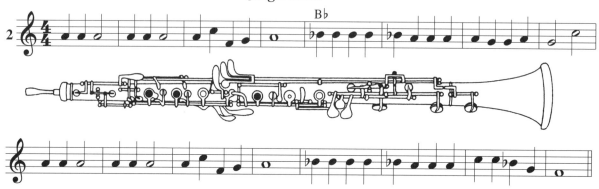

Ode to Joy

A Little Bit Longer

London Bridge

Duet

Troubleshooting the Oboe

PROBLEM	CAUSE	SOLUTIONS
Instrument will not play	1. Instrument	Make sure the instrument is in good, playable condition. The oboe is a delicate instrument, and can easily have a key bent or out of alignment. The quality of the instrument is also very important. The director needs to encourage the parents to spend the extra money necessary to buy or rent a good quality instrument. You get what you pay for, and with the oboe, you may get a lot less than you expect.
	2. Reed	This is a very major concern for double reed instruments. The reed must be in good condition and the right strength for the student. The reed should be soaked in water while the student is assembling the instrument. Do not over-soak the reed. 3–5 minutes is enough time to soften the reed. Though reeds are expensive, students must have a spare new reed at all times. The reed must "crow," or make a sound, in order to play. If you know how to adjust the reed, you may want to do that yourself. Otherwise, you will have to insist on the student's having new reeds at all times. Oboe reeds can be purchased at most music stores or catalog companies. The Appendix of this resource lists some sources and suppliers of quality double reeds. Medium-hard or harder store-purchased reeds are not made to be played without adjustment. Beginners should start on medium-soft and graduate to medium.
Student cannot practice for very long before lips "blow out"	Muscles not developed	(a) Practice. (b) If the student practices but cannot continue because his lips keep "blowing out" or just relaxing, force him to stop. The student needs to practice for a short time but stop before the lips give out. He should take a break for an hour or more and then practice for another 10 or 15 minutes. Each day, he should add a little more time to the first practice session, always trying to stop before the lips "blow out." Once that has happened, the muscles no longer have the strength to continue and that day's practice is over.
Bad intonation	1. Student does not hear the notes in tune	The band director has to insist on good intonation. Have the student match the pitches of another instrument. Help the oboe player notice the difference between notes in tune and notes out of tune. Once a player hears the difference and knows bad intonation when producing it, there is a chance to correct it. This really applies to all instruments, but it is very noticeable when an oboe student is out of tune because of the timbre of the oboe. Work constantly with the player to learn to hear and match pitches. If there

is a piano in the room (and in tune), have the student match the pitches he or she will be using that day. You must develop the student's ability to notice intonation, and to correct it then. Encourage the student to buy a tuner, especially if the student does not have an in-tune piano or keyboard at home.

	2. Low pitch	(a) Put more reed into the mouth. (b) Increase pressure on the reed (without pinching). (c) Bring the oboe closer to the body. (d) Bring tongue to roof of the mouth.
	3. High pitch	(a) Put less reed in the mouth. (b) Loosen embouchure. (c) Move oboe away from body. (d) Lower jaw, making a bigger cavity in the mouth.
Trouble changing notes	Coordination	(a) Practice slowly the two notes in question. Do not add more notes until those two intervals are perfect. Do this slowly and do not gradually speed up. After five times in a row played perfectly, add anther note, and continue in that manner until the passage can be played. (b) Play the notes in backwards order, slowly in a steady rhythm. The rhythm written is not important especially since it is being played backwards. Make all the notes quarter notes, but with a steady slow nonchanging tempo. Do this several times in a row. Then play it in the correct order using the same rhythm. Tell the student to practice it that way at home. If he does, the next day he may be able to play the notes without difficulty.
High pitch, few sounds	1. Embouchure too tight	(a) Relax embouchure. (b) Possibly the player is blowing too hard.
	2. Reed too stiff	(a) Use a softer strength reed. (b) Adjust balance and tip of the reed with a reed knife (not a task for a beginner).
	3. Horn angle	Too close to the body. Should be just above the knees or right at the knees, depending on the size of the student.
Low pitch	1. Lack of support	Blow hard. Make the air go into the oboe faster.
	2. Horn angle too high	Hold the horn at the proper angle. See above.
	3. Reed too soft	Get a stronger reed.

Airy sound	1. Embouchure	Embouchure is too loose. Tighten up so air does not slip out the corners of the mouth.
	2. Air support	Blow harder.
Sound keeps stopping	1. Pinching or biting the reed	(a) Make "oh" shape in lips. (b) Do not squeeze the lips against the reed.
	2. Soft reed	Replace with a stronger or new reed.

Reed Problems: If the teacher is an experienced oboe player and has made good reeds, then it may be a terrific aid to the student if the teacher can quickly adjust the balance and tip strength of the reeds. However, if the teacher is inexperienced and has not worked on oboe reeds or has not had experience adjusting reeds for oboe students, I would not advise the teacher to work on the student's reeds. If the teacher decides to work on the reeds, he/she should use a reed knife. Using an old pocketknife is likely to do more damage than good. I strongly recommend that the students spend the extra money on some of the suggested reeds in the Appendix of this *Kit*. The reeds sound better and play better in tune. They are worth the extra money.

Oboe Fingering Chart

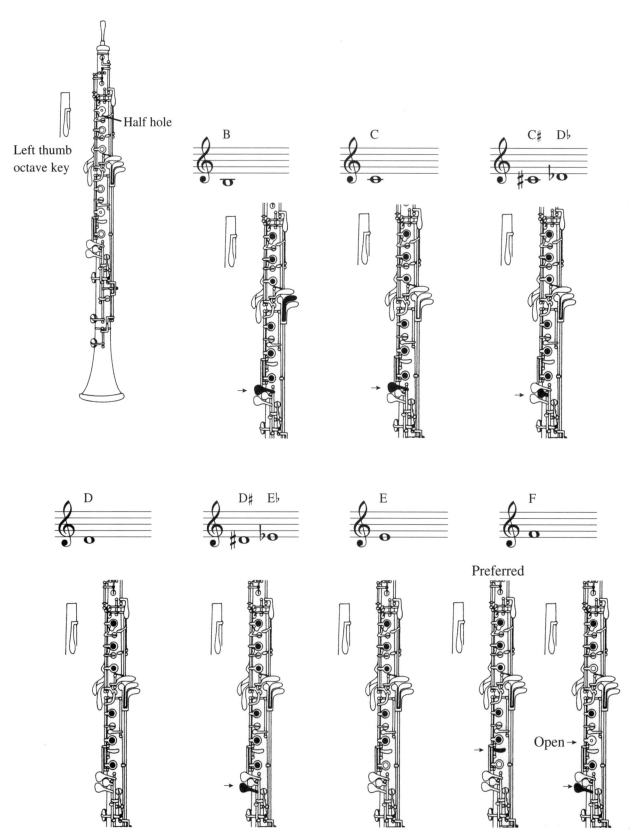

Oboe Fingering Chart, p. 2

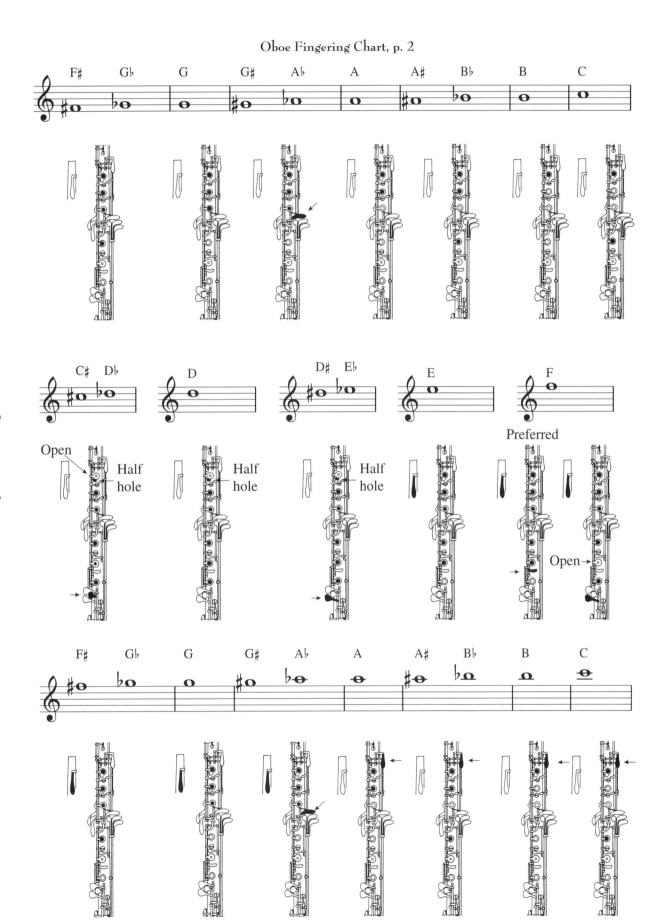

Oboe Lessons Checklist

Lesson 1

- [ ] Choose right student for oboe
- [ ] Choose right class in which to put oboe player if there are not enough oboes for an individual class
- [ ] Chairs set up in advance
- [ ] Name tags on chairs (if applicable)
- [ ] Students with instruments in front row
- [ ] State rules
- [ ] Top of the case
- [ ] Check instrument for quality/repair
- [ ] Instrument assembly
- [ ] Cork grease
- [ ] Soak reed
- [ ] Careful of bridge keys
- [ ] Hand position
- [ ] Good reed
- [ ] Do not oversoak—3 minutes
- [ ] Embouchure—reed on edge of lip—roll in
- [ ] Oboe angle—45 degrees
- [ ] First note B, then A, G
- [ ] First song "Three Blind Mice"
- [ ] Give practice assignment
- [ ] ***Be Enthusiastic!***

Lesson 2

- [ ] Students who played before: Assemble instruments
- [ ] New students: top of the case
- [ ] Advanced students: Play B
- [ ] Assembly of the instrument
- [ ] Check instrument for packing corks, etc.
- [ ] Hand position
- [ ] Beginners: Embouchure
- [ ] Advanced: Play A and G
- [ ] Beginners: Play B
- [ ] Advanced: Look at Lesson 2—discuss reading the notes
- [ ] Play second line
- [ ] Beginners: Play B-A-G
- [ ] Advanced: Play as much of Lesson 2 as possible
- [ ] Specific assignment to advanced and beginning students
- [ ] ***Be Enthusiastic!***

Lesson 3

- [ ] Advanced: Start assembling instruments
- [ ] Beginners: Show top of case
- [ ] Advanced: Play high B, A, G
- [ ] Remind all of good posture
- [ ] Advanced: Review Lesson 2, while instructing other students how to assemble the instrument
- [ ] Students who just learned to assemble instrument: Show hand position

- [ ] Advanced: Continue with Lesson 2
- [ ] New students: Embouchure; play B, A, G
- [ ] Everyone looks at Lesson 3 (or beginning book)
- [ ] Everyone looks at notes; advanced play
- [ ] Quick check for everyone playing instrument
- [ ] Specific assignment
- [ ] ***Be Enthusiastic***—praise their achievement

Lesson 4

- ☐ If new students, you should reschedule them into new class
- ☐ Those who can assemble instrument should start immediately
- ☐ New students: Top of the case and assembly
- ☐ Advanced students: Play B, A, and G
- ☐ New students: Embouchure and B, A, G
- ☐ Review Lesson 2 with Advanced (a few lines)
- ☐ Advanced students: Start to play Lesson 3
- ☐ Beginners: Review B, A, G
- ☐ Watch out for students not reading
- ☐ Look at Lesson 4, play as much as possible
- ☐ Everyone play instrument
- ☐ Specific assignment
- ☐ *Enthusiasm!*

Lesson 5

- ☐ New students should be rescheduled
- ☐ If you must allow new students, spend minimal time with them—show them how to make a sound and move on quickly to others
- ☐ Everyone (advanced): Play "Mary Had a Little Lamb"
- ☐ Instructions for instrument assembly
- ☐ Introduction
- ☐ Playing from book
- ☐ Tapping toes
- ☐ Counting rhythms—watch—make them all count
- ☐ Those who just learned to assemble instrument: Learn to play B, A, and G
- ☐ Advanced: Continue to play Lesson 4
- ☐ Tonguing for those reading
- ☐ Everyone play from book according to where they are musically
- ☐ Quick discussion of Lesson 5
- ☐ Specific assignment
- ☐ *Always be enthusiastic. Compliment their accomplishments!*

BEGINNING BASSOON LESSONS

The bassoon is one of the larger and more difficult instruments on which a beginner may start. Often a student may begin on a smaller instrument, and later change to bassoon, usually in middle or high school. However, now that many schools have two-year kindergarten programs, beginning band students are older and larger, and thus are able to make the bassoon their first instrument.

Like the oboe and the F horn, the bassoon is not an instrument that just anyone should play. Because of its size, many students are not able to handle the bassoon. When a student approaches a band director to play bassoon, certain factors should be considered:

Grades: What kind of grades does the student make? Students should make very good grades, mostly As with a few Bs. As with oboe and F horn, they must be the kind of people who follow directions and listen to themselves and others at the same time.

Academic Attitude: The student should be academically inclined. This is not just a measurement of grades, but a mental attitude. Classroom teachers may be able to advise you about a student's academic attitude.

Singing Ability: Can the student sing and match your pitch?

Personality: The student should have a strong sense of self-confidence.

Size: The student must be large enough to hold and handle this instrument. And the student must have long fingers. The fingers must be able to reach from the back of the instrument to the keys and holes on the front of the bassoon. A petite student will not be able to play the bassoon.

Physical Condition: The student must be in good physical condition. A weak child will not have enough stamina to produce a good tone on the bassoon.

Coordination: The student should be physically coordinated.

The same guidelines should be followed when switching a student from another instrument to bassoon. You do not want to switch the student from clarinet to bassoon if he or she is the worst clarinet player in the band. The student must have a desire to play the bassoon and fit the criteria listed above. Of course, as the band director, you may find a student who fits the description, and then encourage the student to switch. The two instrumentalists most often switched to bassoon are clarinet and saxophone players. The fingerings are somewhat related, and these instrumentalists seem to pick up playing the bassoon more quickly than players of other instruments. However, you may consider anyone who has a desire to play bassoon and fits the description above.

As with the oboe and F horn, this resource provides only instructions on the basics of teaching the bassoon. If the teacher follows the same basic procedure used with other instruments with regard to time management and general approach, he or she should find adequate instructions for teaching the bassoon properly.

Assembly

As with all instruments, the very first step in assembling the instrument is to remove it from the case properly. Before the instrument can be removed, the student must be able to distinguish the top of the case from the bottom of the case. Usually the brand name will be on the top of the case. However, sometimes the name is on both the top and bottom, and in some cases there is no name on it at all. In that situation, the handle is always on the bottom portion of the case. Should the case have handles on both top and bottom portions of the case, the student must notice in which directions the latches move. The latches will move upward if the case is in its proper position. The case should always be placed on the floor or on a flat surface to assemble the instrument. The instrument should not be assembled while the case is in the student's lap. The student should place the instrument on the floor in front of him (or her) with the bottom of the case on the floor. Then the case may be opened.

Before assembling the instrument, have the student take the reed out of the case and soak it in warm water. Soaking the reed in cold water can result in cracking because of the temperature change from the water to the student's mouth. The reed can be placed in a small container, such as a 35mm film canister. Warn the student not to oversoak the reed. A few minutes is all that is necessary. If a reed is oversoaked, it will not play properly. Usually, the time it takes to assemble the instrument will be an adequate time for soaking the reed. On the first day, this may be too long a time period, so keep track of time, and after three to five minutes, have the student remove the reed from the water if the instrument is not assembled.

Photo 2-135

Once the case is opened, the students should grease the corks. The corks should be well lubricated. The student may use cork grease, but Vaseline™ also works very well and does not build up a residue as cork grease will. Each instrument part should be returned to the case after the joints are lubricated.

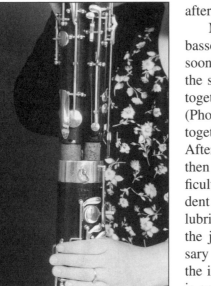

Photo 2-136

Many method books suggest that one start with the boot of the bassoon and then insert the two wing joints separately. Some bassoonists put the two wing joints together first. The keys should face the students during assembly (Photo 2-135). Once the two parts are together, then the student may insert the wing joints into the boot (Photo 2-136). This will make it easier to put these three pieces together and keep the two wing joints aligned properly (Photo 2-137). After the two wing joints are all the way into the boot and lined up, then the joints may be locked into place. If the student is having difficulty inserting the joints, more lubrication is needed. Have the student apply more cork grease or Vaseline™. There must be plenty of lubricant in order to assemble the instrument. The student may twist the joints very slightly if necessary to insert the wing joints into the instrument. However, if there is enough lubricant, that may not be needed. After the wing joints are locked into place, the bell is

placed on the large wing joint. If you prefer to assemble the two wing joints separately, the small wing joint should be attached to the boot first. Be careful to line up the keys of the two wing joints as you insert the larger wing joint into the boot. Then, lock the two joints into position. The student should place his or her hand over the pad of the bell to lift the rod so the two joints will fit together properly without doing damage (Photo 2-138). While assembling the instrument, the student should avoid pushing or gripping too tightly the rods on the bassoon. They can bend and become out of adjustment.

The seat strap hooks into the bottom of the boot. Students should sit on the strap and have the instrument hanging down to their right. An excellent strap and often better than the strap that accompanies the instrument is one made from a belt and an S hook. This homemade   *Photo 2-137* strap is easy to manage, very inexpensive, and does not interfere with the player. One disadvantage of the commercial strap is that the cup of the strap often gets in the way of the key at the bottom of the boot.

The bocal is inserted after the seat strap is in position. It is inserted into the small wing joint. Line up the bocal with the whisper key (Photo 2-139). The whisper key is much like the octave key on the saxophone. It must be lined up in order for the mechanism to function properly. The bocal must not be pulled down when inserting it into the small wing joint. It is fragile and will bend very easily. When not playing, the bocal should be placed in the bell of the bassoon to keep it from being damaged.

The reed is inserted last. Many store-brand reeds are too small for the bocal. In that case, a reamer can be used to enlarge the opening of the reed. This tool can be purchased from music stores that supply reed-making equipment. Adjust the seat strap so the reed is at the student's lips. The student should not be looking up or down, but straight ahead when playing the bassoon (Photo 2-140).

Photo 2-138

Embouchure

Before attempting to play the bassoon, the student should play only the reed. First the teacher should demonstrate and explain how the reed is put into the mouth and how a sound is made. Have the student put his or her finger in the middle of the lower lip (Photo 2-141). The teacher should demonstrate this while explaining it to the student. Tell the student to lower the teeth and pucker (Photo 2-142). No smiling allowed. The top teeth should be over the reed, lips not rolled in, and the teeth should not touch the reed. The student should also drop the jaw to increase the cavity in the mouth (Photo 2-143). The jaw should be in a dropped, relaxed position as if saying the syllable "ooh." The student then holds the reed and blows. After the student is able to make the reed "crow," have the student put the reed on the bocal (Photo 2-144). The first note the student should play is E, third space, bass clef. This is an easy note to play while holding the bassoon.

Sitting Position

Posture is important for playing all musical instruments. Good posture for the bassoon is essential for both producing a good sound and seeing the conductor without the instrument or stand being in the way. The student should sit on the edge of the chair with the left leg forward and the right leg dropped back slightly (Photo 2-145). The bocal should not be put onto the instrument until the student is ready to play. The reed is then inserted and the strap is adjusted so the reed goes straight into the mouth. It should feel as though the reed is resting on the lower lip. The weight of the reed is on the lower lip.

Tonguing

The student should tongue the notes by having the tongue touch the tip of the reed. The tongue goes straight into the opening or the end of the reed. Do not tongue from below the reed. The syllable "tu" usually works with the tongue raised in the mouth. The student may think "ti" if that helps to raise the tongue. You should be careful, however,

Photo 2-139

if you are using "tu" and "ti" to signify rhythms. Tonguing exercises are not necessarily related to rhythmic exercises.

Breathing

Playing double reed instruments takes a great deal of air support. However, as with all instruments, it is best not to mention breathing on the first lesson. The student may be scared and nervous. After a few lessons, as the student becomes more comfortable with the instrument, the breathing will most likely become natural, and the student will breathe properly. If breathing problems continue, then during the fourth or fifth lesson, it may be necessary to discuss breathing. The student should breathe from the bottom, not the top, of the stomach, and not the chest. A deep fast gulp of air is the best and most efficient way to fill the lungs. If the student takes a slow breath, less air will fill the lungs and the student will most likely breathe more from the chest area than from the stomach. A good exercise for air support is to have the student hold a small

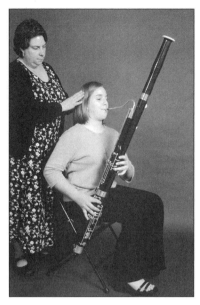

Photo 2-140

piece of paper, about 3 x 5 inches, with the first finger and thumb. Hold the paper at arm's length with the fingers extended to the wall, but the thumb and first finger pointed so the paper is pointed down. Then ask the student to pin the paper against the wall by blowing air directly toward the paper. It will take several tries before the student can accomplish this, but it does allow the student to see and feel how to direct the airstream, and blow with good air support. However, do this only when necessary. If the student is breathing correctly with good air support, do not try to correct something that does not need correcting. And definitely wait at least four lessons before discussing air support.

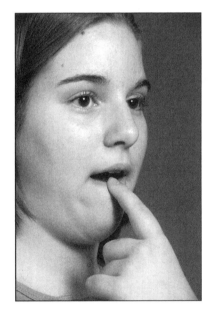

Photo 2-141

Beginning Lessons (Figs. 2-66 to 2-70)

This resource does not give you a detailed description of time management and steps for conducting each beginning bassoon lesson. The basic procedure is the same for all instruments. If you are required to have group lessons and you have only one bassoon player, you may have the bassoon player play along with the low brass or the alto saxophones. The low brass play in the same clef, but the alto saxophone part will transpose automatically to the bass clef by changing only the key signature. The beginning music lessons in the *Kit* are designed specifically for the bassoon and do not match either group exactly. The saxophone section transposes more closely to the bassoon than to the low brass. If you mix groups using the lessons presented here, the students will have to take turns playing. It is manageable, but you must keep track of time so you do not spend too much time with one group.

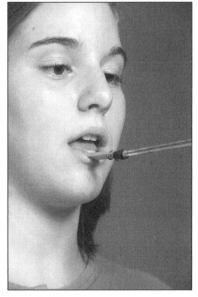

Photo 2-142

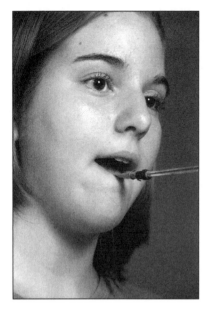

Photo 2-143. Embouchure.

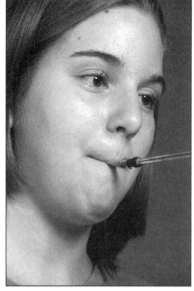

Photo 2-144. Embouchure.

Photo 2-145. Posture.

Hand Positions

Photos 2-146, 2-147, and 2-148 show the students where to place their hands and fingers on the bassoon. It is important that the student's hand reaches around the body of the bassoon so the side keys are not accidentally depressed while she/he is playing the instrument.

Photo 2-146

Photo 2-147

Photo 2-148

Figure 2-66—Music for Bassoon Lesson 1

Teach this lesson without showing the music to the student. Students should concentrate on producing a good sound. Attempting to read music will distract from all that is needed to produce a good sound.

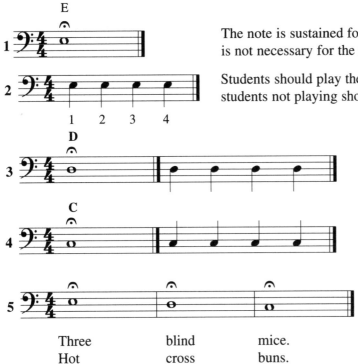

The note is sustained for a comfortable length of time. Counting is not necessary for the first note.

Students should play the note four times in a steady count. All students not playing should count out loud with the band director.

Follow the same procedure as above.

Follow the same procedure as above.

First song. Counting rhythms is not necessary the first time. A quick accomplishment is paramount.

Three   blind   mice.
Hot   cross   buns.

Mary Had a Little Lamb

ASSIGNMENT: First, hold each note, then play each note four times.
Play "Three Blind Mice."
Challenge: Who can play "Mary Had a Little Lamb" using the three notes learned today? Be positive; wish everyone a nice day.
BE ENTHUSIASTIC!

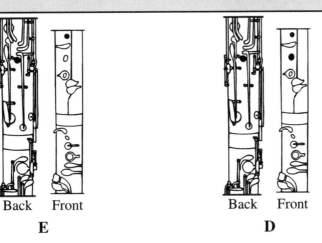

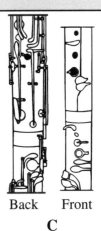

Back   Front   Back   Front   Back   Front

E   **D**   **C**

Figure 2-67
Music for Bassoon Lesson 2
Round One

Lookin' Down

Up and Down

A New One

Three in One

Mary Had a Little Lamb

Tap toes: one foot tap per beat. Start with toes up; heels anchored on floor. Practice tapping toes while playing every line.

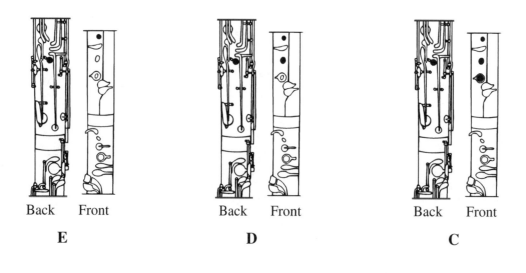

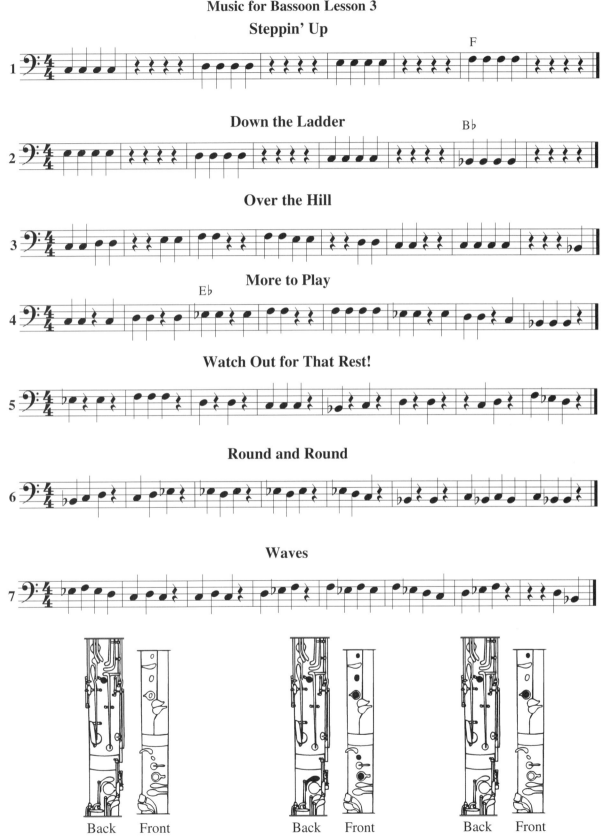

Figure 2-68
Music for Bassoon Lesson 3

Figure 2-69
Music for Bassoon Lesson 4

Golly G!

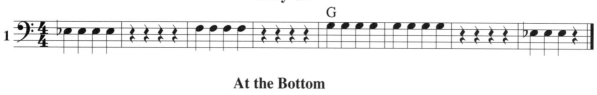

At the Bottom

Twice as Long

Say It Again

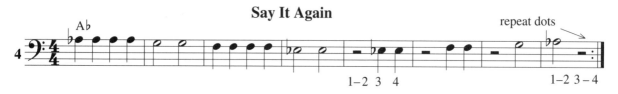

Hot Cross Buns

Go Tell Aunt Rhodie

Skippin' Around

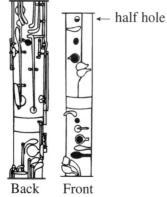

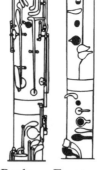

Figure 2-70
Music for Bassoon Lesson 5

Troubleshooting the Bassoon

PROBLEM	CAUSE	SOLUTIONS
Instrument will not play, or plays poorly	1. Poor quality instrument 2. Poor quality reed	(a) The instrument must be of good quality, in good playing condition. Selmer and Yamaha make good beginner instruments. Beware of cheap and unheard-of brands. And, regardless of brand, the instrument must be in a playing condition that makes it easy for a beginner to produce a sound. There is no point in teaching someone when the instrument will not play. (b) The reed must be in good playing condition. Old reeds must be replaced. Most reeds purchased in stores are not of good quality. A few suggested bassoon reeds are discussed in the Appendix under double reeds.
Low notes do not sound clear	1. Covering holes 2. Regulation of keys	(a) Make sure the student is completely covering the holes. A quick test: The teacher may hold his or her hand above the student's fingers. The teacher will be able to feel the air leaking. It is often very helpful to move the student's fingers into position so the holes are completely covered. Then the student can feel the sensation with his fingers, and hear the difference in the sound all at the same time. (b) Make sure all keys are opening and closing properly. (c) Check for springs in the correct position. (d) Water in keys. Blow out water. Check water in boot and small joint. (e) Make sure the embouchure is not too tight: Relax.
Gurgling	Water in instrument	Water in keys. Blow out water. Check water in boot and small joint. Check water in bocal.
Out of tune	Bocal	(a) Adjust bocal. (b) Make sure the reed is in good playing condition. (c) Air support. (d) Sing the notes before playing (this is extremely effective). Students must get used to hearing the notes in tune in the lower octave.
	Playing flat	(a) Put more reed in mouth. (b) Apply more pressure to the reed. (c) Lower head slightly. (d) Raise tongue in mouth. Make the shape of "ee" in mouth with tongue.
	Playing sharp	(a) Less reed in mouth. (b) Loose embouchure—less pressure on the reed. (c) Lower the jaw. (d) Raise head slightly.

All notes not clear	Air support	(a) Tell the student to blow harder.
		(b) If breathing incorrectly, then demonstrate breathing from the diaphragm. Use blow-paper exercise (see p. 241).
		(c) Do not oversoak the reed (3–5 minutes at the most).
		(d) For high notes, more air support (blow harder) and tighten the embouchure.
Octave displacement	1. Air support 2. Reed position	(a) All of the above. (b) Position of the reed on the lip. Low notes: in High notes: on tip of lip
Sound on ½ holes	Approach to playing	Rolling—do not lift fingers.
Finger dexterity	Hand position	(a) Fingers must reach around instrument. (b) Use the nail, not the knuckle, for thumb position.
High notes do not speak	Flicking	When playing the notes between and including A and D, the student should quickly flick the #2 key, as labeled in many fingering charts, or the flicking key (Fig. 2-71; Photo 2-148) just before the moment he or she wants the note to speak. Practicing the following exercise is **crucial** to the success of sound production in this register (Fig. 2-72). The flicking key is similar to an octave key on other woodwind instruments; however, the key is only flicked, not held down continuously. The key should be played quickly like a grace note, but faster.

Photo 2-148

Figure 2-71

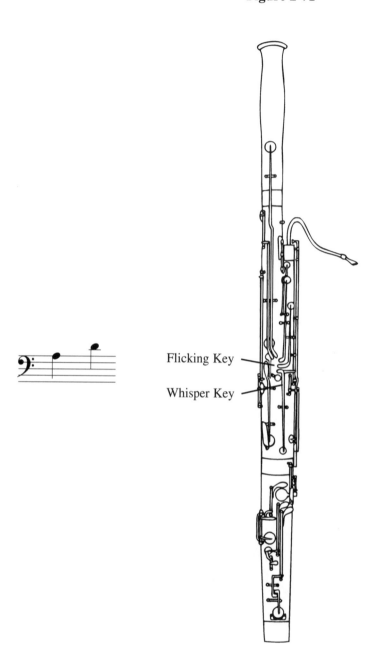

Flicking Key

Whisper Key

Figure 2-72
Flicking Key Exercise

*flick = quickly press and release the flicking key (see Fig. 2-71) just the moment before the note should speak. The note should be played as though it were a grace note, but played faster.

Bassoon Fingering Chart

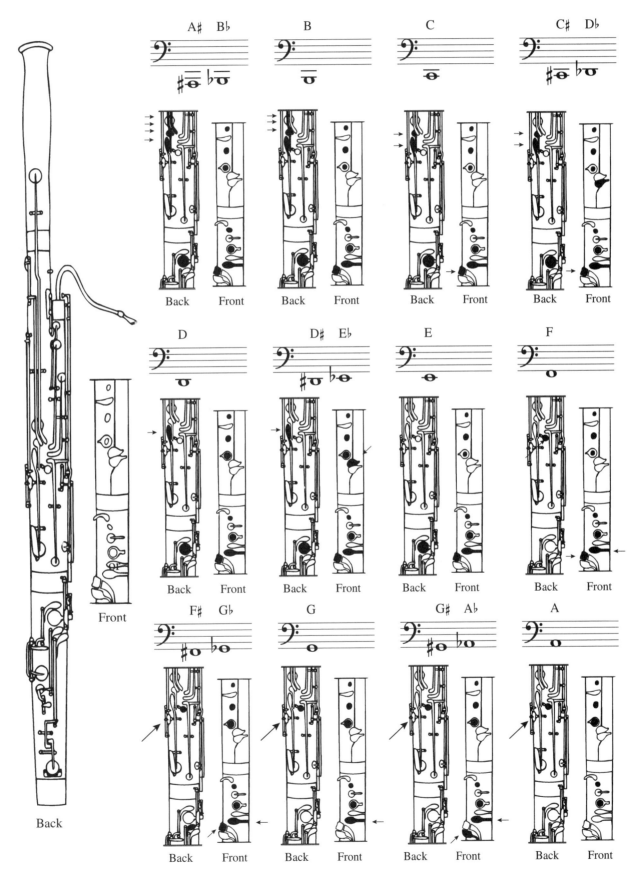

Bassoon Fingering Chart, p. 2

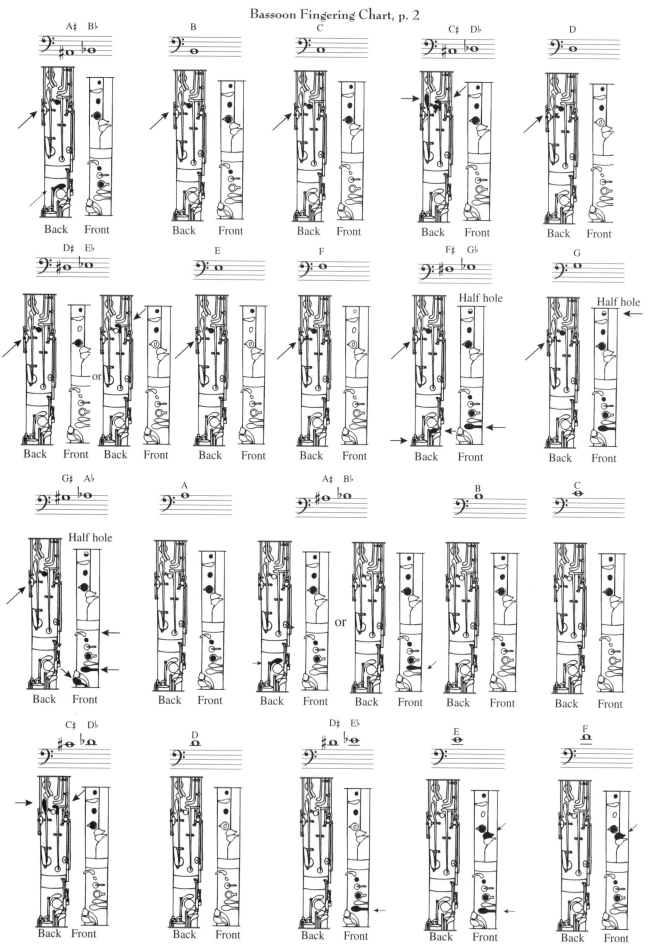

Bassoon Lessons Checklist

Lesson 1

☐ Choosing the right student to play bassoon
☐ What class to put bassoon in if only one player signs up and must have group lessons
☐ Chairs and stands in order
☐ Name tags on chairs
☐ Top of case
☐ How to open
☐ Moisten reed—3–5 minutes
☐ Cork grease
☐ Assembly
☐ Inspect instrument for quality/repair
☐ Posture
☐ Reed to lips without instrument
☐ Embouchure
☐ Reed to bocal
☐ First note: E
☐ Hand position
☐ Sitting position
☐ Tongue the note
☐ Play notes D and C
☐ First song: "Three Blind Mice"
☐ Instructions on how to practice
☐ Disassemble the instrument
☐ Specific assignment
☐ *Be Enthusiastic!*

Lesson 2

☐ Advanced students: Assemble instruments immediately
☐ While advanced are assembling instruments, show new students top of case
☐ Reed check for advanced students
☐ Review notes with advanced students
☐ Continue to show new students how to assemble their instruments
☐ Posture
☐ Advanced: Play "Three Blind Mice"
☐ New students: embouchure, then play E
☐ Advanced students start to play book, beginners follow along
☐ Show beginners D
☐ Advanced: Continue with book
☐ Show beginners C
☐ No book for beginners while playing
☐ Make sure advanced understand how to read the notes—no faking
☐ Only first page for advanced
☐ Beginners: Work on first three notes only
☐ Specific assignment
☐ *Be Enthusiastic!*

Lesson 3

☐ Advanced: Start assembling instruments
☐ New students: Start showing top of case and assembly while advanced students are assembling instruments, reviewing and playing their first notes
☐ Most advanced: Play lesson—reading notes—continue to Lesson 3
☐ Students who just played for the first time last week: Review notes
☐ Continue with beginners, as other students are playing their notes
☐ Keep reviewing all lessons
☐ Use baton/conduct
☐ Point to notes if students are not reading
☐ Have everyone follow along, even when not playing
☐ Posture
☐ Tonguing
☐ If the students are ready, start discussing intonation
☐ Specific assignment
☐ Notice their accomplishments and tell them how they have improved
☐ *Be Enthusiastic!*

Lesson 4

☐ If possible, reschedule new students
☐ Advanced students start assembling instruments as they enter the room
☐ Start showing the new students top of case and assembly
☐ As soon as tones are stabilized, start tuning the instruments
☐ Continue to instruct beginners as you teach the advanced
☐ Counting/toe tapping
☐ Playing the notes (advanced—reading the notes)
☐ Embouchure—Start to be more particular about skin tight against the chin
☐ Posture
☐ Show new notes and rhythms for next lesson
☐ Insist on practice
☐ Give specific assignment
☐ ***Enthusiasm!***

Lesson 5

☐ New students should be rescheduled
☐ Assemble instruments immediately
☐ If you must have new students, teach instrument assembly while teaching the other students
☐ Advanced students: intonation
☐ As advanced play, watch eyes to make sure they are reading
☐ Posture
☐ Tonguing
☐ Breathing in between notes
☐ Discuss chair positions
☐ Embouchure
☐ Try to move as many students as possible to the same page
☐ Keep everyone playing—no more than a 5-minute break for anyone at any time
☐ Specific assignment
☐ ***ENTHUSIASM!!***

## Part 3

Charts and Reports

Accountability is very important for all people involved with the music program. Accountability is not just for teachers, but also for parents and students. Requiring students to turn in practice slips and music report cards with parent signatures helps in evaluation and motivation. It also encourages the parents to be accountable for their child's practice. Using report cards and practice slips helps to keep the parents informed of their child's progress and the reasons for their success or failure. Using lesson charts or schedules helps keep the parents and teachers informed of the lesson day and times. Charts and tables can be a very effective way of keeping the band teacher, classroom teacher, parents, and students organized and informed of the student's progress.

Lesson Schedules

If you are in a situation where you must take students out of class, you may wish to use a rotating schedule such as that shown in Fig. 3-1. This schedule is not for purposes of evaluation, but to set up the lesson groups so a student does not miss the same class time every week he or she has a lesson. Parents and classroom teachers may argue that taking a student out of a class has a harmful effect on the child's schoolwork. However, if you use a rotating schedule, it will be several months before a student misses the same class time. The charts shown in Figs. 3-2 and 3-3 are without group assignments and times, respectively, and you may photocopy either or both charts and use them for your needs. If you have a large number of students and will give lessons all day, the chart in Fig. 3-4 will give you enough lesson times to set the schedule for the entire school day. Some schools may prefer a stationary schedule. In that case, make out a stationary schedule like that shown in Fig. 3-5. A lesson schedule should be given to every band student, teacher, and administrator in the school. Fig. 3-6 shows a blank stationary schedule.

Retrieving Students

When teaching group lessons during the school day, the instrumental teacher may need a quick way to collect missing students. One way to accomplish this is by using the form in Fig. 3-7. Make a list of names of students and have a student go to the classrooms and retrieve the missing students. The more efficient you appear to the classroom teachers, the more cooperation you will receive from them.

Practice Schedules

Students must practice to become successful instrument players. Requiring them to fill out their practice schedules not only encourages students to practice, but also allows parents to easily become involved in the practice time with their children. You may wish to write a note like that shown in Fig. 3-8 to the parents on the first day you hand out practice schedules. Explain the practice slip's purpose, procedures, and penalties for no signature, failure to return the practice slip, or not practicing. Encourage parents to help their child choose a practice time. A student is more likely to practice regularly if he or she practices at the same time every day. Thus, practice becomes routine and a habit. It is not a chore to practice in between other homework. Practicing an instrument is the most enjoyable part of homework a student may experience. Encourage parents to listen to their child play. They do not need to be in the room every minute their child practices. Listening from another room may be a very effective way for parents to monitor their child's practice. Afterwards, the parents may wish to compliment the child on his or her progress. Music teachers are aware of a child's progress each week and compliment and encourage further progress. If a parent takes the time necessary to listen to his or her child play, notices the improvement in tone, and lets the student know that the melodies are recognizable, this will be a great compliment to a young student trying very hard to play a musical instrument. Everyone needs to be rewarded for their efforts, especially young students. Any compliment will encourage a student to continue to play an instrument. The key to a student's success is having the parents involved with the student's practice and noticing and complimenting the student's accomplishments. Fig. 3-9 shows an example of practice records for the students. This may be photocopied and used in your school.

Test

Once students can control the instrument, they should be challenged to see who is the best player. This gives the teacher a chance to see how well each student is playing and encourages the students to play their best. Most likely, this will not take place until the sixth lesson or a little later. However, it is not necessary to wait months or even a year before capitalizing on the competitive spirit. Chair placement works as an incentive to practice, and the students enjoy seeing who is the best in the class. If you allow tryouts for chairs often, it will be an experience the students will look forward to. If possible, have a tryout for chairs before the beginning band concert.

The teacher's attitude sets the atmosphere for chair challenges. You want this to become a friendly challenge, not a vicious contest, in the effort to promote better musicians. If challenges happen often, with the teacher using them as an opportunity to correct mistakes and encourage progress, the students will feel good about these events.

New teachers are often worried about giving tests for chair placement, fearing their ability to judge correctly and the possibility of discouraging the students. However, having tryouts for chairs encourages everyone to practice more. The teacher's ability to listen carefully, judge tone, and correct notes and rhythms is far better than the student's. A teacher can count the number of missed notes and rhythms, and award points for good tones, to make the challenge more objective if he or she is worried about exact accountability. You may consider using the "Performance Judging Sheet" shown in Figure 3-10 as a basic guide for testing and scoring students for grades and chair positions. There may be times you wish to make copies of this chart and have the students make evaluations of performances. Before going to a band contest, make a recording of the band playing one of the compositions. Hand out the evaluation sheets, and have the students score the performance as they listen to the recording. This will help the students hear their own mistakes and greatly improve the contest or concert performance.

Figure 3-11 provides a very effective tool to encourage students to play well enough to perform in the concert. It gives the students a minimum requirement to participate. Award a maximum of four points per composition. Select certain sections of each piece to be played for the test. Require that a student score half of the total maximum points in order to perform with the band in the concert. The student must be able to play at least some of the music very well. If the teacher chooses music with a variety of very easy and somewhat challenging songs, a child will perform in the concert even if he or she can hardly play the most difficult compositions. As long as a child is practicing and trying, he or she will be able to perform in the concert. For example, if there are seven songs to be performed in a concert, a student could score a four on the first song, a four on the second song, a three on the third song, a two on the fourth song, a one on the fifth song, and so on. The maximum possible score is 28. As long as the total score adds up to 14, the student may play in the concert.

This also allows for accountability. The parent can see the progress, or lack thereof, as the preparation for the concert begins. You may require that the parent initial the paper after every test. Then, at the time of the concert, if the child has not been practicing or cannot play any of the songs, and you wish to have that student sit out the concert, the parent cannot accuse you of having given him or her no warning. This may sound like a negative reinforcement, but it is actually a very positive form of encouragement for the students.

Report Cards

Reports cards are not simply tools of measurement and progress, but also tools of encouragement and a means for conveying concern about areas that need attention. Many school report cards only allow for a letter grade or a satisfactory or unsatisfactory. This tells the child and the parent very little. It is important to give grades to band students, and it is important to follow the school's procedures for grades. However, a good report card is designed specifically to help students know their strengths and weaknesses. If you decide to design your own report card or use the report card given in Fig. 3-12, it will be most effective if you have it distributed with the regular report cards at your school. If the teacher gives the band report cards to the students in the band room or at lessons, they will not have the same meaning and effect as they have when they go out with the regular school report cards. Make arrangements ahead of time with the principal to give the report cards to the office so they can be distributed during students' homeroom class or whenever report cards are distributed at your school. This will impress your administrator, and show that you are organized and concerned with the achievement of your students. Also, many principals and the homeroom teacher will be interested to see how the students are doing in band class. The report cards should be returned to the homeroom teacher and then to the band director. This adds to the prestige of the band class and gives further accountability to the students and parents.

Figure 3-1

G. Washington Elementary Band Schedule

DATE	9/6	9/13	9/20	9/27	10/4	10/11	10/18	10/25
8:30	A	G	F	E	D	C	B	A
9:00	B	A	G	F	E	D	C	B
9:30	C	B	A	G	F	E	D	C
10:00	D	C	B	A	G	F	E	D
10:30	E	D	C	B	A	G	F	E
11:00	F	E	D	C	B	A	G	F
11:30	G	F	E	D	C	B	A	G

GROUP A
beginning flutes:
Mary Willis – 4
John Bryant – 4
Jill Smith – 5
Bryan Jones – 5

GROUP B
beginning drums:
Tommy Eubanks – 4
Billy Jones – 4
Maria Johnson – 5

GROUP C
advanced clarinets:
Cynthia McCool – 6
Mary McGill – 7
Robert Parker – 7
Jane Willard – 8
Mollie Navarre – 5

GROUP D
beginning saxes:
Tony Collins – 5
Bret Williams – 4
Samantha Reading – 4
Otis Miller – 5

GROUP E
advanced brass:
Mark Beams – 6
Bradley Jones – 7
Ashley Anton – 8
Bruce Tate – 5

GROUP F
beginning brass:
Phillip Walker – 4
Corey Miller – 5
Caitlin Bruce – 4

GROUP G
beginning clarinets:
Neal Green – 4
Paula Landry – 4
Rita Milano – 5
Billy Abato – 5
Travis Kenner – 6
Diane Welsh – 7

Figure 3-2

Band Schedule

DATE:								
8:30								
9:00								
9:30								
10:00								
10:30								
11:00								
11:30								

Figure 3-3

Band Schedule

DATE:								

Figure 3-4

Band Schedule

Figure 3-5

George Washington Elementary School
Stationary Band Schedule

8:00	Band Rehearsal
8:30	Beginning Flutes
9:00	Beginning Saxes
9:30	Advanced Flutes
10:00	Beginning Drums
10:30	Advanced Brass
11:00	Beginning Clarinets
11:30	Advanced Clarinets and Saxes
12:00	Beginning Brass
12:30	Lunch
1:00	Advanced Drums

Beginning Flutes
Melissa McDaniels – 4
Mollie McGee – 4
Matthew James – 5

Beginning Saxes
Travis Boone – 4
Bryan Sheppard – 5

Advanced Flutes
Jim Buchannan – 6
Mike Mancuso – 5
Diane Cheney – 6
Melinda Clavelle – 7

Beginning Drums
Tony Hillard – 5
Matt Navarre – 4

Advanced Brass
Caitlin Howard – 6
Jason Matte – 7
Nicholas Castillo – 5
Susan Ryan – 6
Anne Kneeles – 8

Beginning Clarinets
Cindy Kendall – 4
Chelsea Trahan – 5

Advanced Clar. and Saxes
Robert Jones – 6
Randy Snyder – 7
James Byrd – 6
Neal Green – 8

Beginning Brass
Josh Hegvik – 4
Emily Nevick – 5
Amanda Newly – 4
Nora Lamer – 5

Advanced Drums
Ashley Clouser – 7
Molly McCarter – 8
Billy Carter – 6
Amy Zackery – 5

Figure 3-6

Stationary Band Schedule

8:00

8:30

9:00

9:30

10:00

10:30

11:00

11:30

12:30

1:00

1:30

2:00

2:30

3:00

3:30

Figure 3-7

Dear Classroom Teacher: date: _____

Please permit the following students to attend their band lesson now in progress.

1.

2.

3.

4.

5.

6.

7.

8.

Thank you very much for your cooperation.
Sincerely,

Band Director

Dear Classroom Teacher: date: _____

Please permit the following students to attend their band lesson now in progress.

1.

2.

3.

4.

5.

6.

7.

8.

Thank you very much for your cooperation.
Sincerely,

Band Director

Dear Classroom Teacher: date: _____

Please permit the following students to attend their band lesson now in progress.

1.

2.

3.

4.

5.

6.

7.

8.

Thank you very much for your cooperation.
Sincerely,

Band Director

Dear Classroom Teacher: date: _____

Please permit the following students to attend their band lesson now in progress.

1.

2.

3.

4.

5.

6.

7.

8.

Thank you very much for your cooperation.
Sincerely,

Band Director

Figure 3-8

Dear Parent:

I am very pleased your child has signed up for the band this year. This should be a fun year in band.

In order for anyone to be successful playing a musical instrument, practice is essential. Enclosed with this letter is a practice slip. Your child's practice time should be recorded each day. If your child does not practice on a particular day, then put a 0 in that box. I expect everyone to practice five days a week with a minimum of thirty minutes per day. That is a total of 2½ hours per week. There will be no benefit if your child tries to practice the entire 2½ hours in one day, and does not practice the rest of the week. One of the purposes of practicing is to develop the muscles needed to play a musical instrument. Only through daily practice will those muscles become strong enough to sustain a good sound on the instrument and maintain a steady rhythm.

I need your cooperation in this matter. Please encourage and require your child to practice daily. A student is more likely to practice if it is a daily routine. Ask your child what time he or she would like to practice. Once your child has picked a practice time, he or she should stick to it. Pretty soon, this will become a routine, and hopefully, you may not have to remind him or her to practice.

The students receive grades for participating in the band. A major portion of the grade comes from practice schedules. Students are required to practice and turn in their practice slips each week. The practice slip must be signed by a parent or guardian in order to be accepted. If your child does not have it signed or forgets the practice slip, he or she will receive a 0 for the homework grade. It would not take very many missed practice slips to seriously affect your child's band grade. Please help us in this matter by requiring your child to practice, and by signing his or her practice schedule each week.

You may further encourage your child to practice by occasionally listening to him or her practice. Notice the improvement. If you hear the tone improve, or the melodies become clearer, mention it. Let your child know you are paying attention, you can hear improvement, and you care.

Thank you, and have a good year.

Sincerely,

Band Director

Figure 3-9

Student's Name _____ Week ending _____

	Sunday	Monday	Tuesday	Wednesday	Thursday	Friday	Saturday
# of minutes							

Required number of minutes to practice _____ Total number of minutes practiced _____

Parent's Signature _____

Student's Name _____ Week ending _____

	Sunday	Monday	Tuesday	Wednesday	Thursday	Friday	Saturday
# of minutes							

Required number of minutes to practice _____ Total number of minutes practiced _____

Parent's Signature _____

Student's Name _____ Week ending _____

	Sunday	Monday	Tuesday	Wednesday	Thursday	Friday	Saturday
# of minutes							

Required number of minutes to practice _____ Total number of minutes practiced _____

Parent's Signature _____

Student's Name _____ Week ending _____

	Sunday	Monday	Tuesday	Wednesday	Thursday	Friday	Saturday
# of minutes							

Required number of minutes to practice _____ Total number of minutes practiced _____

Parent's Signature _____

Student's Name _____ Week ending _____

	Sunday	Monday	Tuesday	Wednesday	Thursday	Friday	Saturday
# of minutes							

Required number of minutes to practice _____ Total number of minutes practiced _____

Parent's Signature _____

Figure 3-10

Performance Judging Sheet

Name of Group _____

Song Performed _____

Date of Performance _____

School _____ Date _____

Evaluation Code:
- 4 = played perfectly
- 3 = played with very few mistakes
- 2 = played with some mistakes
- 1 = played with many mistakes
- 0 = played almost entirely wrong

	Category	4	3	2	1	0	Score
1.	Melody (right notes)						
2.	Intonation (in tune with each other)						
3.	Rhythm						
4.	Dynamics (loud and soft at the right times)						
5.	Tone Quality						
6.	Ensemble (playing together)						
7.	Articulation (tonguing and slurring)						
8.	Balance (for group performance)						
9.	Phrasing (breathing in proper places)						
10.	Smoothness						
11.	Follows the conductor (group performance)						
12.	Emotional response (played with feeling)						
13.	Tempo (too fast or too slow or just right)						
14.	Behavior (stage and performance behavior)						
15.	Audibility (able to hear the notes)						
16.	Posture						

Grand Total _____

Student grading this performance

_____

Figure 3-11

Concert Checklist

CONCERT DATE: _____

To have a really great concert, every person in the entire BAND must do his or her part well. It is up to you to practice your part and contribute to our BAND TEAM effort. You must score at least _____ points to perform in the concert. _____ points is a perfect score.

RATING SYSTEM

4–Perfect Musicianship (notes, rhythms, articulations, dynamics all followed exactly)

3–Good Musicianship (mostly right notes & rhythms, some missed dynamics, phrasing, or articulations)

2–Average Musicianship (some mistakes in notes or rhythms, phrasing, articulations, but not very many)

1–Poor Musicianship (many wrong notes and rhythms)

0–No effort, did not take test or put forth any effort in practice

Song	Test Date	Test Measures	What I Learned in This Song	Points	Parent's Initials

Final Points _____

Student's Name _____

May Perform in the Concert: _____ Yes _____ No

Parent's Signature: _____

Figure 3-12

Band Report Card

Marking Period _____

Name _____ Grade _____ Instrument _____

TONAL RATING (teacher: circle one)
4. Performs correct notes and good intonation
3. Performs with most notes correct, intonation fair
2. Performs with some pitches correct, poor intonation
1. Most pitches incorrect, very poor intonation

TONGUING (teacher: circle one)
4. Uses the tongue consistently and at the right time to separate notes
3. Uses the tongue most of the time when the music indicates tonguing
2. Uses the tongue only occasionally when the music indicates tonguing
1. Never uses the tongue; slurs all notes all the time

CONNECTING NOTES (teacher: circle one)
4. Connects notes smoothly, even when tonguing, all of the time
3. Connects notes smoothly most of the time
2. Connects notes smoothly some of the time
1. Plays very choppily; needs to practice on making a smooth connection in between notes

RHYTHM RATING (teacher: circle one)
4. Performs with correct rhythmic patterns and keeps a steady tempo
3. Performs with most rhythmic patterns correctly, but does not necessarily keep a consistent tempo
2. Performs some rhythms correctly
1. Unable to perform most rhythmic patterns correctly

POSTURE (teacher: circle one)
2. Student sits with good posture: sitting up straight, feet flat on the floor, back is not touching the chair while playing; percussion: standing up straight, feet slightly apart, hands and arms relaxed just above drum or bells
1. Student's posture is poor; see number 2 for good posture

HAND POSITIONS (teacher: circle one)
2. Student uses the correct hand position (stick position for drums and bells)
1. Student does not use the correct hand position

EXPRESSION RATING (teacher: write yes or no, or D for developing)
____ Performs with good tone quality
____ Uses dynamics (plays loudly and softly at the appropriate times)
____ Performs with appropriate phrasing (proper articulation and breathing)
____ Plays expressively and musically

CONDUCT AND ATTENDANCE RATING
(teacher: write yes or no or appropriate number)
____ Demonstrates appropriate behavior (if not, the student's conduct must improve in order to stay in the band)
____ Has good attendance for lessons
____ Has good attendance for rehearsals
____ Is on time to lessons
____ Is on time to rehearsals
____ Brings instrument to class
____ No. of lessons missed
____ No. of rehearsals missed
____ No. of times late to lessons
____ No. of times late to rehearsals
____ No. of times forgot to bring instrument to class

PREPARATION/MUSICAL INDEPENDENCE RATING (teacher: circle all that apply)
4. Learns music independently, with little or no help from the teacher
3. Learns music independently, with some help from the teacher
2. Prepares assigned music
1. Prepares some of the assigned music
0. Prepares little or none of the assigned music; must teach every note of every song, cannot carry one learning experience to another composition

COMPOSITE GRADE _____

(Continue on next page for comments and parent signature)

Figure 3-12 (cont.)

TEACHER'S COMMENTS:

PARENT'S COMMENTS:

PARENT'S SIGNATURE _____ **DATE** _____

Please return to the classroom teacher next week with parent signature and date. Thank you.

Band Director

## Part 4

Conducting

....

Whether you are teaching the entire band or just group lessons, your ability to convey music through your baton and hands will have a major impact on the success of the band program at your school. Conducting is an important part of teaching.

The two major methods of conducting are with a baton and without a baton, using only the hands for cues and gestures. When teaching very young students, I would suggest using a baton. A baton clearly defines the beat. It is not necessary to describe conducting patterns during the first few lessons; just the mere fact that you are indicating every beat will be helpful to the students. You are presenting them with a visual location where each beat begins. One may do this with the hands, but based on my own experience and preference, I have found it easier to convey the beat to young students using a baton.

Conducting should begin in the first lesson. When the student plays his or her first note, conduct it as though a fermata is written over the note. If you do not have a baton in your hands at that time, use your hands to gesture when to start the note and when to end it. By doing this, you will give the student a clear signal to get ready and play the note, and you may cut it off before the student starts to lose control of the pitch. Thus, you have helped the student be more successful on his or her very first attempt to play, and you are already getting the student used to following a conductor. After each student in the class has played the first note, use the baton when all the students play together. This will be fun for the students, and they will experience playing as an ensemble.

As the students progress further and start playing songs from the book, conduct their playing using the correct conducting patterns (Fig. 4-1). Though you may not feel the need to describe the conducting patterns to them, it may be beneficial to let the students know where the down beat is regardless of the number of beats in a measure. Tell the students every time your baton goes straight down, that marks the first beat of the measure. If a student is unsure of the note, or rhythm, at least he or she will have a place where he or she can rejoin the entire group. As the students progress further and feel comfortable with playing the notes on a page, you may then describe your conducting pattern.

One very important technique in conducting, regardless of age group, is to have a stable *ictus plane* (see Fig. 4-1). This is a plane that the baton does not cross when indicating the beats of the measure. When the ictus plane is not stable, the band director may be as guilty of losing time as the people he is conducting.

Figure 4-1

Conducting Patterns

Four-beat pattern

Three-beat pattern

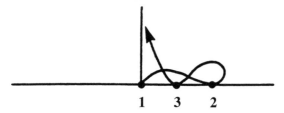

Five-beat pattern (3 + 2)

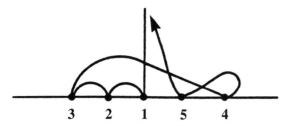

Six-beat pattern

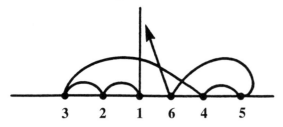

Seven-beat pattern (4 + 3)

Subdivided fourth beat

Two-beat pattern

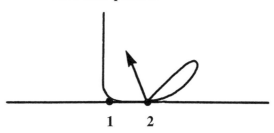

Five-beat pattern (2 + 3)

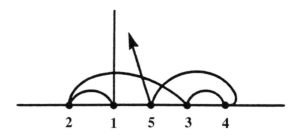

Seven-beat pattern (3 + 4)

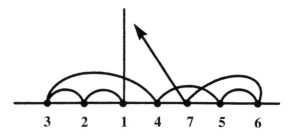

Any variation is acceptable.
For young musicians, a consistent ictus
plane will be very helpful in maintaining a
steady beat.

Cuing is extremely important to beginning students. Even in group lessons, cue the notes, gesture for the rests, and help the students in any way you can. Remember, as discussed previously in this resource, the students are scared. They want and need your help. If your gestures are clear, and you cue when to play and when not to play, you may help them avoid being embarrassed and give them a more enjoyable experience. However, you must also be careful that you are not so clear and always so helpful that the students can get away without reading the music. Watch the students' eyes. If you see a student who is not looking at the page, but only your baton or other students' hands, walk over to that person's stand, and point to the notes with your baton as everyone is playing. It is not necessary to call attention to this person. Simply walk over, point to the notes, and as soon as the student starts to follow the notes and understands what you are doing, resume conducting the entire class. In these early stages, it is a good idea to count out loud so the students hear the beat as well as see it in your conducting.

There are many good conducting books that demonstrate just about every possible variation on conducting any variety of ensemble. Anyone serious about becoming a great conductor should have at least one of these books. This resource provides examples of conducting patterns of the more common time signatures experienced by conducting students in their first year or two of teaching. The one critically important thing is to make every beat very clear so the students always can see your beat and follow it. When teaching beginning band, your primary role as conductor is to help the students as much as possible, keep them playing together, and allow them to enjoy the music. The more aware you are of time, meter, and where every student is in the music, the better the band will sound and the more musically the students will play.

Conducting technique becomes a particular style and signature of every conductor. Every conductor should be expressive and try to bring out as much emotion as possible in the members of the ensemble. However, a simple pattern is the best for young students. Conducting with extra beats and subdivided patterns may confuse the students. If a teacher does this too often for beginning students, they may become too reliant on these gestures for the rhythms. In some cases, it may be so confusing that the students just start to ignore the conductor. This is not to say that one should never subdivide a beat, or indicate a particular rhythm when conducting. However, doing this sparingly may be more effective than "spoonfeeding" every note and rhythm to your students.

As the students progress as young musicians, and you have prepared them to follow you, you will find that your every gesture is important. You will be able to indicate playing softly just by making small smooth gestures with your baton alone. Small but strong, pointed gestures will cause the students to play loudly. This revelation will occur one day when you are conducting and you get a little twitch in your hand. As a result, you will strike a beat a little harder than you meant to, and the band will respond with a much louder, crisper note than you expected. The students will follow you, so be aware that your gestures are critical to your performance. Get the students used to following you from the earliest stages, and not only will they be better musicians, but it will be easier to save a performance when suddenly someone gets lost and a whole section is in the wrong place. If students are used to watching you, they will look up, and you can quickly get them back together before the audience knows anything is wrong.

## Part 5

Surviving the Beginning Band Concert

Performing a beginning band concert as soon as possible is crucial for retaining interest in the band and retaining students in your program. The first concert may be a simple performance of songs from the beginner book. Stock arrangements are not necessary for this concert. As soon as the students can play the first half of the beginner book, they are ready to perform.

The beginning band concert is designed to be educational for the parents as well as a reward for the students' hard work and progress on their instruments. Also, there will be some students who have lost interest in playing their instruments and may be ready to quit the band. There is something special about getting up on the stage with your friends, producing music, sounding good, and getting a great round of applause from very enthusiastic parents. The result may be that many of the students who were going to quit will change their minds because it is now fun, and they want to continue playing their instruments and performing.

For the first concert, you may decide to use the concert presented on pages 279–288 of this resource, or you may choose to use songs from the beginning band method book. The first song played by the band does not have to be a familiar tune. Many contemporary methods have put a name to every line in the book. This is important because it allows the exercises to be more fun for the students, and it can sometimes indicate what is being taught in that lesson or particular line. It is also very convenient for performance purposes. The reason for choosing the first line in the book is because it is the easiest "song" for the students to perform. There is only one note to play, and everyone has the same rhythms at the same time. After the applause has died down from performing the first song, explain to the parents the accomplishment involved in performing this very simple song. You may tell the parents, "Though this sounded very easy, believe me, it did not sound this well the first day we tried it." (There may be chuckles in the audience when you say this. Do not interrupt the audience's laughter. Let them finish and then continue.) "There are several factors in learning to play an instrument. The students not only had to learn what note to play, but when to play it. There are dots and wiggly lines that instruct the students when and what to play. So the students are having to learn a new language as well as play an instrument for the first time in their lives. And that is not all. In addition to learning what and when to play, they have to learn to play it together. So, in addition to looking at the book, holding the instrument, and trying to play the right notes at the right time, they also have to watch the conductor all at the same time in order to play together. And, as if that is not enough, we have to learn to play in tune. Just pushing the buttons will not necessarily make the notes we play sound the same. The students have to learn to listen to each other so they can match the pitches by tightening or loosening their lips so the notes have the correct sound. So, as you can see, there is much more to playing an instrument than just pushing buttons, hitting a drumhead, and blowing air into an instrument. It takes concentration and discipline to make a song sound good and sound easy." The parents probably have never thought of it in that manner. After this has been explained to them, they will have a higher respect for what their own children are accomplishing. Also, because the song was easy, you have just built up the confidence in the students. They played their first song, and it sounded good. The students are feeling good about themselves, and they are beginning to have confidence that this is going to be a good concert.

The next song should be a very simple tune. In the concert provided here, I have selected a song similar to the second line of the second lesson, "Up and Down." It involves only two notes and it is warming them up for their first real song. After the students perform "Up and Down," or the second song from the book, explain to the parents that the students have now learned to read more notes, and they must move their fingers in order to play the right note at the right time. "The students are developing coordination while having fun playing music."

Usually, the third song the students play may be "Mary Had a Little Lamb." Before the students play the song, explain to the parents that the students have learned three notes and a rest, so they can now play a "very famous song" we have all heard before. You may wish to ask the parents if they can name the tune after the students play it. This provides for audience involvement and is more fun for everyone. A formal concert, where the conductor says nothing during the entire concert, is not ideal for this situation. The audience wants to hear from you. You will make the concert more interesting as well as increase the parents' appreciation for the children's accomplishments. If you get the audience involved, it will be more fun for everyone, and the students will relax and play better.

After "Mary Had a Little Lamb," have the students play solos, duets, trios, or quartets. They may pick any song from the book, or any source they wish. The director should audition the students' songs, to make sure they can play them well enough to stand in front of an audience and play them. It is not necessary that they play perfectly, but you should make sure that they play well enough not to be embarrassed in front of their parents. Students may wish to play the same line together. Even though the students are playing unison, that is acceptable. Going out in front of an audience and showing off to their parents and friends can be the biggest morale booster some of these children may ever have. Give them this moment. It will lengthen your concert while giving the band a chance to rest before playing the next song. If you have a huge beginning band, you may have to limit the number of solos and ensembles. You should limit the students to four solos or ensembles between the songs the band plays. For the sake of variety, tell the students that they may pick any song except those the band is performing.

After the first group of solos and ensembles, have the band play another song together. It is advisable to pick something that is very easy but involves all the notes they have learned in the first two to three lessons. The concert included in this resource uses the song, "Over the Hill." This song starts on an easy note and moves stepwise up to the highest note, and then back down. It is easy, and allows the parents to hear all the new notes they have learned. It also allows the parents to hear the progress in which one learns to play a musical instrument. When introducing this song, inform the parents what is involved in playing it. It is up to the band director to educate the audience on the accomplishment of their children.

After the band has played "Over the Hill," allow more solos or ensembles to be performed. Introduce each student and announce the name of the song. Do not keep the audience guessing, especially since many of the songs from the beginner books are exercises and not familiar songs.

The next song should still be easy, but maybe a little bit trickier. Most beginning books will have a song with a rest that changes positions in the measure. This is important, because you want to keep the children counting. In the song, "Watch Out for That Rest!," if the students do not count, someone will play an unintentional solo. Announce to the parents that the next song is a bit trickier than the previous songs the band has played. "It is very important that students know when not to play as well as when to play. When not to play is indicated by what musicians call 'a rest.' In the next song, everyone plays together, but the rest is not always where we may expect it to be. If we do this right, we will play as an ensemble. If we goof, there may be an unexpected soloist." And this solo could very well take place in the concert. Practice this line often enough so the students know what to expect. Also, your conducting gestures will pull them through this song together. Your concern is not how you look to the audience. Your job is to get the students through the concert playing as well as possible, so if big gestures are needed to show when to play, and small gestures to show when not to play, use them. Gesture in such a way that the band can easily follow you. And, if a student gets nervous and plays in a rest, it is not a big deal. The audience will give him or her an extra big round of applause for trying. The point of this song, however, is to keep the music progressing in an orderly and slightly more difficult pattern to the end of the concert.

After this song has been performed, allow more students to play solos or ensembles. Two to four such performances between band songs is an adequate break for the band.

Before playing the next song with the entire band, discuss with the parents what new accomplishments the students had to learn before they could perform the next song. "So far, the students have learned to play several different notes and have played several songs, but all the rhythms have been the same. In order to play the next song, they had to learn to see and play notes that last twice as long as the notes and rests they had played before. Also, the students had to learn to read a symbol that means to play the entire song again, called repeat dots. So, now your children are looking at a page with all kinds of symbols meaning to hold notes and rests for one or two beats, and to play a song again. At the same time, they are tapping their toes, pushing and lifting fingers, listening to each other, and watching the director. They are doing a lot of things in order to make music for you, and the wonderful thing is, they are making it sound easy." Usually the next song to play is "Hot Cross Buns." You may choose to introduce it before or after the band plays.

Allow a few more students to play solos and ensembles after the completion of the previous song. It is a good idea to have different instruments play between the band songs. You do not want the parents comparing sounds of one flute player to another. Have a saxophone student play a song, then a flute, then trumpet, and so on. It will keep a variety of instruments in sight, and prevent parents or students from realizing that one student plays better than another.

A familiar song in most books is Beethoven's "Ode to Joy." The students like this song, and because the notes all progress stepwise, it is very easy to play. You may, of course, choose any song from the beginner book, but it would be advisable to choose a song that is easy, sounds familiar, and continues to build confidence in the students.

Continue to have more solos and ensembles after each song. A good program plan will have the students who play well play their solos first, then the weaker students play their songs in the middle of the concert, and the best students play last. The overall impression of the concert will be much better. First impressions are very important, but people also remember best what they heard last. So, give them a good first impression, and save the very best for last. At the end of the concert, the parents may declare you a miracle worker.

The next song you may choose to play is one a little longer with more skips or leaps in the intervals. Students love to play "Jingle Bells." Even if it is not Christmas, the students enjoy playing this song. It is easy and familiar to everyone. You may wish to explain to parents that playing this song involves longer notes and a longer song, so more concentration is needed to perform it.

The final song of the concert usually involves some harmony. Most of the contemporary methods have some very good beginning band arrangements throughout the book. If your students are ready for such an arrangement, you may wish to program it. However, if they are not ready, play a simple duet such as "London Bridge."

At some point during the concert, be sure to acknowledge the cooperation of the principal, teachers, staff, custodian, parents, students, and anyone else who may have helped you during the school year and in the planning of this concert. Let the students know how proud you are of them. At the end of the concert, have the students stand and take a bow. Get out of the way so the parents may take pictures.

Do not wait until the end of the school year to perform this concert. Perform as soon as possible. The longer you wait for the beginning band concert, the more students will drop out of the band. The students do not have to play perfectly. However, they should play well. If you have been tuning the students at every lesson and rehearsal, they will play fairly well in tune during the concert. When rehearsing, if you have demanded that they play together, and worked on ensemble performance, they will play well. As soon as the students can perform, play this concert. Then perform as often as possible. Ask your principal if you may start assemblies with the band playing a song. You do not want to take up a lot of time— just have the band seated at the bottom of the stage, play one song, and return to the audience. The exposure will be a great morale booster, and it is a great recruiting tool.

Conductor
Concert pitch/percussion

First Concert
PREMIERE SONG

UP AND DOWN

MARY HAD A LITTLE LAMB

OVER THE HILL

WATCH OUT FOR THAT REST!

HOT CROSS BUNS

Conductor
Concert pitch/percussion

ODE TO JOY

JINGLE BELLS

LONDON BRIDGE
(DUET)

sus. cymbal

B♭ Instruments   **First Concert**
(Clarinets, T. Sax, Trumpets, TC Baritone)

E♭ Instruments
(E♭ Saxophones & E♭ Clarinets)

First Concert

PREMIERE SONG

UP AND DOWN

MARY HAD A LITTLE LAMB

OVER THE HILL

`WATCH OUT FOR THAT REST!

HOT CROSS BUNS

ODE TO JOY

JINGLE BELLS

LONDON BRIDGE
(DUET)

C Instruments
(Trombones/Baritones/Bassoons) 𝄢: **First Concert**

Tuba   **First Concert**

## Part 6

Band Method
Review

....

This section offers a short review of some of the contemporary band method books on the market today. It is not an attempt to review all methods currently available. The methods listed below are methods with which the author is familiar and which he recommends. There is no rule that a teacher must start with one band method and continue with it all the way through the band's development or studies. You may find it very effective to use Book I by one publisher, Book II by another, and the supplementary series of another. A band method is a tool by which the teacher instructs the students how to play an instrument. The band method may make the process of teaching easier for the instructor, but it is the creativity, knowledge, and understanding of how to play and teach the instruments that will make the teacher a success. The following methods are listed in alphabetical order by title.

Accent on Achievement, by John O'Reilly and Mark Williams (Van Nuys, CA: Alfred Publishing Company, 1997).

This method is presented in a very colorful book that uses graphics to indicate new musical instructions. Color photographs give good examples of students playing their instruments utilizing good posture and embouchure. Brass instruments start on concert D and play up to Concert F in the first pages of the book. There are lots of fun songs and arrangements by the authors. Books I, II, and III are now available. A *Teacher's Resource Kit* is available for Books I and II. The kits contain flash cards, CDs, fact sheets on composers, worksheets and more. Alfred Publishing Company has a broad range of band arrangements and theory methods to supplement studies.

Belwin 21st Century Band Method, by Jack Bullock and Anthony Maiello (Belwin-Mills Publishing Corp., 1996). Administered by Warner Bros. Publ., Miami, FL.

Here is a band method that uses the latest technology available as of the printing of this resource. In addition to using color on all the pages of each book, it is accompanied by a very good video of how to assemble and play each instrument and CDs and cassettes of the music. The entire band method is available for

SmartMusic™ by Coda Music Technology. The first notes in Book I start with concert D and move up to concert F. All three methods contain both classical and popular songs in full band arrangements that are familiar to most students.

Essential Elements 2000, by Tim Lautzenheiser, John Higgins, Charles Menghini, Paul Lavender, Tom Rhodes, and Don Bierschenk (Milwaukee, WI: Hal Leonard Corp., 1999).

Essential Elements is the only method that comes with a CD included in the price of the book. It is also one of the few methods that starts with quarter notes rather than whole notes. The flutes start their first note with an F and brass instruments start with a G and work down the scale. The book does contain full band arrangements that may be used in concerts. Book II uses some of the Rubank® studies and solos. *Essential Elements* continues its studies with an excellent technique book that works with scales and other technical developments.

Now Go Home and Practice, by Jim Probasco, David Grable, and Dan Meeks (Dayton, OH: Heritage Music Press, A Division of the Lorenz Corporation, 1994).

I love this title! It does not necessarily make students go home and practice, but at least the title reminds them of what they are supposed to do. This is one of the very few books that starts the students playing quarter notes. The notes of the first page are concert F, G, and E♭. This starts the instruments on higher notes for the beginning lessons, which can be an advantage for instruments that need to develop stronger embouchures from the very first lessons. There are letters to parents, practice charts, teaching tips, and a place on each page for parents to acknowledge their child's progress. This is the only book (of which I am aware) that licenses the band teacher to make duplicate copies of the accompanying tapes and CDs for the students at no charge. The series consists of Book I, Book II, and *Technicises For Band.* Full band arrangements are integrated throughout the first two methods. The *Technicises For Band* is a series of scales, arpeggios, and chorales that will develop the technical abilities of your students. Though the book is not supported by computer programs and other multimedia aids, it is a good basic band program and most students progress quickly using it.

Premier Performance, by Ed Sueta (Rockaway, NJ: Ed Sueta Music Publications, Inc., 1999).

Ed Sueta's original band method called the *Ed Sueta Band Method* has been a well-known book for more than 20 years. This is his new band method. At the time of writing, only the flute and clarinet books were available. The design of this method is to have a four-page "pre-lesson" section where the notes used should be better suited for those instruments. Since all the books were not available, a judgment cannot be made about the effectiveness of "pre-lessons," but it is an idea that is not used often in contemporary band methods. The flute book starts on low B, A, and G. Students may be instructed to play the lines sounding up an octave if you wish to have them play the higher tones first. The book does contain fun songs and full band arrangements.

Sound Spectacular, by Andrew Balent (New York: Carl Fischer, 1992).

This is a good basic band method. The first book has one pre-lesson for each instrument before starting its heterogeneous lessons. Book I contains two full band arrangements and Book II has one full band arrangement. Photographs of students sitting with good posture and embouchure playing their instruments are featured at the beginning of each student book. The brass starts on concert F and plays down immediately to concert B♭. At the end of Book I, the author gives teacher aids such as lesson plans and sample letters. The series also has additional supplements for solos, ensembles, a first Concert Folio, which has several beginning band arrangements, and a book of theory concepts.

Standard of Excellence, by Bruce Pearson (San Diego: Neil A. Kjos Music Company, 1996).

This book uses color and other graphic techniques to teach new notes and musical concepts to the students. Books I and II have accompanying CDs available. Drawings are used to demonstrate assembling and playing of the instruments. At the beginning of Book I, the brass instruments start on concert B♭, and work up the scale to concert F. The teacher's editions contain excellent teacher aids such as checklists for instruments, a curriculum outline, troubleshooting tips, and drum rudiments. Book III gives historical information on some of the music and composers which the students are playing. Computer software by Amadeus Al Fine is available as a teaching assessment tool for students and teachers. Individual arrangements and musical collections are also available with this series.

## Part 7

Final Tips
and Suggestions

Education

There are several ways in which a music instructor may continue to learn and grow as a teacher. One way is to pursue advanced degrees. As you continue with your education, I strongly advise that you take music courses that interest you. If you pursue advanced education degrees, do not forget about what made you become a music teacher in the first place: your love for music. As you take the required courses for your next degree, take courses in music that are of particular interest to you. If you like the Romantic era, then take an analytical or historical course in the subject. Theory may be of a special interest to you. Take a course in Schenkerian analysis. You may never communicate any of this knowledge directly to your students, but because you have a greater understanding of music, they will see and feel your excitement about music. In short, make sure you continue to learn about music and increase your own love for music.

Many of the state music educators' conventions have wonderful workshops and clinics that are of great benefit to new and experienced music teachers. Attend these conventions. You may wish to attend more than just the one in your own state each year. By hearing other bands play and watching other conductors, you may pick up a lot of hints about improving your own situation. Also, at many of these state conventions, a large portion of the music industry is there to show you their products. This is a great place to look at the music before you purchase it. Many stores and publishers attend these conferences. Take your time and look through the music. Find what songs and arrangements are scored at just the level for your band, and pick music that will be fun and exciting. Other products, such as musical instruments, computer music software, and uniforms, from just about every aspect of the music business, are represented at these meetings. The conferences also provide a very good forum for discussions as to what others may do in your particular situation. Do not be afraid to ask questions. Many people are more than willing to share their experiences with you. Take what is valuable to you and discard what does not apply. Just be ready to learn, no matter from what source.

Performance

Have your band perform as often as possible. Do not wait until spring for the first concert with your beginners. Perform as soon as your band can play half of the first book. Then perform a spring concert and more. Ask your principal if you may start assemblies with a song. The song does not have to relate to the particular assembly. Start the programs with a pop tune or some song that will be fun for the band students to play and for the audience to listen to. You need only one song, not an entire concert. This will improve your final concert of the year because you have performed the song before, and it will continually bring attention to the band. Your band will grow if you perform often. This is a great building and retention tool, but it also builds strength in the band program.

Perform in public as often as possible. This builds pride in both the band program and the school. If your band is a viable part of the community, it will be harder for a school board to eliminate the band from the school day.

Retention

Once we have recruited students, we need to keep them in the band. This is a multi-level task.

Be a good teacher. That is the first order of business. You may be very good at getting the kids excited about joining the band, but you have to be able to teach them to play well and sound good quickly. No matter what instrument is your own personal favorite, or your major, learn to play them all. You need to know what the student is feeling in order to understand how to make suggestions to correct a situation. However, do not learn in front of the students. Do not play a note on an instrument in front of the children unless you can produce a good sound using the correct embouchure. Practice at home until you are ready to give your students a good example. Once you can play an instrument well, bring in your own mouthpiece, and when a student is having a problem try to duplicate the problem on his or her instrument (with your mouthpiece, of course). Then you can tell the student why he or she was having a problem producing a sound or playing a phrase, and how to correct the situation. Of course, you must check out the student's mouthpiece and reed before you attempt to play the student's instrument. If the mouthpiece is chipped or the reed broken, there is no point in going any further. That is the problem!

Perform often. That cannot be overstated. The more you perform, the more students will want to stay in the band. After all, that is the joy of playing music: performing for an audience. Otherwise, we just get tired of practicing. Perform in parades, take trips to fun places, and do whatever your budget will allow. It costs nothing to perform often for your school and local community.

Make band fun! Play a variety of music. Take requests as much as possible (stay within the realm of good taste, however). Whenever you program a concert, do not play only the hardest music possible. Program a few easy songs that are fun that the children and the audience will enjoy. In most cases you will want to program some music that is challenging, but do not overburden your band or your audience. Band should be challenging, changing, and fun all the time. A great program has a variety of classical, pop, rock, jazz, and/or movie themes.

And, as I have said throughout this resource, **be enthusiastic!** No one will want to stay in your band if you are not having a good time. Let the students see your emotions. If you like a song, let them know it. For the most part, it is not necessary to play music you do not like. Though you may feel the need to play a particular classical or rock piece (for the kids) that you do not care for, make most of the music you program compositions that you like. You are not going to get a musical performance on something you halfheartedly conduct. Enjoy your job. Enjoy teaching. The kids want to be with someone who is having a good time. Don't be afraid to let them see your joy and concern for them.

Keeping the Band Program

Do not think that because you live in an affluent community, or because your administration loves your program, that your program is safe from a budget-slashing school board. Very wealthy communities have lost their bands and entire music programs because a school board decided to save money on the music program. There are organizations such as CAT (Citizens Against Taxes) and others that would like to do away with public schools, never mind viable band programs. You must be prepared to defend your program at any time during your career regardless of how well established your situation may be.

One of the first things you must do to keep the band is to be a part of the community. Play in the parades and festivals in your city or town park. Make sure the entire community sees the band as an important part of your town. Your band should play a major part in building pride in your city. And that is not just going to contests and winning first divisions, but participating in your community celebrations. Play for political events. Do not choose sides, just play for whoever is in office. If it comes to a school board battle, you will need more than the band parents at a board meeting to keep your band program alive. You will need the support of your entire town.

When you have done all this—by performing often in the community and being as visible as possible—and the school board is still ready to remove your program from the budget, there is one final argument you may make. Much wonderful research in recent years has shown that music can increase intelligence, facilitate learning, and more. But a hostile school board will take away your argument by telling you other courses provide the same service. There is one argument that a school board cannot dispute: Band is the only organization that builds pride in the school, while educating the children, in which anyone in school may participate. In order to play on an athletic team, one must be talented in that area. To play on the chess team, one must have talent and ability to use strategy in order to win and bring pride to the school. However, to play in the band and be a viable member, talent is not necessary. Anyone who wants to play an instrument and is willing to practice may participate and become a very important part of the organization. The self-esteem of the child will increase, his or her grade will improve, the entire school will feel good about the band whether they are band members or not, and **no** other organization in the school is open to the entire school body. This is an argument you must present to the school board in open session and closed session. You are not fighting for your life or career, but for the welfare of your school and community.

How to Practice

Teaching students how to practice can be one of the most valuable assets you can give musicians. Just practicing and rehearsing a passage over and over again may never achieve the desired result for which the student or the band director is looking. The following are some suggestions for practicing alone and rehearsing with the entire ensemble.

Isolate the Problem (Fig. 7-1)

As mentioned above, simply playing the same passage over and over again is a waste of time. The problem which is keeping the passage from being played correctly may never be solved in this manner, and if it improves, it may never reach a point of being played consistently correctly. One must be patient enough to figure out where the problem is and how to correct it.

If the student or teacher is not sure which note or notes are not being played correctly, or which note is causing the problem, start where the passage began to have a problem. Play two notes, slowly and in absolutely correct rhythm. *Slowly* and *correctly* are the key words. Playing a passage fast when it cannot be played correctly is a waste of time. Nothing will improve, because the performer does not understand rhythmically what is causing the problem. After the first two notes are played correctly, then add one more note, in rhythm. Play it several times in a row correctly before adding another note. Continue in this

Figure 7-1
Isolate the Problem

Step 1
Isolate the problem passage.

Step 2
Play the first two notes only.
(Always add a minimum of two beats rest before you repeat a passage.)

Step 3
Subdivide the rhythm if necessary.
(First, play all the notes tongued; then tie the three Fs together, then slur the 4 notes as written.)

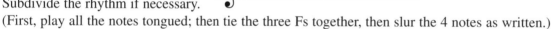

Step 4
Add one more note.
(Repeat each step at least five times correctly before continuing to the next step.)

Step 5
Add one more note.
(Remember not to speed up—keep the same steady slow tempo; this is key to making the pattern consistently correct.)

Step 6
Add one more note and repeat the measure over and over again.

etc.

The passage is taken from "Distant Castles," by Randy Navarre, published by Northeastern Music Publications, Inc., 1997. Used with permission.

pattern until the passage is played correctly. However, do not speed up the passage. Play the passage several days in a row correctly at exactly the same tempo. If the student is advanced enough to use a metronome, then he or she should use it. If you are conducting the band or an ensemble, keep the tempo slow and steady. Do not gradually increase the tempo. You want the performer(s) to feel and understand exactly where every note lies within every beat.

Accent the Problem

Many times the problem note is the note that is rushed or played too quickly. Often it is the note that is easy to play just before a difficult fingering that causes the passage to be played incorrectly. This is why a passage must be played very slowly so the student and/or the teacher can hear the note that is being rushed. Once that note is found, the student should then accent that note (see the example in Fig. 7-2). While practicing, it is okay to overaccent the note in question. This will make the performer hold on to the note a little longer which will usually be the appropriate duration for the note. Again, the performer should practice this slowly before increasing the tempo. After practicing this to the point of perfection, the student will soon forget to exaggerate the emphasis on the note in question, and the passage will sound musical. However, the student will always be aware of that particular passage and will be careful not to rush to the next note too quickly. If necessary, instruct the student to accent the note even in performance. The audience will most likely never notice the accent, and the passage will be played correctly. This technique may be used with the entire band, or section, as well as with an individual.

Figure 7-2
Accent the Problem

Often the problem is with the easy note. In anticipation of the more difficult fingering, the student will rush the note before. Accenting the note before will often take care of the problem.

This passage is from "Distant Castles," by Randy Navarre, published by Northeastern Music Publications, Inc., 1997. Used with permission.

Keep It Slow

Sometimes there may be a passage in a song that is very fast and hard to play quickly. There may not be a particular problem note, but the performer simply cannot play the passage without slowing down. This may seem like a contradiction, but in this case, slow the entire passage down tremendously. The passage must be played slowly enough so that the performer knows and hears exactly where every note is within every beat. And the passage must be played at a tempo that the student can play over and over again without a mistake of note or rhythm. Do not gradually increase the tempo. This is often taught as a way to learn how to play a phrase up to the marked tempo; however, this will never make it consistent. The student must play the passage every day at the same extremely slow tempo and be exactly correct several times a day. Though it will be tempting to increase the tempo, do not! If one is practicing alone or having a lesson one on one, use a metronome. This technique may be used with the entire band. It is then the responsibility of the conductor to not allow the band to increase the tempo. After a week of practicing the passage in this manner, start the song in an early section at the correct tempo and hear how well the passage will be played. This will happen because the performer(s) will know exactly where every note lies within every beat of the song. (See the example in Fig. 7-3.)

Figure 7-3
Slow Practice

Practice very slowly and repeat over and over again. Do not gradually speed up. Keep the same slow tempo for at least seven days in a row. Use a metronome if possible.

This passage is taken from "Pride of the Lancers," by Randy Navarre, published by Northeastern Music Publications, Inc., 2000. Used with permission.

Changing the Rhythms

Some passages will have very difficult fingerings, and the student's fingers may have a problem moving quickly from one note to the next note. One may then apply the dotted-eighth/sixteenth pattern to get the fingers to move quickly and cleanly from note to note. See the passage in the first example in Fig. 7-4. If a student cannot play the two notes without playing extra notes in between those notes, isolate the third

Figure 7-4
Dotted Pattern

Example 1

Example 2

Change the rhythm to the dotted pattern. Start very slowly, but play the rhythm accurately.

Example 3
Reverse pattern.

Example 4

Add the first note of the phrase. Remember to always put at least two beats of rest in between the repeated patterns.

Example from "Penguins on Parade," by Bob Lowden, published by Northeastern Music Publications, Inc., 1994. Used with permission.

and fourth notes of the phrase. Take the first two notes and play them as dotted-eighth/sixteenth notes with a quarter note to follow, as shown in example 2. Play this very slowly at first. Then gradually increase the tempo; however, do not increase the tempo until the three notes are played perfectly at least five times in a row. Once that can be accomplished up to the marked tempo, or faster, reverse the rhythmic pattern. Play first the sixteenth note, then the dotted-eighth note, followed by the quarter, as in example 3. Finally, add one more note to complete the pattern in the dotted-eighth/sixteenth note pattern, as shown in example 4. It is always best to use a metronome while practicing a passage in this manner. Again, if you are practicing this with an ensemble, the conductor must be a very good metronome. This will get the "glups"—extra notes—out of most difficult passages.

Phrasing

Emphasizing good phrasing is not only the musical thing to do, but it also helps technique tremendously. A simple rule to remember is: A short note followed by a long note always gets the accent. No matter how short the long note is, the shorter note must be emphasized. This helps the performer move the fingers and also helps the performer hear where he or she is in the beat. (Perhaps now you are beginning to realize that rhythm is extremely crucial to technique. Understanding where one is rhythmically is helpful in placing the notes and coordinating the fingers at exactly the right time.)

Whenever one hears an artist perform, whether the person is an instrumentalist or a vocalist, this type of phrasing is occurring. It is musical to emphasize a phrase. Most listeners are very lazy and pay little attention to what the artist is really doing. The artist must get the phrasing across to the audience. There is always a slight or even sometimes an exaggerated accent on most if not all phrases in a song. This, of course, can be overdone, but there is no reason not to overemphasize the beginning of a phrase while practicing so the start of the passage is rhythmically in the correct place. Once the performer is comfortable playing a passage, the accent subsides to a more natural volume.

Fig. 7-5 gives some examples of where to accent the short note followed by the long note.

Three examples:

Figure 7-5
Accented Phrasing

Example 1
"Distant Castles" 1997*
by Randy Navarre

Example 2
"Jazz Cats" 1993*
by Larry McKenna

Example 3
"Victory on Parade"
2000*
by Robert Geisler

*Published by Northeastern Music Publications, Inc. Used with permission.

Repairs

It is not necessary for a band director or private music teacher to be a complete walking repair shop. However, it is important that the teacher be able to make some very minor repairs very quickly.

The teacher need not send an instrument to the repair shop for every little mishap that may happen to the instrument. Many repairs can be made in the classroom in front of the student. Some suggestions have already been made in Part 2 of this resource. I will include a few more here.

Woodwinds occasionally have the keys stick to the tone holes. Most of the time this is easy to repair. Take a dollar bill (domination does not matter) from your wallet, place the bill between the tone hole and the key. Close the key with one hand and press it down with enough pressure so the key is pressing against the bill, but is still allowing you to slide the bill out from under the key. This will remove the sticky residue that collects while the student is playing. You may need to do this procedure a few times in a row, but it should get the key working properly again.

Also, on woodwinds, check the springs. Sometimes a key will not lift off the tone hole because the spring that works the mechanism has come off its location. Find the key that is not working properly and follow the lever to the spring. If the spring is sticking out and not attached to the lever, simply push the spring back in place.

Sometimes the saxophone octave key does not open or close properly or to the correct degree needed to produce the higher or lower sound. If the octave key will not open when the octave key is pressed, hold the saxophone at the bottom of the neck where the neck meets the body of the saxophone, holding the octave key so the part with the pad is up. Then, push the key up very slightly with your other hand (thumb). Then release the key and see if the octave key functions properly. You may need to do this in increments until the key works. Do not bend the key a great deal at a time. The key can break! If the octave pad will not close even when the octave key is not being pressed, then follow the same procedure and push the key down, very slightly, so the pad will stay over the tone hole. With experience, you will be able to do this quickly. This is an easy repair and a waste of time for a repair shop, not to mention a waste of money for your student's parents.

Some pads on woodwinds are very easy to replace. Small repair kits that have glue and a small selection of pads are available. Heat the bottom of the key with a match to melt the glue, remove the old pad, and put in the new pad. Make sure it is the right size pad for that key. You do not want a pad that is too small or too large for the key and tone hole. Usually the register key or octave keys are the first to go on most woodwind instruments, and these are easy to replace. I do not suggest taking an instrument apart to repair or replace difficult-to-reach keys—leave that for the professionals. You should do quick and easy jobs. If you start taking keys off a woodwind instrument, you may not be able to figure out where they go again. A repair person will charge you a lot of money if you go to him with a bag of keys and pads in one hand and a clarinet in the other and ask him to make it work again.

Before a trumpet, baritone, or tuba is sent to the shop because the valves will not move up and down, you should check the valves first. Sometimes the valves are in sideways. Also, after awhile, there will be a buildup of a residue along the walls of the valves. Remove the valve from the cylinder, take a soft damp towel (do not use any type of abrasive cleaners, only water), and clean the sides of the piston and the inside of the cylinder. Once it is clean, apply valve oil to it and return it into the cylinder. Do this for each valve on the instrument. The same thing may apply to the trombone slide. Remove the outside slide, clean the inner slide with a damp towel, place slide oil on the instrument, and replace the outer slide.

Drumheads are easy to replace. Just remember to tighten the lugs across from each other just as in tuning the drums. (See page 205 where tuning is discussed.) Never tighten the lugs side by side all across the drum. That could result in the head ripping or at least becoming weaker in certain sections of the drum. Soon, you will have another broken drumhead to replace.

Many colleges offer summer repair courses that are one to two weeks in length. These provide an excellent means of learning quick repairs that will greatly help your students when a sudden crisis appears. The college course and repair kits are well worth the money you spend on them and will save you much more money and aggravation in the long run. (Just imagine, you're at festival or contest. Your first chair clarinetist with the wonderful, beautiful solo in the first song suddenly comes up to you and says his clarinet will not work. You get out your trusty set of little screwdrivers, tighten the rods on the stack, put in a new octave key pad, and the student says, "Thanks." You just about had a heart attack, but you saved the day. If you hadn't known what to do . . .) You may also purchase repair kits that have a large variety of pads and tools for such repairs. They are available through many music stores and music catalog companies. At least carry a set of small screwdrivers, an assortment of pads, key oil, and several clean towels with you whenever you teach or go to festivals and contests.

Interviewing for the Job

Developing good interviewing skills is essential if you want to get a good position teaching music. This is an area in which many teachers fail. A prospective teacher must come off as enthusiastic, willing to work, and knowledgeable about his or her subject, how to teach, and how to handle children. And many times the principal knows little to nothing about music, and may be a very poor interviewer. It is your job to let the interviewer know that you know how to teach, and that you have the knowledge to be successful even when the interviewer is not asking the right questions.

Before you ever come into an interview, be prepared. If you are new to teaching, review all the basics to teaching all of the instruments. Know the fingerings for all of the notes that students will learn in the first year of study. If a music supervisor is a part of the search-and-interview panel, it is very likely you will be asked how to play certain notes and what fingerings are used to produce certain notes on all of the instruments. You will not impress anyone if you do not know the basic fingerings for playing the instrument.

Look and act professional. Wear a suit and tie if you are a male, and dress professionally if you are a female. Regardless of what the daily attire may be during the school year, you must make a good impression at first sight. Casual clothing will immediately put you at a disadvantage. Be neat, sit with good posture, and above all be polite. Do not interrupt your interviewer.

It is important that you get across to the interviewer that you have lots of ideas as to how to teach and that you can come up with new ones quickly when you are teaching. The interviewer may ask questions that are not related to teaching music. It is your job to answer the question asked, and then continue in such a way that you relate that question to a musical answer. Make sure the principal or supervisor knows by the end of the interview that you have a great knowledge of music and creative ways of teaching music to the students.

Keep track of the discussion. Take notes as you talk if necessary. If the phone rings, write a note on the pad as to what the discussion was before the phone rang. The principal will be most impressed if you can continue the conservation as if there had been no interruption. Show the interviewer that you are organized. This will be very impressive regardless of whether the interviewer is a musical person or not. Good teachers must be organized.

Finally, be enthusiastic. You are more likely to get a job offer if you indicate that you really want the job. No one wants to hire a reluctant employee, no matter how knowledgeable he or she may be about the subject. Enthusiasm is a large portion of teaching. If you cannot convince the principal or music supervisor that you really want the job, chances are that you will not get the offer. Not all principals may know a lot about music or teaching music, but most people admire and respect someone's enthusiasm for the subject that he or she may teach. Let the interviewer or panel know that you want the job.

Immediately after the interview, write a thank-you letter. Let the school personnel know that you appreciate the time they took to interview you, and that you would look forward to being a part of this school. If the school has a fax machine, fax the letter either the same day or the following day. Then send the hard copy by mail.

It is okay and a good idea to call once to see if the principal or music supervisor has any additional questions about you. This is your chance to offer more of your musical knowledge that may not have been revealed during the interview. Call only once, however. Do not be a pest. However, more than once I have hired someone because he or she took the time to give me a call a few days later to further show his or her desire for the position.

I wish you good luck and hope you will not have to give many interviews in your teaching career!

Appendix

This appendix gives instrumental music teachers valuable resources to further aid in their success.

The major, harmonic, and melodic minor scales are included for both treble clef and bass clef instruments. All twelve scales are included for each mode, but not all the enharmonic spellings. I have used the more common spellings of the scales and the ones musicians are more likely to encounter while performing and sight-reading music.

Also included is a short list of additional musical studies for the instruments discussed in the *Kit*. The list is designed to give you a few additional teaching resources. You may wish to offer them as an alternative to the music lessons in the beginning band methods.

Finding good reeds for double reed instruments is always a difficult chore for young students. Included here are recommendations for some good books on buying and making double reeds. Also listed are a few suppliers you can contact for these products if you can't find what you're looking for in your local music store.

The final section of the appendix lists music stores that carry both sheet music and music-related books. Other music stores in your area may also carry these same products.

Major Scales

Start at ♩ = 60, eventually play at faster tempos

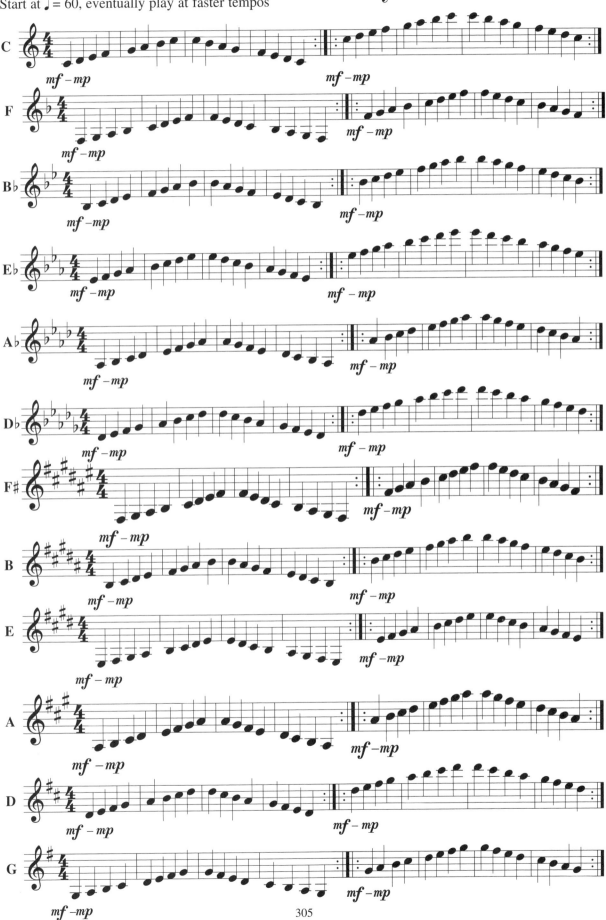

Harmonic Minor Scales

Start at ♩ = 60, eventually play at faster tempos

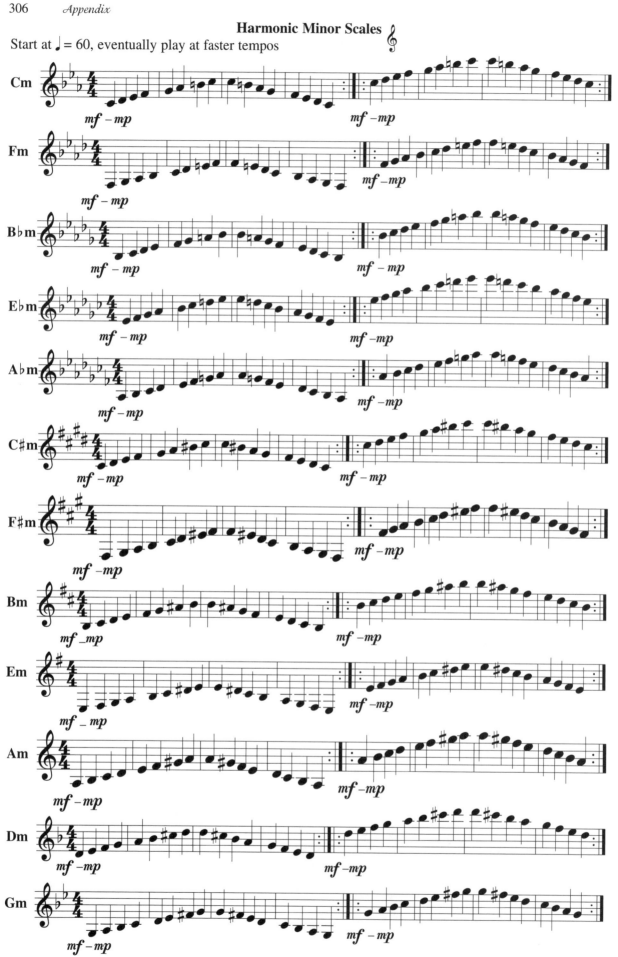

Melodic Minor Scales

Start at ♩ = 60, eventually play at faster tempos

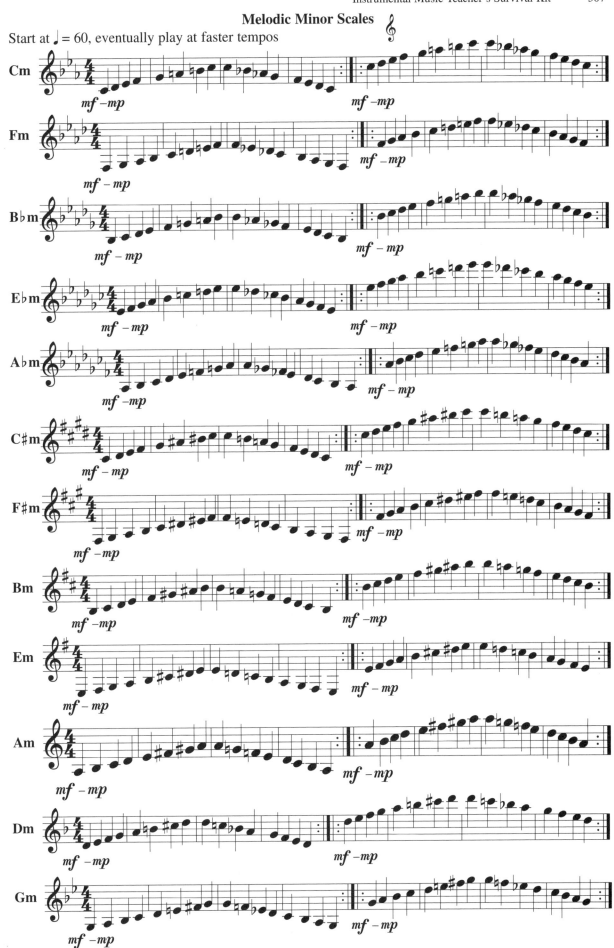

Major Scales

Start at ♩ = 60, eventually play at faster tempos

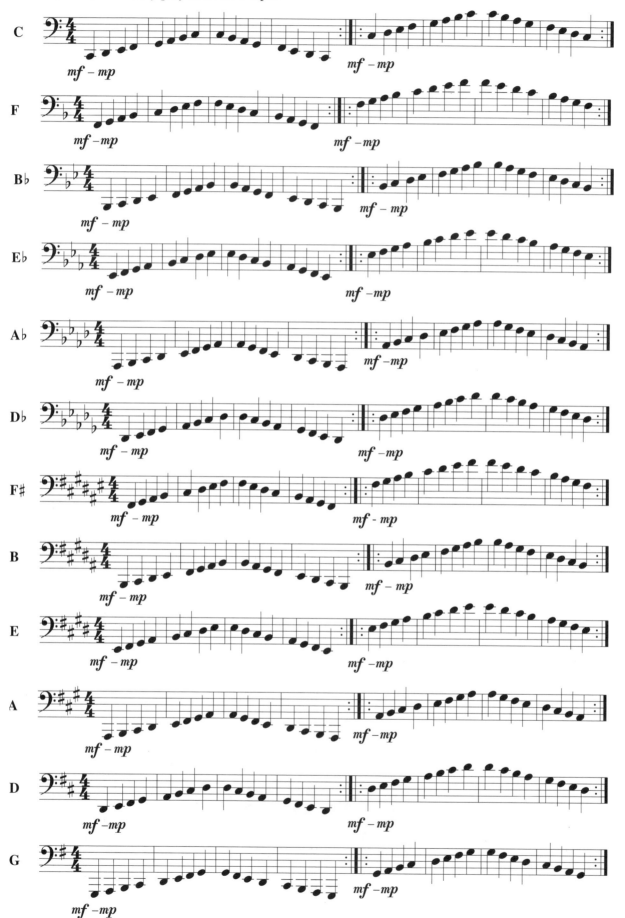

Harmonic Minor Scales 𝄢:

Start at ♩ = 60, eventually play at faster tempos

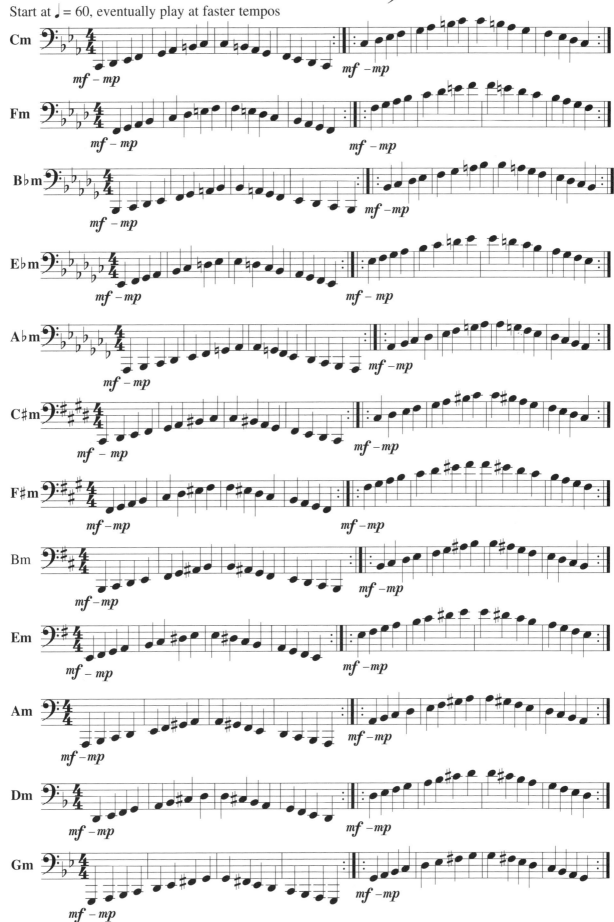

Appendix

Melodic Minor Scales 𝄢

Start at ♩ = 60, eventually play at faster tempos

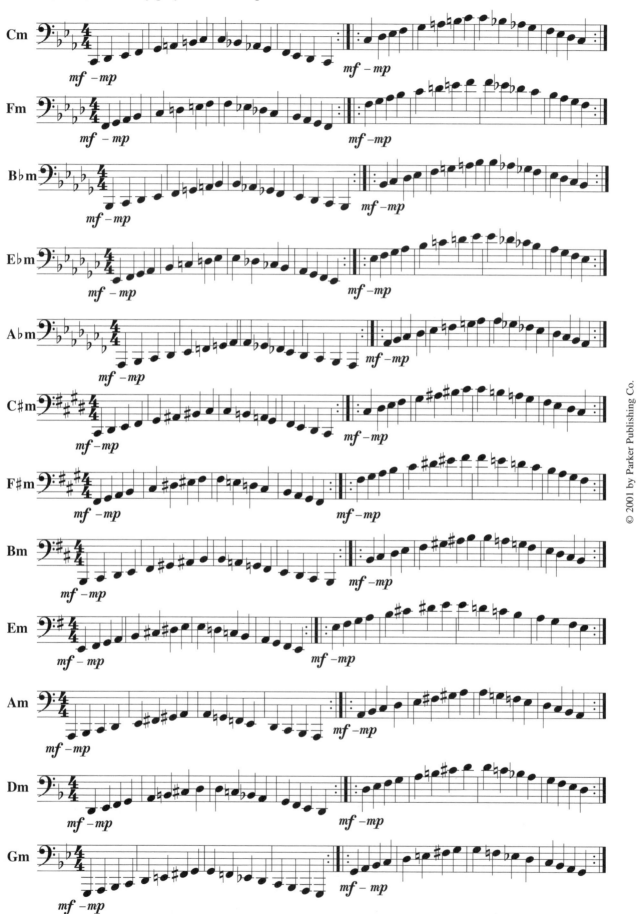

Suggested Books for Additional Studies

Flute:

Rubank® Methods (boring, but very good—The Rubank® Methods are very good for all the instruments, but must be mixed with other studies. They are boring, but anyone who has studied and completed the Rubank Methods is a good player!)

Concert and Contest Collection for Flute. Rubank, 1969.

Solos for the Flute Player, by Louis Moyse. Schirmer/Hal Leonard, 1961.

Forty Little Pieces in Progressive Order for Beginning Flutist, by Louis Moyse. Schirmer/Hal Leonard, 1965.

Oboe:

Gekeler Method for Oboe I, by Kenneth Gekeler. Belwin Mills, 1940.

Barrett Oboe Method, by Boosey & Hawkes (no date on publication).

Ferling Studies for Oboe & Saxophone, by Southern Music Company, 1958.

Rubank® Methods (boring, but very good).

Bassoon:

Rubank® Methods (boring, but very good).

Clarinet:

The Working Clarinetist, by Peter Hadcock. Roncorp, Inc. (advanced).

Clarinet Articulation, by Allen Sigel. Roncorp, Inc.

Rubank® Methods (boring, but effective).

Saxophone:

Selected Studies, by Voxman-Hal Leonard.

The Art of Saxophone, by Larry Teal. Summy-Burchard, 1963. Dist. by Warner Bros.

The Saxophonist Workbook, by Larry Teal. University Music Press, 1958.

Rubank® Methods (boring, but effective).

Trumpet:

Rubank® Methods (boring, but a very good study).

Concert & Contest Collection for Trumpet, by H. Voxman. Rubank/Hal Leonard, 1967.

Belwin Master Duets—easy—intermediate—advanced. Vol. 1. Belwin-Mills, 1986.

F Horn:

Deux Cents Etudes Nouvelles, Vol. 2 & 3, by Maxime-Alphonse. Leduc, 1920.

335 Selected Melodious, Progressive, and Technical Studies, Vol. 1, by Pottag-Andraud. Southern Music, 1955.

Embouchure Building for Horn, by Joseph Singer. Published by Belwin. No date available.

Rubank® Methods

Trombone:

The Trombonist's Handbook, by Reginald Fink.
Studies in Legato for Trombone, by Reginald H. Fink. Carl Fischer, 1967.
Rubank® Methods

Tuba:

The Legacy of a Master, by Arnold Jacobs. The Instrumentalist Publishing Co., 1987.
Rubank® Methods

Snare Drum (Percussion):

Alfred Drum Method, Alfred Publishing Co., 1987.
Stick Control, by George Stone. George B. Stone & Son, 1935. Distributed by Ludwig.
Progressive Steps to Modern Syncopation, by Ted Reed. Copyright assigned to Alfred Publishing Co., 1996.
Roy Burns Beginning Drum Method, Warner Bros., 1962.

Bells (Mallet Percussion):

Fundamentals Methods for Mallets Book 1 (& 2), by Mitch Peters. Alfred Publishing Co., 1995.
Fundamental Studies for Mallets, by Garwood Whaley. J. R. Publications, 1974.

Double Reeds and Books on Buying and Making Double Reeds

Top quality reed makers:

Jones Reeds—oboe and bassoon

Artist Lesher Reeds—oboe and bassoon (the Artist reeds have a darker tone than the "regular" Lesher reeds)

Evans Reeds—oboe and bassoon

Diener Reeds—bassoon only (guaranteed to play—a premium reed; not necessarily for beginners)

Reed-making books:

Bassoon Reed Making, by Mark Popkons and Loren Glickman. Instrumentalist (available at Muncy Winds)

The Oboe Reed Book, by Jay Light

Suppliers and catalogues:

Muncy Winds: 1-800-333-6415, fax: 1-828-963-8990, www.muncywinds.com

Forrests: 1-800-322-6263, www.forrestsmusic.com

Midwest Musical Imports: 1-800-926-5587, mmi@mmimports.com

The Woodwind & Brasswind: 1-800-348-5003, www.wwandbw.com

Repair Book

A Guide to Repairing Woodwinds, by Ronald Saska. Roncorp, Inc.

Sources

Some Music Stores That Carry Sheet Music and Books

This is not meant to be a complete list of stores. Try your local music store for music and accessories.

Bookmark
307 Forest Ave.
Pacific Grove, CA 93950

Brook Mays Print Music
5756 LBJ Freeway
Dallas, Texas 75240
1-800-432-2676

Florida Music Service
2017 E. Fowler Avenue
Tampa, FL 33612
1-800-229-8863

J. W. Pepper & Son Inc.
P.O. Box 850
Valley Forge, PA 19482
1-800-345-6296

Malecki Music, Inc.
4500 Broadmoor SE
Grand Rapids, MI 49501
1-800-253-9692

Mannerino Sheet Music, Inc.
7605 Hamilton Avenue
Cincinnati, OH 45231
1-800-466-8863

Northwest Music Services
1991 Main Street
Vancouver, BC V5T-3C1
Canada
1-800-663-6797

Pender's Music Company
314 S. Elm Street
Denton, Texas 76201
1-800-772-5918

RBC Music Company, Inc.
P.O. Box 29128
San Antonio, Texas 78229
1-800-548-0917

Senseney Music, Inc.
2300 E. Lincoln
Wichita, KS 67211
1-800-362-1060

Shattinger Music Co.
1810 S. Broadway
St. Louis, MO 63104
1-800-444-2408

Southern Music Company
1248 Austin Hwy #212
San Antonio, Texas 78209
1-800-284-5443

Stanton's Sheet Music, Inc.
330 S. Fourth Street
Columbus, OH 43215
1-800-42MUSIC

Theodore Presser Music Stores
One Presser Place
Bryn Mawr, PA 19010
610-527-4242

Ward-Brodt Music Mall
2200 West Beltline Highway
Madison, WI 53725
1-800-369-6255

Wingert-Jones Music Inc.
11225 Colorado Street
Kansas City, MO 64137
1-800-258-9566

Index